In Search of the Primitive

SHERMAN PAUL

In Search

of the Primitive

REREADING DAVID ANTIN, JEROME ROTHENBERG,

AND GARY SNYDER

Louisiana State University Press

Baton Rouge and London

Copyright © 1986 by Louisiana State University Press
All rights reserved
Manufactured in the United States of America

Designer: Patricia Douglas Crowder
Typeface: Linotron 202 Trump Medieval
Typesetter: G & S Typesetters, Inc.

LIBRARY OF CONGRESS CATALOGING-IN-PUBLICATION DATA

Paul, Sherman.
    In search of the primitive.

    1. American poetry—20th century—History and
criticism.   2. Primitivism in literature.   3. Antin,
David—Criticism and interpretation.   4. Rothenberg,
Jerome, 1931–   —Criticism and interpretation.
5. Snyder, Gary—Criticism and interpretation.   I. Title.
PS310.P68P38   1986   811'.54'091   86-2873
ISBN 0-8071-1292-5

6387

Contents

Preface

Even at the risk of the usual misunderstanding of *primitive*, I have chosen to call these rereadings *In Search of the Primitive* for several compelling reasons. I want to acknowledge Stanley Diamond, an anthropologist whose own major work is covered by this title. His thought has directly contributed to the work of Antin, Rothenberg, and Snyder—in fact, *Alcheringa*, the magazine with which all have been associated, reprinted a portion of Diamond's title essay in its second issue. Among others whose names are on his honor roll of critics of civilization, he has given intellectual legitimacy to the concept of the primitive and, in terms of the model he has constructed, attempted, as he says approvingly of Ruth Benedict's critical use of anthropology, "to educate a chaotic and narrowing society to a more spacious view of human possibilities." He speaks of this as involving "a deeper vision of man," but he might also have said a more inclusive one. For he does not propose to replace civilization with the primitive so much as teach us to spare the primitive and incorporate what we may still learn from it in our present way of life. It is in this sense, I think, that the search for the primitive has become one of the notable projects of recent poetry—poetry since World War II—though the primitive, a legacy of Romanticism, has been a conspicuous element of the avant-garde arts throughout this century.

Primitive simply means first, earliest, original, basic. Historically it refers to a way of life prior to civilization—that is, the city-state—but to evoke it now is, as Kenneth Burke says, to temporalize the essence, essence, in this instance, being the fuller human nature, the first nature, to which we aspire. Since it asks us to view ourselves in light of all human history, it is a term of manifold critical uses. Many of these are evident in the work of the poets treated here. But if any is focal, perhaps it is the political, for the good reason that these poets, dedicated to *poesis*, have entered the public realm and, to that extent, reclaimed the *polis*, the place of speech and act, that Plato tried to abolish. Plato also tried to banish the poets, and this, with the abolition of the *polis*, is a direct attack on the primitive, on the *muthologos*, as Olson says in *The Maximus Poems*, on the shaman, on the trickster. Politics, as we have come to know it, follows Plato in wishing to be rid of contradiction, opposing voices; and the poet, who by virtue of his vocation never loses connection with the primitive, is of necessity often at war with the state. The primitive, in being prior to the city-state, may have been nonpolitical, but to those who now search for the primitive, the search is clearly political. Diamond's most important essays, it should be noted, were initially published in the 1960s when this generation of poets emerged.

I chose this title, then, to emphasize this radical conflict in history, but also because, in being equally true of the poets treated in *The Lost America of Love*, it indicates the insistence that makes the present study a sequel. Or, since *The Lost America of Love* was said to be a sequel to *Olson's Push*, perhaps I should say the third volume of an informal account of what, to my mind, is most interesting and significant in recent American poetry. Happily, I find, I am not alone in thinking this. There is, for example, Reinhold Schiffer, whose

"Ethnopoetics: Some Aspects of American Avant-Garde Primitivism" (*Dutch Quarterly Review of Anglo-American Letters,* 1979) focuses on Snyder, Rothenberg, and Antin—I cite his order because in his case it indicates an ascending order of endorsement—and offers a tolerant yet skeptical assessment of the political value of their work.

Methodologically, however, this study is a sequel in following the meditative practice of *The Lost America of Love.* The only innovation is "the thwarting of ends" (Rothenberg's good phrase)—the letters that make such open criticism demonstrably dialogical and keep it open.

The poets treated here have been generous in their response, as has Marjorie Perloff, and I am especially grateful to them for permitting me to use their letters. I am also grateful to Gavin Selerie, who initially published the section on David Antin at the Binnacle Press in London; to George F. Butterick and Cid Corman for sustaining and informative correspondence; to my students for continuing conversation about poetry; and to the Department of English and the Graduate College of the University of Iowa for material assistance. My outstanding debt is still to Jim.

I. So to Speak

DAVID ANTIN

Even so, begin—with irritation.

Here is a writer who is interesting. *Interest:* Antin uses this
word to define an artist's *raison d'être* and a situation, the presentation of an artwork, that "forces questioning." An artist is
interesting when he is at the boundary searching out questions and when he provokes us to do the same. When he has
"striking power" (perhaps what Cage considers the "power to
irritate"?). When he takes the next move in the game of chess
that figures for him the "advance" of art. Not the "fundamentally trivial representation of reality" of our game, which represents a struggle for power with no option but conflict, but
an earlier game, the Indian game of *shantrandji,* which was
"built up out of the human experiences of its time"—the fact,
for example, that the division of people into social classes
is arbitrary, that chance invades such boundaries—and was
"thought to teach humility to rulers."

Antin says that "changes in the structure of the game can
only be judged in terms of whether they are 'interesting' and
how 'interesting.'" Mere fashions, innovations that are a dead
end don't count. Only changes that have "profound consequences that reverberate throughout the entire system." *And,*
as he says in "Art Chronicle," where he addresses the critical

situation of art criticism, the players, not the critics, determine these changes.

Antin is a superb critic who can say this because he is an artist whose art is notable for its critical intelligence, and for changing the rules of the game. His first talk poem, "talking at pomona," is the result of a course of improvisatory experiment, and it rehearses much of the critical work he was then doing for *Art News.* The talk poems become his art and his criticism, an art to be cherished for its quality of mind, for bringing into art the present act of mind, or, better, to cite Cage, for letting "life obscure the difference between life and art."

Remember: the great critics have often themselves been "interesting" artists. Who has helped us understand modernism and postmodernism better than Cage, Olson, Duncan, Creeley, Antin, Rothenberg, etc.?

10 March 1981

Profound consequences. His work proposes such consequences. Like Olson, he wants an art more responsive, more adequate to the real; an art that more *truly represents* it, cracks and all, and is made (repeat) "out of the character of human experiences in our world." A human universe, defined not humanistically by anthropocentrism but by the characteristics evoked by such cognates as *human, humane, humanity.* Antin—and the remarkable group of poets associated with him on *some/thing*—would recover this (no: *the*) scope of poetry by recovering the full (often forgotten) human resources of language. What Rothenberg has been doing in those thick, rich anthologies of his, in his work, with Dennis Tedlock, in *Alcheringa,* where Antin, a lifelong friend, is a contributing editor. Where, in the landmark issue on ethnopoetics, Antin defines ethnopoetics as "Human Poetics," "People's Poetics or the poetics of natural language."

"My interest," he reports in *Contemporary Authors*, is "in the human significance of language structures." "I am interested in the lethal implications of socially debased language." This, certainly, contributes to his interest.

The real: "The terrible thing Gedaliah said would be if all our ideas of reality were based on the evidence of 200 years of experimentation and measurement and the constitution of the universe was changing all this time" (Antin, "Autobiography 2"). *The full(y) human resources of language:* "the language is a Whole System accessible to everyone: the *only* such Whole System" (Hugh Kenner, in *Vort*).

Isn't the fact of neglect—that a poet of such intelligence and accomplishment is neglected—cause for irritation? Antin might simply shrug it off, muttering "trivial," his obsessive word of reprobation. After all, hasn't he shown in his art criticism that neglect *is* more often than not the reality of the case? Didn't he have to come forward with reappraisals of such "interesting" artists as Warhol and Robert Morris; have to sort out the scrambled minds of Max Kozloff and Thomas Hess; have to remind us, in "talking at pomona," of how shoddy the art world is, how badly served it is—we are—by "painting relators" who "have sometimes been thought of as critics" and sometimes are "hustlers called dealers"?

Painting relators (*realtors?*) are those who relate one painting to another and so define what a painting is. They assimilate the innovative, the new and interesting, to the old. They constitute what George Quasha calls the "concensus," and they

11 March 1981

threaten the new (the out of bounds) by absorbing it. Kenner, adapting the designation, says: "In the practical world of discussion—at its most expensively practical, the world of curricula—we come down to assenting when a poetry-relator tells us that he and his fellow-relators have agreed that men shall call *this* 'poetry' and not *that*." Men *and* women.

But don't they accomplish most by outright neglect, by not noticing an interesting poet even after others have noticed him? Those who have noticed him are for the most part those Antin calls contemporaries (the "truly contemporaneous artists of our time are known primarily to a community consisting of themselves"). Olson's *polis*, the "few American poets," the "careful ones" he speaks of in *Maximus III*. So Antin is recognized in Barry Alpert's *Vort* (with Rothenberg, in 1975) and Bill Spanos' *Boundary 2* (again with Rothenberg, in 1975). And in that incredibly open and inclusive anthology by Ronald Gross and George Quasha, *Open Poetry* (1973), devoted, as Quasha says, to showing us "the variety of means being employed now in putting language to new communicative uses."

Even overlooked are such challenging and brilliant essays on the *situation in poetry* as "Modernism and Postmodernism: Approaching the Present in American Poetry," in the first issue of *Boundary 2*, and the follow-up, "Some Questions About Modernism," in *Occident* (1974)—both, incidentally, little magazines supported by academic institutions. These position papers, intended to provoke response, received very little as far as I know; none, in any case, in *APR*, the trade journal in which Antin appeared in the first issue, in 1972. A measure of what's interesting in a decade of poetry? Why didn't those issues of *Vort* and *Boundary 2*, the Gross-Quasha anthology, the anthologies of Rothenberg (*Revolution of the Word, Technicians of the Sacred, Shaking the Pumpkin,*

America a Prophecy), especially the last edited with Quasha, and the special ethnopoetics issue of *Alcheringa* (1976) ignite something? Approaching the Present in American Poetry, indeed!

And *some/thing* (1965–66), not to be confused with, though not without relation to, Dick Higgins' Something Else Press. Has anyone in speaking of the recent history of American poetry mentioned a magazine in its way as significant—as striking in its three issues—as *Origin* and the *Black Mountain Review* in the previous decade? And to be noted, if only for its last issue, "A Vietnam Assemblage," which is as interesting politically as it is poetically, and reminds us (will our present administration remind us?) that poets are sometimes political and write, as Antin says he did, out of "intense feeling about this war"?

Antin and Rothenberg, who earlier had been involved with the "deep image," used *some/thing* "to coalesce and . . . crystallize the new concerns." As Cage said of the advance in new music (in *Silence*, 1961), "one does not . . . make just any experiment but does what must be done. . . . One does something else." One is "active according to present necessities."

I note immediately its labyrinthine emblem because I have been reading *Alcheringa*, where it also appears as a signature.

It is a Pima drawing of "the pathways: searchings: stopping-places: where-the-god-has-stopped: a wave length: energy: cessation: strife: emergence into: something." It already announces a project beyond the scope of a single magazine or the different views of its editors; the project of a generation of poets, *something*, you might say, in which poets as different as Olson, Snyder, Duncan, MacLow, and Schwerner join, as in fact they do in ethnopoetics.

Ethnopoetics is neither an exotic nor an antiquarian concern, and it is not, for all of its dependence on such studies, anthropological. Rothenberg opens the first issue of *some/thing* with "Aztec Definitions: Found Poems From The Florentine Codex." What he has found are poems, as he says in a prefatorial manifesto (he is a man of pre-faces, one of the pedagogical poets who has become pedagogical out of need, the necessities of poetry)—what he has found are not "poetry proper—the songs and hymns" but definitions in which we hear the sound of poetry and recognize a poetics "not far from our own." Rothenberg turns to the Aztec as Olson turned to the Maya, but his sense of the human universe is informed by their predicament (and ours), by "what's to be done when the shape of the real falls apart?" He writes of a vanishing civilization. In these definitions of some things he finds the mind released from system, entered on the wonderful freedom "of preparing chaos for the birth of something real." So isn't the allusion to Duchamp in "found poetry" appropriate? Appropriate also because he sees the connection between the oldest ("primitive") poetries and the new?

Ethnopoetics. See Quasha's definition, cited by Sylvia Wynter:

> At root, "Ethnopoetics" has to do with the essentially "local" incidence of "poesis" or acts of "making." The

word *Ethno* derives from Indo-European *seu* which the American Heritage dictionary lists as "people," our "people," we "ourselves," "of our kind"—and it lives on in the word "self" and in the reflexive pronouns of French and Spanish. So Ethnopoetics is rooted in "self-poetics," "our kind" of poetics, which by an inevitable extension of *poesis* becomes that activity which has gradually become conscious of itself since the Romantics—Self-making. What does "ethno" do? That question translates as: What does any local band of people living together do in their poetry? Answer: They say themselves. They say who they are. They speak their name in what they do. (How many names of peoples mean simply, the People?) They heal themselves and keep themselves whole. They know who they are.

And see the elaboration of this definition (definition seems to be the business at hand) in "The Age of The Open Secret," a definition large and pertinent enough to include many of the poetries of our time—those, of course, that belong to what Snyder calls the Great Subculture and that have been excluded from the "mainstream of Western intellectual tradition."

The first issue of *some/thing* ends with another manifesto, this one by Antin. It is almost entirely set in CAPS, and already is a talk poem, not so much because the breath phrase determines the space breaks, as because the space breaks and spacing deliver the utterance ("SPEECH IS BOUNDED ON BOTH SIDES BY SILENCE"). He calls it "SILENCE/NOISE," after the limiting conditions that for him define language, and even though he modifies Cage's notion of silence, adopts (adapts) some of his verbal tactics. Rothenberg's manifesto is subdued, more explanatory than declarative, in keeping with its unobtrusive format. Not Antin's, which is a kind of Antin sampler. He begins in his adversarial way: "THIS IS NOT GOING TO BE AN ARTICLE ON ESTHETICS   THERE ARE VERY FEW THINGS WE NEED LESS THAN ESTHET-

13 March 1981

ICS PERHAPS ONLY TASTE." He is a partisan not of beauty but of truth, of more adequate representations of the case (human life). There is no need, he believes, to distinguish poetry and prose, and he subsumes both in language, which he addresses as "A SURVIVAL TOOL." Why? Because a *human* community cannot survive without its language: "LANGUAGE IS WHAT MAKES IT HUMAN." (And language is utterance, as here.) Then, when he addresses the fact that language is public, he adduces instances that propose the experiments in *Talking:* it's hard, he says, to imagine a linguistic community smaller than two people or one man and a tape recorder. (So even now, in a recent talk poem, "whos listening out there," the pathos that evokes for him such nostalgia arises from the extremity of isolation requisite to broadcasting.)

Having defined language by its limits, he exemplifies silence/noise in terms of his own experience in South Brooklyn—*he tells a story,* and it is set in lowercase type, and is more responsive to the breath phrase. It is a story about a window, which admits noise when open and when closed (aided by an air-conditioner) brings silence. These terms equate with disorder and order, and are necessary to his argument—an argument introducing ideas and terminology from physics, linguistics, communications theory, philosophy of language, etc. But remembering how much attention he gives to Duchamp's windows, I am taken by the example of the window. And in what follows I especially note his important footnote from Wittgenstein ("An utterance is an image of reality"), his concern with speech as "AN ATTEMPT TO CREATE AND TO RECOVER OR DISCOVER AND TRANSMIT SOME ORDER," which is what he himself is enacting here, and his belief that the occasion and condition of poetry in our time (*ground* in two senses: "THE NEED TO GAIN GROUND") is the unreality of what in the last few centuries we have taken for the most significant aspects of reality. He shares with Rothenberg the feeling that a civilization is vanishing. "THE FEELING THAT SOME/THING LIES OUT THERE THAT WE CANNOT LAY HOLD OF IS THE FEELING OF THE INADEQUACY OF THE EXISTING ORDER." *And:* "IT IS THE DEMAND FOR A DIFFERENT ORDER."

Isn't this evident in the difference between the old and new poetries? Doesn't this measure the magnitude of the task? Nothing trivial here. Isn't this evident in *some/thing*, that repertoire of experiments, of formats and type sizes and typefaces? That gathering of "interesting" poets, among them Blackburn, Schwerner, MacLow, Wakoski, Owens, Enslin, Eshleman, Schneemann?

I do not find Antin in the anthologies of poetry or the anthologies of American literature, and anthologies tell us who's in and who's out. I do not find him in such accounts of the ground as Howard's or Vendler's. *American Literary Scholarship*, which cites only the issues of *Vort* and *Boundary 2*, tells of the general neglect. He was not admitted to *Parnassus*, and is curiously absent (considering some who are present) in the *Dictionary of Literary Biography*. Reviews of his work have been sparse, and the most substantial has been by Marjorie Perloff in the *New Republic* (5 March 1977). She also supplied the entry on Antin in *Contemporary Poets* (1980) and at the recent convention brought him to the attention of MLA.

14 March 1981

Perloff, incidentally, opens her review of *talking at the boundaries* by citing Antin's challenging remarks ("i had always had mixed feelings about being considered a poet   'if robert lowell is a poet i dont want to be a poet   if robert frost was a poet i dont want to be a poet   if socrates was a poet ill consider it'"). This is a good way in and defines him nicely, though the

seemingly casual throwaway nature of these remarks may also
be used to dismiss him. Come on! How can anyone (in his
right mind) say such things! In any case, Perloff begins at a
boundary—recognizes the boundary but doesn't cross it. Always a thorough scholar (she relies on the special issues of
Vort and *Boundary 2*), she seems to have missed the essay on
modernism and postmodernism in which Antin fully explains
the not unjustifiable reasons for placing himself in this way.
She also seems to have missed remarks equally provocative—
and undoubtedly playful, for he is nothing if not playful, and
playfulness is not accorded the seriousness due it, is not privileged, as we say—remarks such as "Williams is a total clod"
and "I've always loved Duncan because he's a fraudulent poet."
But the point is this: that Antin had clearly stated in 1972
what was at stake in his criticism of Lowell, and as far as I
know, none of the scholar-critics who have written on Lowell
has mentioned him, let alone tried to engage him.

("If we were talking about modern painting, you wouldn't
throw Burchfield & Grant Wood at me & expect a serious discussion."—Rothenberg to Spanos, in *Boundary 2*)

"The academic or literary mind fantasizes a cultish conspir-
acy behind what it doesn't understand, and it continues to demand critical data on its own terms. In doing so it tries to
convert the open to the closed, because it doesn't see that
open poetics is precise in a way that is fundamentally different
from closed poetics" (Quasha, in *Alcheringa*).

We *are* talking at the boundaries!

15 March
1981

"Anyone interested in the 'boundaries' of contemporary 'poetry' should begin by reading the heated exchange between
William Spanos and Robert Kroetsch, the editors of *Boundary*

2, as to whether 'what i am doing here' deserved publication."
Good advice. But why are *boundaries* and *poetry* set off in
quotes? This exchange, part of a three-way correspondence
that includes Antin, is serious and lively, and more lively than
heated, the heat arising mostly from Antin's resistance to
Spanos' advocacy of Heidegger. Perloff, whom I'm citing, sides
with Kroetsch's "conservative position" in respect to the "lack
of form" in Antin's talk poems. She dismisses Spanos' placement of Antin's work in the context of contemporary issues as
"surely extravagant" (earlier she questioned Antin's concern
with the visible form of the talk poems as "pretentious nonsense," questioned what in fact may first "trouble" us on opening the book). What is the conservative position? She cites
Kroetsch as arguing that "to write at all is somehow to create
art," that is, to select and thereby create a form, and that in
failing to do this, Antin's work is a poem (merely) of "pure
content." Can it be that the Olson-Creeley notion of form as
the extension of content has gone unheard? And Ginsberg's
"Mind is shapely"? Or that Perloff has forgotten Frank
O'Hara's distinction between *design* (look or format) and *form*
(interior structure, movement), and his remark that "where
design is weak, oddly enough, the form is usually strong and
may even be the reason why the design is weak"? (And didn't
O'Hara speak for a generation of poets when he said that poets
should not be "stifled" and poems should not be "prevented
from breathing"? A remark that reminds me that as early as
1944, Cage spoke of the *time arts*—dance, music, poetry—as
having the "life structure," the rhythmic structure, of the
breath, and that Antin in the *Occident* article says that modernism was *smothered* by the closed poetics of the New
Critics.)

So much for the rich content of *Boundary 2*, to which we
may turn if we heed her throwaway "but Spanos understands

what Antin is up to." She won't tell us. (See Lita Hornick's *David Antin/Debunker of the "Real"* for a good introductory, straight-out account.) And the equally rich issue of *Vort?* We learn only that David Bromige inevitably remarked the difference between the spoken poem and the printed poem; that this—does it compromise Antin's demonstration?—constitutes the "real problem" (not the problem of the "real"); that the printed talk poems bore her (does she hear them?); and, most important for her, that the talk poems (a performative art, remember) are "not . . . likely to serve as a useful model for other poets."

Model = Paradigm = FORM.

Much of the review is given over to an inspection and rehearsal of the poems, and Antin is shown, after all, to have a "principle of selection" and to have produced work with "orderly structure." It seems that though he works in "a wholly nontraditional way," he does the right thing, and so the fact that he has produced "one of the most challenging 'art works' of the mid-'70s" need not disturb us. It is comforting to know that this artwork "sounds as if Gertrude Stein had collaborated with Mark Twain." (According to what tradition, then, is he "non-traditional"? isn't the modernist tradition nontraditional? isn't the vernacular tradition nontraditional?) It wouldn't do to mention Cage, who is as much an influence as Stein, and who, with Stein, Antin considers "fundamental," more important to him than Pound and Williams.*

The desideratum of Perloff's criticism is form, about which Antin writes so tellingly in his essay on modernism and post-

---

*In *The Poetics of Indeterminacy*, published after this entry was written, Perloff writes of Cage and Antin.

modernism. Here he reminds us of the fact that the generation of poets preceding his own (the generation of Olson,
Duncan, Ginsberg, O'Hara) was neglected by the New Critics
and easily dismissed on formal grounds. He cites an essay of
Tate's, in 1968(!), in which Tate refers to the work of this generation of poets as "so-called poetry," an "anti-poetry, a para-
site on the body of positive poetry," and makes a last-ditch
stand against the barbarians ("primitives") in the open field by
insisting on "formal versification [as] the primary structure of
poetic order," where "poetic order," we know, stands for civilization (the civilization that is vanishing), for the Culture
that art would save from Anarchy.

When Perloff writes the entry for *Contemporary Poets* (1980),
she defends Antin's "extraordinary improvisations" against
the "hostility in establishment quarters." (Who in the establishment *cares*, has so greeted him?)* But form is still the
issue. "As scores of actual talks, these texts obviously lack
verse form: they do away not only with meter, but even with
the last stronghold of free verse—lineation"—an issue compounded now ("to make matters worse") by Antin's rejection
of lyric emotion. Yet, by using Frye, she is able to show that
Antin is "a perfectly traditional poet," albeit of a tradition not
now in repute. She claims that Antin is not a Romanticist,
but how does this square with his belief that by talking he
discovers a self, that utterance, as important to him as to
Whitman, is saying who you are, a song of the self? How does
this square with the acknowledgment of his "process-oriented
art"? It is true that Antin disavows song and emotion, but
though he lacks song, it would be foolish to think that he
lacks emotion. ("I'm hostile to the vocabulary of 'emotion'

*Harold Bloom. See the talk poem, "the search for the pres-
ent," Iowa City, 11 April 1981.

and its role in social discourse. It is almost always introduced as an alibi for something else.") "Definitions for Mendy," cited as an elegy by Perloff, is not an elegy and, in consequence of its attack on elegy, delivers an emotion more intense and truer (as Antin sees it) than elegiac emotion. This poem is excruciating because in it Antin recognizes the cracks in reality and refuses the comfort—and falsity—of elegiac form (conventions). Or isn't it rather that in the collision of language systems, he has opened the cracks in reality? Antin is a poet whose chief concern is with the truth of the case: of reality and feeling. As Rothenberg says, he wants to keep language and reality together.

The question Antin asks us to ask of him—the question Perloff avoids—involves his central concern, reality and its representation. He explains to Michael Davidson that

> I am very concerned with the 17th century form of the axiom that extends beyond art: *what is the domain of the human mind and its relation to the world*—which the 17th century framed as *what is the domain of human knowledge, its relation to truth* (the object of knowledge) *and what are the appropriate methods for discovering it, representing it and communicating it.* I think the difficulty in framing this question which was normally underestimated by 17th century science and never really approached by art—is the fundamental one. Any redefinition axiom I would want to aim into this predicament or difficulty. Therefore the Wittgenstein relation, the relation to Socratic dialectic, etc. I reject Kant out of hand as the victim of the language of human reality through poetry.* I claim all of that for poetry. I think we can only approach this problem by going back to the more basic language acts like "talk-

*See Antin's letter of 25 June 1981 for his correction of this misprinted statement.

ing" (it is not necessarily the only one but the one I'm trying—"asking," "formulating," "asking oneself," "explaining," "narrating"). My attraction to fundamental human genres is the extent of my "modernism"—like "telling a story," "asking a question," "giving directions," "trying to remember," etc.

if robert lowell is a poet i dont want to be a poet   This is a considered statement, backed by thorough knowledge of the situation in poetry, and intended to place Antin in respect to it. He made it in 1973, having recently published the essay on modernism and postmodernism in which Lowell figures as the representative of all that Antin rejects. It is a remarkable essay, recovering a tradition for allegiance, scoring a host of poets (a poetics and a sensibility), explaining the lack of attraction to the new poetry, and showing the ongoing direction, of advance. As I said, a position paper—and still needed, alas, at this late date! That may account for the stringent judgments, for the unremitting (unnecessary?) harshness—though this may·be a style of mind, the edge of a mind characteristically dialectical, and an act of mind not to be dismissed but to be acknowledged as such and encountered. Don't we take acts of thought—critical activity—too lightly? Haven't we forgotten what serious (nontrivial) intellectual engagement is? So, in its way, performative.

18 March 1981

Antin doesn't make a sharp distinction between modernism and postmodernism. For him postmodernism simply names the fact that modernism, once open to the fullness of experience, has become closed and that a new generation of poets, aware of this, is at work recovering and advancing its open possibilities. Antin's essays (this essay and the follow-up in *Occident*) belong with such notable learned reassessments of modernism as Duncan's in *The H.D. Book* and Rothenberg's in the interview in *Boundary 2*.

30 March 1981

The distinction is one of generations, and chiefly involves
what the second generation, that of Jarrell, Roethke, Schwartz,
Shapiro, and Lowell, made of the work of their elders, Pound,
Eliot, Williams, etc. "It was pathetic," Antin says elsewhere.
"A single lawn that covered America from suburb to suburb."
How modernism, mediated for them by Auden, was closed
(out) and, as Antin has it, ran out in Lowell, whose eminence,
of course, derived from being at the end of a line and so much
the exemplary poet of the New Criticism. Put it this way:
what Lowell did as a poet represents the critical diminish-
ment of modernism (chiefly) by Tate and Cleanth Brooks.
(There are several current assessments of this, *i.e.*, Grant
Webster's *The Republic of Letters*. By now the assessment has
the substantial weight of history, though it should be recognized that historical treatment is a way of killing off something that may be still alive—in the extremities, anyway.
Otherwise, why this vehemence?) Antin's treatment of Jarrell
and Lowell is devastating. It will be hard to reread these poets,
and their followers, and not be troubled by Antin's conviction
of their triviality, their intellectual shallowness.

Closed. By a formal concern for moral order (form as its signature) and by the reduction of "collage modernism" to irony,
"monodimensional contrast."

> This persistent tendency to project any feature from
> any plane of human experience onto a single moral axis
> is an underlying characteristic of the particular branch
> of "modernism" developed by Eliot, Tate and Brooks. It
> is not a characteristic of Pound or Williams, and it
> is why Eliot and Tate will lead to Lowell . . . , while
> Pound and Williams will lead to Rexroth, Zukofsky,
> Olson, Duncan, Creeley. . . .
>
> The effect . . . was largely to reduce the idea of complex
> poems to an idea of ironic poems, which is to reduce

the complex "hyperspace" of modernist collage (Pound, Williams, Olson, Zukofsky) to the nearly trivial, single-dimensional ironic and moral space of Eliot, Tate, Lowell, and so on. This is the reason for not recognizing Olson. It was the same reason for not recognizing Zukofsky. They do not occupy a trivial moral space.

According to Antin, this restricted poetry is also pornographic because it "offers neither intellectual nor emotional experience but a fantasy of controlled intensity." He goes on to exemplify this in Lowell's work, and blames not Lowell but "the decadence of the metrical-moral tradition." And this brings him to the crucial issue: "The idea of a metrics as a 'moral' or 'ideal' traditional order against which the 'emotional' human impulses of a poet struggle in the form of his real speech is a transparently trivial paradigm."

(See his "Notes For an Ultimate Prosody," the gist given in the epigraph: "The Contribution of Meter to the Sound Structure of Poetry is and has been Trivial.")

The form of his real speech. I think of Williams' preface to *The Wedge*. But this prefaces Antin's brilliant account of Olson's poetics ("Projective Verse") and practice ("As the Dead Prey Upon Us"), both of which figure here as the primary example of the recovery of poetic possibilities. Antin himself did not know of the *Black Mountain Review* and *Origin* until sometime around 1959–1960; Olson was not an early mentor. But here, in this history of traditions, he is fully acknowledged and generously given the prominence he deserves. "The appearance of Olson and the Black Mountain poets," he says, "was the beginning of the end for the Metaphysical Modernist tradition."

What does he consider important? That the recovery of collage modernism meant "a return to the semantic complexities of normal human discourse in the full 'hyperspace' of real language" and the end of those musical tendencies he dismisses as song ("'hurdy gurdy' music," the respective eloquence, "'dime store'" and "'general store,'" of Yeats and Frost, and "the mechanical organ of Dylan Thomas"). Olson went to school to Pound but goes beyond Pound, locating the music of poetry in the breath, "in the origins of human utterance." His expressivist poetics treats poetry as "well-formed utterance" ("an adequate traversal of the poet's various energy states") and recognizes the well-formedness of language itself, its manifold possibilities enabling poets to sustain long poems "with unerring, abundant and casual subtleties."

Isn't he describing the talk poems here, and again when he says of Olson's long poems that "the large curve of music subsumes without blurring many sequences of intricately various detail whose sequential relations form a large part of Olson's poetics"?

One thing more. Olson (and Duncan) shift "the whole emphasis [Pound's effort to recover the cultural heritage of poetry] into an attempt to recover the cultural heritage of humanity, 'The Human Universe.'"

31 March 1981   Antin's assessment of modernism is especially fine for the good reason that his allegiance from the start has been cosmopolitan. His earliest concerns had been with European poetry (he translated Breton and Apollinaire) and with anti-formalist philosophers like Heidegger. "I was all over the place," he says, "looking for a poetry with a serious engagement with the mind." This allegiance is evident everywhere in his essay, most conspicuously in his remarks on the provin-

cialism of Pound and Eliot and his citation of the truly modern work of Blaise Cendrars. It is not coincidental that the
Cendrars poem is not "carved" but a racy talk poem, an example of what Pound and Eliot, behind the times, were inca-
pable of recognizing: that their contemporaries in France were
trying to get out of "literature" and had found in Whitman
someone to lead them out. Antin, it seems, found Whitman in
France—a not unlikely place, considering the tutelage in poetry at American universities at this time. What this means
for a generation of poets is summarily stated: "American poetry had not had this kind of modernism since Whitman, and
the Pound-Eliot tradition does not contain it."

By putting Olson with Cendrars, Antin strikes up for international modernism. In his account of the various groups that
contributed to "the great explosion of American poetry" in
the 1960s (is there anything explosive now?)—in this account,
the differences between the Black Mountain, the Beat, and the
New York poets are of little importance. What matters is their
common schooling in European poetry, their cosmopolitan-
ism, the fact, as he remarks of the Beats (his account of the
establishment response to Ginsberg's work covers his own neglect), that "a major factor that separated the Beat Poets from
the Academic Poets was education, which the Beat Poets had
and the Academic Poets did not have." Even more, what matters is their "contempt for the trivial poetry of the last phase
of the 'closed verse' tradition and more significantly the underlying conviction that poetry was made by a man [or woman]
on his [or her] feet, talking."

This essay, clearly, is also personal history. When he wrote
it—in that year, anyway—he had published his first talk poem.
So he places himself in respect to Olson by noting that
though poetry now is enactment, an activity, it is not yet oral,

has not itself, as with him, become performance. If Lowell is at the end of a (played-out) line, Antin is at the advancing end of another: "literature" → the poem as notation or score (Olson, Ginsberg) → the oral poem (Antin).

When Antin entered the scene, the field had been opened, much had been recovered (and more would be recovered by his generation of poets). The concluding paragraph of his essay is both summary and prospectus. There is an agenda here. What he says of the oral poem proposes the issue of *Boundary 2* on the oral impulse in contemporary American poetry in which he figures with Rothenberg. With this, of most importance are matters of special concern to him: that "phenomenological reality is 'discovered' and 'constructed' by poets" (the Romantic metaphysic and epistemology still sustain poetry); that poetry is a representation of reality (Wittgenstein); that the aspiration of Romantic poetry, like his and that of his generation, is "to a poetry broad enough and deep enough to embody the universal human condition"; and that poets now are searching out the poetries of "non-literate and partially literate cultures" and reevaluating the genres (the work of *Alcheringa* and its successor, *New Wilderness Letter*).

The talk poems both exemplify and address these themes. They are examples of the "'exemplary' presentation" he speaks of in the essay in *Occident*.

1 April
1981

Considering these essays, which are rehearsals of Antin's education, prompts the thought that human beings themselves contribute much of the resistance to their own liberation. Modernism was (is) a movement of liberation—and didn't the aesthetics of liberation David Porter treats in his book on Emerson find its greatest achievement in lectures, lectures as much poems as Cage's, talk poems that bear some resem-

blance to Antin's? Don't forget the oral culture of the Tran-
scendentalist period, the predilection for conversation, lectures, oratory. Olson's *Reading at Berkeley* is not the first talk
poem, just one more example of the fact this partisan of
muthos recognized—that, to cite Tzara (cited by Antin),
"thought is made in the mouth," though Olson would not,
liké Antin, appreciate its applicability to Socrates! Everything
in Antin's account of modernism is directed toward liberation:
the rejection of arbitrary systems of representation and the
aesthetics of arrangement, the recovery of linguistic playfulness and the appreciation of "ordinary talk" as inclusive of
verse and prose. And in his work, ordinary talk (which we find
so extraordinary) is the means by which he enters the domain
of all human experience. The talk poems fulfill his demands;
in their open space he is permitted to say "a lot of things"
(what he has to say, so to speak) "in their full energy and
perspicuity."

Yet he came to the talk poems late. Because he resisted what
Olson calls the "lyrical interference of the individual as ego,"
what he himself speaks of as "the Romantic domain assumptions of psychological motivation of personal expression supposed to underlie construction." His work through 1971—
*Definitions, Autobiography, Code of Flag Behavior, Medita-
tions*—belongs with that of poets like Cage and MacLow who
give over to chance operations the once directive power of the
ego. Of course the improvisatory nature of the talk poems
allows for chance, though not the previous methodological
kind, or the kind one finds in Cage, which provides a fixed
structure. And what's to be noted, since even a lowercase *i* is
an ego, is that the ego is now present, though neither especially interfering nor lyrical.

The most significant omission in this account of education is
Duchamp, the master in the modernist generation to whom
Antin most readily turns and who becomes the subject of
articles and an early talk poem. You can read a great deal of
Antin in what he says of Duchamp, this "artist of the mind,"
given to provocation, whose work recalls us to "polemical art
. . . the work itself . . . an argument and a struggle for its
own existence in the teeth of fraud and taste." His remarks on
Duchamp's playfulness are also pertinent: "the word 'produced' is a curiously inappropriate term for Duchamp, as inappropriate as the word 'work.' For while labor may or may
not have been involved in any given 'piece' of Duchamp's, it
all seemed much less relevant than the idea of 'a piece being
offered' in a kind of uninsistent gambit. 'Play' instead of 'work'
and a 'game' instead of the seriousness of 'art.'" Chess, and
Duchamp "the Clausewitz of the '60s avantgarde." Of course,
what matters most to Antin are the tactics, Duchamp's stratagems, "stratagems involving complete systems that he puts
into some degree of disarray"—the collision of systems that
Antin himself practices, in "Stanzas," for example, where the
stanza takes the syllogistic form and, as Toby Olson says,
"speech force erodes logical force," and speech, which is primary, proves itself to be both more sensible and wiser.

All of Antin's work, as he says, "assaults" conventional form.
Don't the titles of his works name genres? Definition. Autobiography. Code. Meditation. Talking.

Take *Definitions* (1967). The title defines a primary activity, a
concern with language; and both title and format—a spiral
notebook, graph paper, typewriting, not a slim volume of
verse—suggest a "scientific" (cool) approach, concern for ob-
jectivity and precision. Incidentally, Duchamp used graph
paper for some of his writing on language, and in the talk poem

"duchamp and language," Antin considers the implications of definitions when he speaks of the fact that "a language does not consist of words" and that "dictionaries are not natural parts of language activity among human beings."

The three long poems of this volume treat loss, personal, then social, the enormity of the one continuous with that of the others, the Vietnam War, the murder of young men working for civil rights. He sums it up when he says that what he felt was more terrible than grief and that "the structure of the society in which the elegy belongs was not my society."

These are sound poems, best appreciated when read aloud according to the scoring. Their power resides in this necessity to speak, in the way single words and scientific statement are forced by this necessity to come into and contribute to the humanity of utterance. And in the way, as Donald Phelps observes, the "very mechanisms with which he pretends to affectless art—the computations of phrase, the repetitions—. . . admit that *music* which confirms his own emotional resource." Yes, Phelps reminds us at the start that though Antin defends against emotion, it does slip through, "as smoke through the interstices of all the hard words." And he characterizes this volume and much in the others when he says of this work that it "agonize[s] the heart by wringing the mind."

Of the three poems, I think "Definitions for Mendy" the most successful—that is, I like it best, appreciate what it does, and do not feel the tedium I do in the others, these in every way as interesting experimentally and perhaps utilizing tedium, as in Cage, for good reason.

Definitions assaults definition, and "Definitions for Mendy" assaults the elegy. Can you understand death by defining the word *death?* Even if "definitions" by definition are exact, unambiguous, direct—definite and definitive—it doesn't mean that they cover—are adequate to—experienced reality. Definitions aren't language, that is, the words defined in the dictionary have not yet found their human use, their occasion. By bringing words to their human use, Antin gives us a representation of reality.

The definitions of *loss* and of *value,* from which "Definitions for Mendy" unfolds,* come from an insurance handbook and Webster's dictionary. They have the neutrality of the words in Schwerner and Kaplan's *Domesday Dictionary.* They themselves are not *the* definition of *death,* though they help to define it. That is, *loss* is so general a case, and *value* so valuable, these definitions do apply. They enter the language system, and it is within this all-inclusive system that they help us define what especially needs defining: what it means to be human.

The poem is generated by Antin's overwhelming experience of the death of his friend—he is still powerfully moved, almost overcome when he recovers the poem's occasion in the *Vort* interview—and by his fierce determination to avoid the refuge of feeling and sentiment afforded by elegy, by a conventional form and image of reality. To assault the elegy is one way of showing us the cracks in reality, to represent the fact that reality is not confined to our representations of it. What is especially interesting is that the poem, as he explains, has meaning at stake, that he wrote it nearly eight years after Mendy's death because in all that time he was unable to "ap-

*Fugally, he told me, noting his study of music.

prehend" or find a way to "handle" it (*apprehend* is better
than *understand* because we never quite understand, that
is, attain congruence, and *apprehend* suggests that we must
handle this among the matters at hand). The poem, then,
arose not out of the desire to assuage grief but out of the need
to understand: to find death intelligible, and, if not, to acknowledge its unintelligibility. By virtue of his honesty, by
means of the poem's agitated movement and closure in the
"blinding light" of truth that leaves us in the darkness of
the unintelligible, the poem represents reality. Conventional
forms, like the elegy, take us "on bridges past the cracks in
the real," and he, as he says, "wanted to deal with cracks."

Yes, and open them. The languages of the poem—physics and
physical bodies, and ordinary human experience—collide, are
at their boundaries, all the while, as he says, "I kept trying
to find the answers through the language." The answers? The
truth. That death cracks our "realities" and exposes the real;
that loss (to redefine it) is of the nature of the real; what does
indeed occur when one experiences reality; and that language,
as it is used here (I think of Duchamp's windows when I read
"find the answers *through* the language"), is the activity that
helps us realize this.

Rereading *Autobiography* (1967) reminds me that a poem like   3 April
"Definitions for Mendy" is not as impersonal as it seems, that   1981
though we come to know Antin through his activity of mind,
the personal is included in the poem and may have generated
it. I am thinking especially of the verse paragraph in which he
tells of Mendy's visit and his mention of the concert—parts
of the poem that in the later talk poems would probably be
stories. I am thinking of his inappropriate and inadequate response to the news of Mendy's fatal sickness and the evident
importance of this experience in his rehearsal of it in the *Vort*

interview. Why do I think of it now? Because, beyond his belief that the personal in an autobiography resides in the way it
is told, in the structure of its representation of reality, there is
much that is personal in the forty-five disparate entries that
compose it. And: whatever the method, whatever the structure of representation, *he wants to tell his story*, and here, by
means of these narrative fragments, he is on the way to the
oral poetry of dis-closure, of self-discovery, he comes to in the
talk poems. It is true that he assaults the autobiographical
genre by denying its assumptions of narrative continuity and
continuity of the self. Fifteen pages or so, supplemented by
biographical and bibliographical notes, may be enough to tell
the story—essential autobiography?—of a man in his mid-
thirties, yet they make light of the genre.

The method is improvisatory and recalls Williams' *Kora in
Hell*, and, like Williams' work, it challenges our normal habits of reading, of making sense of what we read. Even so, we
look for connections, we piece things together, which may be
the reason Dick Higgins thinks it collage. And some things
seem to be insistent. The autobiography begins with the idea
of autobiography and crisis, and concerns crises: for example,
the childhood experience in which he became "suspicious and
gave up art" and a later episode in which he experiences his
unreality and, correlatively, an inability to feel. In one entry
he speaks of taking his glove off to think, and in another,
a mere snatch of speech about hunting, the "primitive" seems
to answer the need for contact, and for jeopardy and recovered
feeling. ("Primitive" = oral = contact with feelings and
things?) Moreover, the man depicted by means of these fragments is not especially attractive. He is easily bored and feels
pestered by others and is not very responsive; in a fragment of
conversation (is he overhearing the young woman whose sui-
cidal tendencies trouble him but whose erotic needs he over-

looks?), he is said to be selfish. He is critical of his remote-
ness and self-absorption, his cruelty ("I had to stop seeing her
because my face hurt from smiling"), his cleverness. Here,
when he tells of others' lives, it is to suggest how few openings we have, how little we know of the full range of human
life, to show how sentimental and easily ridiculed most human relations (profound needs) are, and to indicate the kind of
emotions and dependencies he'd avoid. He is also troubled by
the question—it seems to characterize a generation—of being
in the right place.

Creeley defines autobiography as life tracking life. Chronology may not be essential, just the tracks. Self is also the
reality of which autobiography is the representation. How do
you make a self out of all these fragments? Don't you do it, as
here, by writing, or, as later on, by talking? Doesn't the self
inhere in the activity? These are aspects of a self, and there
are more, always more. The self collects/is its experience, as
in Whitman? You go on talking?

Consider "Autobiography 2" in *Code of Flag Behavior* (1968).
Is an autobiography anything one remembers, only what one
remembers, to be defined by memory? By chance, by what one
remembers *now*, without the help of diaries, notebooks, etc.?
So we have autobiographies, versions of the self *in time*, sections, as it were, cut through, this specimen and that, this collage and that? Doesn't the form represent this, that one's autobiography is essentially here/now, always of the present
perspective? and always incomplete? Is the "true" form of
autobiography the absence of form, or the form our recollections take? The fragments here are not necessarily episodes of
Antin's own experience—I mean that much of what he remembers is the experience of others, their actions, not his.
What, then, is to be made of the fact that some episodes are

his and can be verified—like the recollection of the image of
his father in the bathroom and the business of gum and comic
strips, which figure in the talk poems?

You get some sense of the "narrator," how he realizes his "in-
consequentiality," his humor, his predilection for stories—and
his impulse to autobiography, which is something more, finally, than a desire to assault the form. He is looking for an
open space large enough to permit him to treat this essential
matter in his way, serially, one frame, so to speak, at a time.
And without embarrassment? Perhaps not. To make autobiography *interesting* again. Just as in the talk poems he would
make discourse interesting again; yes, make teaching and
lecturing interesting again by reminding us that their generative power, hence human value, resides in talk, talk as he exemplifies it.

12 April
1981

As he indeed (in fact) does. Did, at the conference here on the
avant-garde. I had always wondered at the monologist aspect
of the talk poems and his own remarks on not wanting to be
interrupted. But the talk he gave made me appreciate the fact
that its making was a response to—a dialogue with—all that
had occurred; it was quick with resonances of the (heady) occasion. This is not so readily evident on a tape, still less so in
the printed score, which, incidentally, I now see (say) is composed of utterances. He says in "Dialogue," a recent talk poem
which he gave me, that "we speak in utterances with little
tunes   not even sentences."

And "Dialogue," where dialogue is told pictorially by the
photographs that enclose the talk, addresses any misapprehen-
sion of the monological we might have. No one can meet Antin
without immediate engagement; he is not reserved. And not
reserved in the talk poems. He does, as he says, engage people

in these poems—and wins them by his exuberance. The talk
poems are dialogical not only because he provokes us (kindly,
with the generous burden of his deep human concern: they
are notably about people whose lives he shares in their
stories, stories of how they live, their lives, we find, having no
intentional course but only the waywardness of the way, this
accepted as the human condition and the condition of being
human. And human, we find, is not narrowly construed; his
stories are often about women). The talk poems are also dialogical because, in Buber's sense, he meets us. Reality—perhaps the poems represent this reality, too—reality, real living,
is meeting. The poems are relational events (Buber's phrase).
As Dick Higgins, who was there, says of exemplative art, "the
action is always between."

No one I know, except Duncan, is such a great talker. Are they
our Coleridges? And no one is so much one of those people
who, as Olson said of Apollonius (Olson), talks to live. "He
craved to talk, as any live man does, to get at things by talking
about them." Talking as discovery.

He is most alive in his talk? Yes, wholly present, rapt, like
Rothenberg later, chanting Amer-indian poems, himself a
"shaman." The experiences belong together because both were
relational events notable for generosity and energy, that generativity. Antin says in "Dialogue" of the stories he once collected that most of them were dead "because the tellers had
no energy to bring them to life and no special desire or need
to." Poems now, as Olson proposed in 1950, are often not only
energy-constructs ("the going energy of content toward its
form") but an energy-discharge ("a poem is energy transferred
from where the poet got it . . . by way of the poem itself to
. . . the reader"). And we do not (or do we?) need to be reminded that the "secret of a poem's energy" is speech ("speech

is the 'solid' of verse"), and that drama, "all act," as Olson says, springs from the "place where breath comes from."

Olson notes that a poet's energy will have several causations. Isn't one, for Antin, the dialogue already under way before the talk poem begins, and the dialogue that actually continues as he speaks, the evident fact that at least some of the energy he gives back is ours—taken from the audience itself? And isn't another causation the special desire or need to tell his story? The autobiographical impulse is narrative. We want to tell a story, not, as he says in "Dialogue," merely to give an account of something but "to bring the present to the past   and let that past unfold there as the present between the two of you listener and teller as it is unfolding." Bring the present to the past? Isn't it usually the past to the present? We bring the present to the past when we bring our concern, when we speak of it, when, as he says, we *let that past unfold there.* The talk poems are not only dialectical, working in terms of polar words (*i.e., professional* and *amateur*); they work by *unfolding,* and what they unfold are stories. Does this unfolding permit him to return to a meadow, the "eternal pasture folded in all thought" (Duncan)? Isn't the autobiographical impulse of the talk poems prompted by the desire to return, to make present a past life? How can he speak of *unfold* and not recall Whitman, who said, "What a history [his story] is folded inward and inward again in the single word I"? Hence, in meditation, as Olson said, you go round and round the subject (*subject!*); you unpeel the onion or, projectively, turn the inside out.

The present is also a gift; narrative is a human transaction in which "people try to exchange realities." Like the distressed woman in "talking fit," he wants to tell his story (stories) in order to make sense of his life—and ours. Isn't the beautiful human transaction that confirms Antin in "Dialogue" the exchange between David and the goldsmith whose story exemplifies the meaning of *friend*? *"hello david,"* his story begins, *"this is yakov."*

Life stories are not life studies. Though he is "a personal poet," he is quick to add, "the most impersonal of personal poets." His stories are most often other peoples' stories. He is not a confessional poet: he doesn't privilege sickness (so easily done in a therapeutic society) and he isn't locked within his own subjectivity, where the experience of confessional poets is gathered and (again) privileged, so that other peoples' stories are no longer their own, but appropriations by the poet. For confessional poets, one might say, as Buber says of Heidegger, "'existence' is monological," and thus understand better why Antin is dialogical. Why Yakov's story is italicized.

I cannot read "Dialogue," which treats the words *professional* and *amateur*, without the insistent recollection of Williams' "The Desert Music," where Williams rehearses in making a poem (and in order to make it and to continue making poems) much of his essential autobiography. Writing to live—to affirm "I *am* a poet! I / am." In "Dialogue"—and who shall say under what necessity, though it seems exigent—Antin affirms his *vocation* or *calling*. Like his friend Walter, who gives up studying for the ministry, he carries on not only the dialogue of Christianity ("the collision of the idea of christ and the idea of jesus") but several of the many dialogues of our culture. Like Walter, he is not a *professional* ("a profession assumes a world you want to continue"), and, in not being one, he ministers to the culture. He stands with the poets of culture, with Whitman, Pound, Williams, Eliot, H.D., Olson,

Duncan, Ginsberg. And doesn't he offer us, as some of them do, an ontological possibility?

By chance, in leafing through *The Poetics of The New American Poetry*, I come on Stein, who, in addressing narration, reminds us that in the beginning (and the beginning of talking), there was no difference between poetry and prose: "in poetry they tried to say what they knew as they knew it." She is speaking of the way it is in the Old Testament.

14 April
1981

Of course there are professional poets. (If so-and-so is a professional poet, I don't want to be one.) At the conference on the avant-garde, the avant-garde was distinguished from the decadent and/or academic. It might also have been distinguished from the professional, not so much because it gets so little money as because it wants neither the world as it is nor the literature that represents (accepts) it to continue.

some/thing is (was) avant-garde, uniting formal (antiformal) experiment and politics—not ideology so much as resistance and the will to change. The title of the last issue (why did it close?) is "A Vietnam Assemblage." This names both concerns. See the note: "in a special sense it is a communal effort—an overall structure made up of words, a language trap to close-with a state, a process, a system—something afflicting & evading all of us." Assemblage as communal. I like that. It reminds me of what Rothenberg says of the "collective" voice in *Code of Flag Behavior* and *Meditations*.

Now isn't *Code of Flag Behavior* a single-handed assemblage directed to a similar end? Why entitle the book after a poem made up of literal instructions from the code of flag behavior if not to put the code as he deploys it (in a found poem) in col-

lision with itself? To undermine at the same time as he pro-
claims a sacred patriotism ("always aloft and free"). To remind
us in "burning" (which calls up Vietnam) that when the flag
is no longer fit for use it should be destroyed in a dignified
way. To remind us that when flown "with the union down," as
he flies it, it is a sign of distress. Elsewhere he considers allegory as figurative replacement, as a way of re-moving, distanc-
ing things ("say that it is an allegory and that the sunlight was
a memory of a glass of water"—so much for having stated the
case in "Definitions for Mendy"); now he exploits the code,
our symbolic sense of the flag.

Did anyone in the 1960s consider Antin a political poet, and
this book an exemplary text? "the marchers," a collage that
visually represents the marchers and their signs in a fairly
solid block of words and wonderfully alters/repeats many of
its components to make an appropriate music, was probably
not taken seriously. The line that frames the poem also underscores the profound reason for such protest marches: "by walking together   they will not feel   all alone." The sympathy
here seems critical, the poet himself at a distance from the
event. His representation is also humorous, sadly so, like Jewish humor: "ALL YOU NEED TO MAKE LOVE   IS THE
LOVERS." There is a series of syntactically parallel statements involving THE PLAYERS, THE JOYFUL, THE WORK-
ERS, PEOPLE, so that in response to what's needed, there is
this little gathering that makes a ritual, as the poem does, too.
Representation of reality? What is rendered here is the very
genesis of protest marches ("ALL YOU NEED TO MAKE
PROTEST   IS PEOPLE")—the inevitable genesis of politics in
human need, politics as a human activity, however sad and in-
effectual in the drizzle at dusk. And just as important, politics—or, better, protest? speech?—as a human activity con-

tinuous with, inseparable from, other human activities. This is dramatized in "the london march" (*Talking*), where Antin and Ely, his wife, play cards, hoping in this way to ensure or encourage the success of an anti-Vietnam protest march thousands of miles away, their commitment clear enough but, as the game goes on, entangled in much besides, in the mesh of their "personal" lives.

The fact that politics, and so much so in our time, is (of) our daily lives may, for some readers, diminish its importance, especially so as presented here, in "cool," experimental forms. But this, I think, is the distinction of the book and a distinction of Antin's work, which is not political in such obviously recognizable, demonstrable forms as Baraka's, or even Dorn's and Duncan's, but political throughout, politics caught up everywhere in its rich and various human texture, in this way made significant. Take "a list of the delusions of the insane," which soon enough destroys our immunity by calling up much that is not delusional ("that children are burning") and by rendering our own secret, or not so secret, fear of apocalyptic conflagration and "suicide of the soul." Or "who are my friends," which may pretend to simplicity or naïveté, but, even so, in its play on President Johnson's "we must help our frehnds in veetnaehm," works to the fact of foes in Washington; gets there in the circuitous way of the talk poems, with stories too, and—it is worth noting—with much that reminds us of Ginsberg, a poet whom Antin (rightly) admires. Or "W. S. Male": is this characterization an intelligence report? Or "history," which, like some other poems here, puts languages in collision, puts in question the concept of history by reducing history to a chronological list of assassinations, cataclysms, disappearances, the lines of the poem for the most part headlines, history now news of this kind, significant matters, like "a school burned in little rock," swamped in the flow of events.

Doesn't this poem thereby represent reality, give us our
history?

Even the subsequent sections of the book contribute to the
overall sense of politics by reflecting much of our culture in
its fragments. (Lita Hornick says that Antin attacks "the
whole sphere of civilized culture.") In the context of this
book, "Autobiography 2" offers us the testimony of another
(questionable) form of history, and that organized in terms of a
no longer stable, continuous self, a self itself composed of/in-
formed by, among other things, recollections of what others
have said of the Bolsheviks, the Spanish civil war, the Nazis,
the Korean War, Sputnik, Vietnam. The last section, "novel
poem," is a poem that is indeed novel, its eleven chapters
having been composed of materials taken from novels quickly
flipped through. These novel poems, as Antin says, "are first
derivative novels" and "characterize the inflections of the novels they're derivatives of." The poem is novel, of course, in
making light of novelistic narrative continuity. It gives us the
gist of novels and lets us have the novelistic pleasure of imaginatively filling them out. It is also parodic. Nevertheless,
since novels depict social life, the poem reminds us of the
various textures of human life of which politics is a part. Notable here is the juxtaposition of a chapter on the decadence
of the international set and a chapter that rehearses a Dr.
Strangelove situation. Also a "concluding" chapter, parodying
Hemingway's style and attitudes, yet an anecdote of life as
it is:

> 'we'll take a chance' said the man
> 'we'll take a chance' said Andrei
> 'as long as one can walk' said Andrei
> 'one walks' said the man
> then the man fell

20 April
1981

Meditations (1971). In the plural because there are many, of various kinds. The book is not like the others, unusual in format, and its quiet appearance and gray cover are appropriate. I think immediately of Charles Altieri's reservations about the talk poems, having recently received, through the kindness of the editor, an issue of *Par Rapport* on postmodernism: "I tend to want more focus and to base my admiration precisely on traditional notions of meditative poetry which he wants to call into question." Now the meditative poems of this book— and the talk poems—may be untraditional, but in their way they involve us in customary meditative concerns, bring us to them with renewed interest. Antin is a moralist (so is Cage), and he may be experimental for the good reason that nothing is so difficult in our time as to credibly speak moral truth. To attend and speak such truth is one of the eminently *human* things to which he devotes his work. His work bears out Olson's remark that life is preoccupation with itself—that we are concerned with our lives. Were it not for the fact that the talk poems belong to a trajectory of experiment and, accordingly, propose and demonstrate a disturbing poetics, would we find them anything but the brilliant talk of a poet deeply moved to speech by his awareness of our human predicaments? Isn't that their accomplishment? And among the boundaries he talks at, don't we find—though it is easy to distinguish his work from them—those of such popular moral appeal as soap opera and stand-up comedy? Which is only another way of showing us what talk is about. Surely a man who named his son Blaise did so for the good reason that he admired *both* Cendrars and Pascal. Some of the meditations are *pensées*.

The meditative act in *Meditations* involves language, is essentially an act of attention to words. Kerouac would say that

they are the jewel center. "The meditative act, as I was defining it in the work," Antin says, "was to respond to those
givens [arbitrary word sets, for example], work with them, because the world is full of such givens and I was reenacting the
sense of this givenness." Nothing new in such practice, as he
knows, citing the practice of MacLow and Wakoski. Nothing
new, not even such practice put to such meditative use—used
because, as he says of "The Separation Meditations," he wanted
to meditate upon the war ("the place I was coming from was
an intense feeling about this war. There was no way of talking
about it").

I am impressed most by "scenario for a beginning meditation," "Stanzas," and "The Separation Meditations." The "scenario," which opens the book, reminds us that meditation is
interior *talking*, self-dialogue to the end of self-discovery. The
scenario for a *beginning meditation* is also one for *beginning
a meditation*. This involves the problem posed by "supposing
you think of your life / where does it begin?" where *it* refers
to both life and meditation, to the fact that it is hard to begin
meditating on one's life because one's life has long been under
way and also one's thought about it, which is connected with
yet different from the decisive act of *beginning* to write one's
thoughts, make that beginning. How interruptive of the deep
continuum of being is the wide spacing (duration) between utterances! This makes us realize how factitious beginning is
and also belongs with the fact that in disturbing the self to interrogate it, we talk to ourselves, create an other. The occasion is sufficiently disturbing to suggest the dark night of the
soul. And in a special sense it may be said to locate the beginning of the talk poems. Antin is already talking here and talking about such insistences as the right time and place for beginning (that is, entering on self-aware present life: "i wanted

to begin for a long time") and the difficulty of doing this hon-
estly. Moreover, our realization of the excruciating loneliness
of such self-preoccupation makes us appreciate the way in
which Antin goes on to ameliorate it in the talk poems, not
only by talking of private concerns in a public place (this nullifies the separation of private and public), but by proposing
marriage as an essential public place, realizing in this relation
("its impossible to speak a language alone") the assurance of a
common language. (See *talking at the boundaries*, 228.)

21 April   Some of the entries in the first section propose "Stanzas"—
1981   "consideration 3," for example:

> 1. it was interesting
> 2. it was also practical

These are not mutually exclusive declarations and, as *also*
tells us, may be accommodated by both/and. So we become
aware of our habits (forms) of thought and their systematic nature; habits of thought (rationality) of which "Stanzas" is the
reductio ad absurdum.

The syllogism is a tristich. There are ninety-five such stanzas
involving repetition and variation, some bearing out the as-
sertions, others denying them or concluding with silly, ridiculous, or nonsensical statements. Logic, obviously, is not
foolproof. The poetry of repetition and variation is Steinesque;
it also resides in the native linguistic and experiential prover-
bial wisdom (in sum: humanity) with which we test the claims
of logic. The stanzas deny either/or, exclusive categories of
thought, and they are especially telling because some, while
hypothetical, are burdened by history:

> all Germans are white men
> all civilized men are white
> all Germans are civilized
> *(#73)*

if they need food we will give them money
they do not need food
we give them money
        (#76)

Repetition in "Stanzas" promotes expectation and prompts
shock: deconstructs. But in "The Separation Meditations,"
repetition augments the chance operation and educes truths
that seem to be inherent in language itself. One of the entries
reads: "I WOULD RATHER BELIEVE ALL THE FABLES OF
THE LEGEND THE TALMUD AND THE ALCORAN THAN
THAT THIS UNIVERSAL FRAME IS WITHOUT A MIND."

Are they "Separation Meditations" because he wished to separate himself from the war? stand over against it? Wanting to
meditate on the war, he found a model in Epictetus, a "well
educated Hellenistic slave" who had a "strong sense of his inability to force anything on the world," yet "a fierce quality
in his gentleness and concern." (The characterization establishes an identity.) Then, using as givens the footnotes to a
nineteenth-century edition of this Stoic philosopher, he
worked rapidly through the text and chose phrases that caught
his attention—did this thirteen times and composed thirteen
meditations. (Not finding this edition, I am unable to "repeat"
the experiment.)

These meditations begin with the enabling discovery of how
to begin: "The places where you are now." And one essential
of meditation soon emerges: "The notion is of a man returning to himself or turning his attention to his true self." This
is shortly followed by "That there is a spiritual relation between them." Later on, another round produces

    1. which is divine
    2. that we will put our highest self
    3. in our world.

There are also such telling finds as

    1. authority
    2. tyrants
    3. a ravine into which corpses were thrown

and

    1. the truth is
    2. of many alternatives
    3. only a corner
    4. where a fact happens to stand

These meditations take various forms, some numbered and in caps, others in a somewhat stanzaic form, or in run-on lists, the last in prose paragraphs—each in its way putting lines in association or freeing them for multiphasic association. All contribute to the sense of a world of system and totalitarian violence, where one is under the necessity to maintain oneself, hold out, escape. And they have an incremental power, as, for example, the variously repeated "you perform the acts fitting and appropriate" or such singly placed words as "love" and "spirit." There are many Antin takes—"who is unskilled in the art of living," "get a grasp on reality," "go beyond the accepted code," "discover what forces / are good and evil," "there is no real contradiction."

In its entirety the book might take an epigraph from the last meditation: "Reality suggests an acrobatic feat."

22 April 1981   "The November Exercises" that opens *Talking* (1972) belongs with the previous books. The daily improvisations were prompted by picking phrases from a book written to instruct foreigners in English. Antin says that he had in mind the example of Rothko—each page is a canvas—but that he improved on Rothko by adding time markings to indicate the "casualness." These markings add little, I think, because they

intermit reading—the *instanter* Olson talks about. Improvisation, of course, reminds me of Kandinsky—is this work a matter of inner necessity?—and of Williams' *Kora in Hell.* Williams (after Stein) might very well have written the entry for Saturday, November 21:

> (1:25 AM) In Canada there's plenty of snow.
> In Canada there are many lakes.
> Here is her raincoat. Here are
> her rubbers. There's no space for
> the box. There are four windows
> in the room. There's only one
> apple on the table. There are
> others in the bag. Here's my
> paper. Here are my answers.
> There's not enough bread
> for toast. There are no eggs in
> the refrigerator. Here are two
> nickels on the sofa. Here's a
> fine situation.

I think of Williams, too, because Antin knows that this journal is not the usual kind and he calls the entries "exercises," thinking, he says, of "the whole meaning of daily exercises."

Inner necessity? The entries are not uncharacteristic and touch many of his bases. At the start, one retells the anecdote of Yung Kiang and Hung Mung and thereby acknowledges Cage, whose work comes to mind later in the controlled improvisations for two voices. At the end—the journal doesn't run the entire month—the entry picks up an insistence of other work, that of driving a car, only to employ it here as a representation of reality:

> Before the automobile has noticed it's
> carrying a beginner it's out on the
> roadway. The instruction book gives
> a false impression of a real
> picture. Everything you expected to

> handle with patient acceptance is now
> speeded up and scattered. Relax,
> hold onto the steering wheel and
> pretend that you're driving.

This, though inimitably Antin, recalls Williams' "To Elsie":

> No one
> to witness
> and adjust, no one to drive the car

Talking is a book of improvisations, moving from the interior voice of "The November Exercises" through the controlled improvisations of the tri-logue/dialogue of "in place of a lecture: 3 musics for 2 voices" and "the london march" to the single, public voice of "talking at pomona," the first talk poem (a found poem in its way, since he recognized it, or Ely did, as a poem after the fact) and a wholly improvisatory work. The book may be said to chart the difficult work of turning the mind inside out in a poem (I cite Williams, in *Kora in Hell*), the projective need to come into the open. Now Antin forgoes chance operations or Cage-like controls, the fixed formal structures within which Cage seems to be able to work freely and happily. He has put himself in the open and, as Olson says, "can go by no track other than the one under hand declares, for itself." Now form is (only) the extension of content. Now chance is risk, the ever-present risk of the ongoing proceeding. Now, yes, *now* is where he wants to be, in the present, the present to which so much modern and postmodern art aspires, "the exact moment," Williams says, "that he is."

Writing is a present, and so is talking. And talking—fittingly participial—keeps the present present, which is as long (to answer the question of another recent talk poem, "how long is the present?") as the talking itself, and as intensely a present as the moment when he amputated his finger in the door of his van and his "present erupted." Talking, which he enjoys ("im not worried about what im going to say at all   im a talking animal and i have things on my mind   and i will have no trouble saying what i want to say")—talking is a pleasant jeopardy that puts him fully in touch with himself and the world (his audience, other).

Puts him in jeopardy but not always pleasantly? Doesn't this account for the brief and unsatisfactory talk poem at the Los Angeles Book Fair? Wasn't that present too dismal and too long? Doesn't this account for the prologue that accompanies it, and for his concern with discourse groups ("it is impossible to discourse with anyone you believe to be fundamentally other")?

Inside (private) out (public). He fulfills a social need. Isn't this represented by the cover photographs, 35mm filmstrips of urban/suburban San Diego, that enclose all this talking? That's the ambience, the context of his life, as in Creeley's *Contexts of Poetry.*

"in place of a lecture: 3 musics for 2 voices." What would the lecture have been about? The inhumanity of science, of any system concerned only with itself, whose abstractions discount the fullness of experience? This performance piece is charming and reminds me of the routines of Elaine May and Mike Nichols. It enacts the way we con-verse, how dialogue, in its waywardness, advances, humanizes a situation by imaginatively filling it out; how talking does indeed get us somewhere, is a human activity because of its seemingly irrelevant questionings and digressions. The score—the voices are in different typefaces—suggests the way each of us is limited by a script, by an (almost) inviolable subjectivity; but there are

moments when the scripts intersect, when talking breaks the boundaries.

This is also the case in "the london march," which, as the talk goes on ("i was just talking"), recovers the 1950s as the depressing background of the present ineffective activism. 1950s: the background of *talking at the boundaries.*

Speaking of *Talking.* Barry Alpert notes that "Antin always displays an ego wrestling with an intellectual and emotional problem, rather than the ego's struggle to eliminate itself and to come into as close a relation to nature as humanly possible." Is he a poet of society more than a poet of cosmos? Is his human universe primarily social because he early discovered cracks in reality?

"I find a great excitement in art. I mean the thing about poetry is that it's a kind of . . . war . . . over reality. I know it can have many other aspects, but it's often a struggle over reality. It may be an attempt to infiltrate, encircle, or acquire or construct—a reality."

Poetry is also a way (in every sense) of discovering the self. And at the same time isn't oral poetry—oral (open) poetry over against written (closed) poetry—a way into the world, as Rothenberg says, a way to participate in the world, not master it?

"I want to know 'how it stands with the world,' not the *spiritual* world, or not *especially* the 'spiritual world.' Because it was in that trip that came to a divide at that place that we lost too much world."

Talk poems. Antin's inevitable form.   24 April
                                                        1981

"O. [oral] poetry long played an integral role in the life of human beings and social communities; its practice provided that
spiritual activity necessary to man's [and woman's] existence;
its bonds with everyday life were manifold and close" (*Prince-
ton Encyclopedia of Poetry and Poetics*, 593).

> progress
> is beginning   ("Man is, He acts."—Olson)
> man's activity
>
> even if the description is a delusion
> it is worth
> while
>
> for the value
> he wishes to speak
> stands in the world
>   *   *   *
>
> take what comes
> what is given
> is used
>
> the extreme
> is used
>
> express
> its sense
>   *   *   *
>
> words
> in the ceremony of manumission
>   ("*5th separation meditation*")

In this meditation I am reminded by

> the central mind
> seems out of place

of Rothenberg's "The Dreamers," dedicated to Antin. It concerns the powers hidden in language that "the action of the

poem brings . . . to light"; how the "deva in us" is a "divus
(deus)," and David sounds like deva, this poet who

> forces them out of the one mind
> in mything
> mouthing the grains of language

Myth/muthos. Jane Harrison: "A *mythos* to the Greek was
primarily just a thing spoken, uttered by the *mouth.*" I take
this from Olson, *The Special View of History,* where he reminds us that both *muthos* and *logos* mean "what is said,"
and that the poet, the *muthologos,* undertakes "the practice of
life as story." I note that in the margin I had written *Antin.*

And he, of course, knows Olson's definition, though he doesn't
mention Olson in "what am i doing here?," the initial talk
poem of *talking at the boundaries* (1976). The title of the
talk should not be misread as a question about his presence
here (he's in the right place); it directs us to his talking, to the
mything/mouthing he is doing here. In the course of running
through the meaning of *myth,* he mentions Duncan, who,
it seems, omitted the telling definition of *myth* as talk. Yet
Duncan knows it ("sweet muthos   our mouth's telling") and
cites Jane Harrison in the etymologies that preface *The Truth
& Life of Myth,* the title, incidentally, having some bearing on
Antin's concern with the ways in which our stories may be
said to be true. Olson connected *muthos* with a historio-
graphical concern for facts: he wanted to know the facts of the
case, "how it stands with the world."

Duncan cites another definition that applies to Antin's story-
telling: "myth is the truth of the fact." How our stories *represent* the case, not necessarily the scientific "truth" but, as in
the instance of Candy, essential history (as Aristotle defines
poetry), "the structure of her life . . . the existence that she

lived." How our stories *fit*—and sometimes by fitting imperil our lives, as he explains in "talking fit."

You can see how *myth/muthos* generates later talks, how this very talking is his way of "thinking into and among important things"; for example, how, having said that talking preceded writing, he will eventually spell out the differences between oral and literal cultures (in the fuller account of what he is doing here in "the sociology of art").

The talks are seamless: episodes in a discourse without boundaries, or whose boundaries are known only when talking/thinking discovers them and then talks *at* and/or *against* them. The form of the talks—and the context he provides for them in the book—suggests that there is no beginning or end to talk, that though his personal discourse has limits and may, in fact, be wrong, it is part and parcel of the endless discourse by means of which humanity tries to say itself. And there is no need to impose form: talk itself creates coherence.

Doubly performative: a poet speaking, demonstrating his declarations, enacting his ideas.

> I want to restore the idea of the centrality of speech genres or discourse genres to any human poetics.
>
> *   *   *
>
> In a monologue . . . you're conducting a discourse.
>
> *   *   *
>
> I assume that in all language acts there is always an other, even when it is only the self alone.
>   (*"Talking To Discover"*)

26 April
1981

"Ignatow is much too framed a poet for me to identify with fully . . . I am . . . moving away from that conscious framing.

The only framing I will allow is the framing that the attentive
mind produces by its intensive concentration on the task at
hand—and I will also insist on allowing all that looseness that
there is before the intensity finds its path or rises from discovering that there is a path, where before it was just walking and is now walking somewhere. That's why I'm glad you
[William Spanos] had so strong a take on the American voice.
Implausible as it may seem I feel a strong identity with Twain
and Kerouac and Whitman, without their lyricism maybe [yes:
maybe], and without the folksiness, but I was never plain
folks, nor are my neighbors [yes: he's a conceptual poet who
by talking keeps in touch with life]."

>   ill tell you a story about this   i mean its
>   not like i needed this story   because
>   i could have gone on in the other direction
>   but i wanted to come around the edge and
>   i remembered this story

In talking straight ahead—"not after the establishment,"
Williams says, "but speaking straight ahead. I would gladly
have traded what I have tried to say, for what came off my
tongue, naturally"—he talks roundabout. Verse, he notes in
an essay on Duchamp, comes from *vertere*, to turn, and is
"turned talk."

In "Radical Coherency" (1981) he addresses the development
of his work, from *Meditations* to the talk poems, in terms of
organizing principles. The early work employs collage, takes
pieces of language out of the matrix of continuous discourse
and reassembles them. This, he says, gave him pleasure, though
he was dissatisfied to find that his knowledge of the sources
did not make him what he likes to be, his own best audience.
It is evident that in the talk poems he has himself produced
continuous discourse and for the reason that the example of

the collage organization of a Sears shopping center makes
clear: that such "simultaneous incoherent coherency" is not,
as he finds when he takes his mother shopping, necessarily
pleasant. He hilariously describes the Sears store—he is as
conversant with brand names as with the various termi-
nologies of linguistics, mathematics, physics, cybernetics, art,
literature, and philosophy—but his recognition of its order
is not apprehended by his mother, who is unfamiliar with
such places, doesn't know how to read them and move about
in them. Her disorientation, furthered by aging, is sad enough,
as anyone who has taken such filial excursions knows, and
this proposes what now concerns him: "the kinds of coherency that develop sometimes rather startlingly   out of the
way the human mind works as it faces the exigencies of everyday life." The example of this, which closes the talk at a still
deeper depth, is the *story* of his grandmother's dying in which
he formulates the radical (root) coherency, the sense (the context) of his grandmother's incoherent words, that, if acted on,
would, he believes, have saved her life.

"When people are very old, and there is the consciousness of
death coming upon them," Creeley says in "Inside Out," "a
very marked impulse to tell what their lives have been occurs.
. . . The grandfathers, and grandmothers, are the great story
tellers—and in societies alert to that human need they are of
course so used." But not only the old:

> I am telling you a
> story to let myself
> think about it.

And I'm talking it, not writing it, because I need, I respond to
the urgency of speech (see "and ive called this talk tuning"),
and my talk represents the way the human mind works as it
faces exigencies. In "real estate," he says that the "natural

habitat" of poets is performance and "in performance improvisation has always been   a response to some very specific set of urgencies."

What continues in Antin's work is improvisation, the desire to acknowledge the instant in the choice of possibilities (to "get on with it, keep moving, keep in, speed, the nerves, their speed, the perceptions, theirs, the acts, the split second acts, the whole business, keep it moving as fast as you can."— Olson). He wants to arrive not at the foreknown but the new, and to arrive there rapidly. Improvisation is a way of talking at the boundaries.

27 April 1981   *Boundaries.* So many of them. Margins, which are not justified and he refuses to justify ("the word forms / on the left: you must / stand in line. Speech / is as swift as synapse."— Olson, "ABCs"). Forms, molds, containers, frames, meter, etc. ("I would strip my poetry of every characteristic that could be taken as a formal consideration.") Closed systems and "mechanical truth" (*i.e.*, "science is its own enterprise   its such a closed world"). Between art and life ("a painted border   there is this ambiguity about where the painting ends and the world begins"). Between people, between cultures, between systems ("A door without a wall is ridiculous" and a wall without a door? "I was trying to open something"). An interface. A window. The edge, where he acknowledges both sides. The edge, and the "dialectic with life and the moment": Emerson's onward way, beyond the circumference; Williams' unbound thinking; Duncan's Whiteheadian primordial ("the characteristic of an artist is the gift of being ready to do something for which youre not prepared"). Etc. Etc.

> (there is always a field,
> for the strong there is always

an alternative)
        (*Olson, "In Cold Hell, In Thicket"*)

When Bateson considers boundaries, he's most concerned
to question "inside" and "outside" in respect to the self.
("i wanted to talk not to myself and thats why i came
out   out?   what was i in that i came out of?") "Relationship," Bateson says, "is not internal to the single person."

Talking and walking (Heidegger), picked up and demonstrated
in a letter to Spanos: "I can imagine my impulse to speak, to
move through language to some formulation, to some new
place as being like a kind of walk." The kind of walk for which
the walking instructions of an oral culture rather than the
map of a literal culture provide an example. The kind of movement within space of which a *periplum* is the record

        periplum, not as land looks on a map
        but as sea bord seen by men sailing
                (*Pound, Canto LIX*)

What Olson means by mapping as metric; and walking in the
world, as Williams has it, and as these walkers do it, by "foot
travel" (Antin's mode of thinking/talking), to discover, make it
new. "I'm really looking for the right situation for discovery
and invention," Antin says, "and I'm more interested in looking and discovering than in convincing or explaining."

Discovering, among other things (among things), the self.
That is certainly an insistence of *talking at the boundaries,*
and "Talking To Discover" (in *Alcheringa*) names it: "The invention of the self is an outcome of talking to discover, the
outcome of a discourse genre." Or, as the "10th separation
meditation" puts it:

> occasionally
> he speaks
> to possess his soul.

Why? Because "the self is a preliterate society   because it doesnt proceed by writing   and it has no absolute repository of any past event   . . . it has only the memory   which is a way of proceeding and not a treasure trove." Memory. Mnemosyne: mother of the Muses, forgotten in the "patriarchal poetry" (Stein's phrase) of literalism? "Story," as Duncan says, "Herself a mother of sorts"? So, in §V of *Song of Myself*, by remembering, by telling a story, Whitman re-discovers what elsewhere he calls "the divinity of the mouth"—discovers (and isn't this why speech is the twin of his vision?) the profundity of utterance, how, as Olson says of the projective poet, he goes "down through the workings of his own throat to that place where breath comes from, where breath has its beginnings." So Antin remembers, tells stories—for more than entertaining anecdotal reasons. And remarks on the fact that speech is inalienable ("it would be funny to hear me talking like a poet with an english accent").

George Economou summarizes this aspect of the talk poems as well as anyone has:

> Antin—seems to be autobiographical and personal in exactly the ways Rothenberg is not. The *Talking* poems . . . confront us with a man interested in, defying us to prove his talking is not poetry. He talks about artists and the art world, the university, poetry, trips related to those activities and institutions, he satirizes, analyzes, applies mathematical theory to life-experience, he recollects, and more recently talks about marriage, the death of friends [and still more recently, childhood and family], but all the time he is really talking about himself, as a person and as poet, because to think is to talk

is to make poetry. This "talking" is finally an act of intense self-definition and because it is a personal act performed in public it breaks down the public-private barrier [boundary] and arouses not embarrassment but fellow-feeling.

Fellow-feeling, like Whitman, and why both are not confessional poets, and why he confirms again, as Whitman had, the authenticity of the personal.

That's Creeley's phrase in praise of Whitman, and I think of Creeley because in the following I also hear his agitation.

> who speaks for me when i speak?   do i
> have a quorum?   im here in this public place talking in
>   the context of some old friends some new ones and
>   people who have come here with expectations
> maybe of what a poet is   you know?
>   what a poet will do   what hell talk
>   about   and i come here with my
>   private thing so to speak   and i tell
>   you im here to define myself and im
>   telling you who i am and what im doing
> it for

Such talk is notable for its animation. To use Olson's distinctions, it is "language as the act of the instant" not "as the act of thought about the instant." So, as Antin says when he takes up the matter of form in "the sociology of art," you don't halt, you don't stop the action to interrogate it, you don't "convert the act of meaning into the object of meaning." And form—if you must use a notion he finds "stupid"—is nothing but the extension of content. And shapely, as Ginsberg says thought is, because discourse forms itself.

29 April
1981

And isn't it all, finally, a matter of energy, the work, "measured out in energy" (where measure isn't meter), itself a "high energy-construct" (Olson), the "organized energy" Antin speaks of, energy that the work transfers?

Energeia. Think of Wilhelm von Humboldt's introduction to the study of the Kwai (Javanese) language: "Language is not a work (*ergon*) but an activity (*energeia*)." And the sentence prior to this: "writing is only an incomplete mummified depository which needs, for full understanding, an imaginative oral reconstitution." Animated speech! Following von Humboldt's account of language as "the ever-repetitive work of the spirit," Jerry [Gerald Bruns] summarizes: "Language is not an artifact of the spirit but the very form in which the life of the spirit is realized."

"I suppose I take that ongoing impulse, von Humboldt's generative force of language, to be the center of poetry. And because I think we've gotten too far from the center, too far from the generative force of discourse as it forms itself in the mouth and mind, I'm willing to give up just about everything else to get it" (Antin to Spanos).

Speech itself is poetry, not the vehicle *for* poetry.

The talk poems are not only poems of an occasion they themselves are the occasion ("some action taken in some place"):

> come in   come in   this is nothing
> terribly formal and what poem there is
> will be built about whatever happens

They are, to use Rothenberg's term (adapted from Whitehead?) "language events," irreducible poems-in-process. Their form, as Duncan says of Whitman's, is an organic, evolving form of "the ever flowing, ever Self-creative ground of a process."

It is tempting to think of them, as Antin seems to, as "sacred bundles"—perhaps because this reminds me of Olson's notion of the poem as *conjecture*, things thrown together. Collage? Rothenberg considers his work (say, in *Poland/1931*) collage, and in some respects, in the way he keeps it going, it may be considered a *lineated* talk poem. But Antin rejects the notion of collage because "everything here [in the talk poems] seems less disjunctive than fluid." Yes, fluidity is their hallmark, and not since Whitman have we had a poetry so fluid. "I want the flow of talk." So he does away with punctuation, paragraphing, lineation. Such notation is "too precisely conceived for real human discourse"—just as meters were both too simple in their scoring and too restrictive for Whitman.

He may disagree with Snyder over song, but what of Vāk, or Sarasvati, "the flowing one," goddess of poetry?

The talk poems restore the primacy of speech and demonstrate some of the things that enable us to live in a human universe. As the titles of some of them tell us, there is the need to be (in the) present, in the here/now of one's occasion; to live one's life now and not, as Thoreau would say, postpone it. We are always in the right place; it is always the right time. And we can have our lives by contacting them, by talking about them.

2 May
1981

This also involves the decisive matter of vocation, how we stand in respect to professionalism and money and commoditization (of art, for example, which is as much the target of Antin's catharsis of concepts as science, medicine, or linguistics). In his demonstration the artist is the exemplary person, one whose vocation is to risk the open, attend the particulars of the moment, and find the way without recourse to maps. He is like the potter in an oral culture, who makes things of communal use not by consulting a prototype but by following a way of proceeding. Think of how Antin proceeds, warms up, works in, elaborates, closes (form as proceeding); how he goes by feel, follows the impulse; how the work is always different but always recognizably his.

This is not to be estranged, as Olson cites Heraclitus to tell us we have been, from the familiar world. This is not to be done out of the world by Idealism. "what theyve done [the literalists who make maps] is to isolate a space   outside of the one theyre in   they have in some sense to alienate themselves and their world   which they have always been inside of." Literalism comes with writing, with the desire for transcendence, the wish to place "meaning outside of mind," and the "career of literalism" is the history of Western thought, begun when Plato wrote down, fixed forever, what Socrates spoke. Literalism is the "disease of mind" (MIND). Antin turns from it, turns back to the preliterate (oral), because literalism is authoritarian, denies freedom. Literate societies, he says, are rigid and inflexible; oral societies are changing and fluid.

How much is at stake in telling stories! No wonder postmodern poets appreciate oral cultures! The story—as we have it in Antin—is the acme of openness, the correlative of this fluidity, his representation of reality. Where the map spatializes, the story temporalizes. "a 'story' is never present all at once   its beginning and end cant be surveyed at the same time   so that it never has the isolated and bounded content of a drawing or map."

Talking is beyond boundaries—and boundless.

And the matter of freedom is crucial. Lita Hornick says of Antin's work, "There emerges a belief in a fluid continuum, which is life, and which had best be as little regulated and as little deformed as possible." Consider this in respect to the self. What better example of the kind of fit the artist resists in literal societies than the marine in "talking at the boundaries"—this young man confronted by so many of the crises, the life decisions treated in the talk poems; this young man so representative of a generation of students, who can't find the right place, whose "life had no form" and who entered the marines in order to give it a "shape." "what he knew [Antin says] was that he had taken the matter of his life   grey amorphous and soft as an oyster   but still pulsating   ticking with life   and placed it in some other hands   so that they would put it into some kind of container that would shape it for him   hold it together   this ticking thing."

Isn't the military (as you should know) preeminently patriarchal? Duncan says that evil is *over us,* is coercion, denies our volition, the very pulse and impulse to be obeyed in poetry.

Had the marine talked more, as he talked to Antin, would he have decided to yield his life? See Tillie Olsen's *Silences.*

Antin attends to exigencies of this profoundly vital kind. He knows that the self whose liberation is essential (talk is self-originative) is soft and vulnerable. He makes no exorbitant claims for the self. I can't recall any story in which the life history (I say "history" to exclude the instance of Gene, the artist who had not postponed his life) fulfills the paradigm of "happiness." But unsatisfactory as life may be in these literal terms, he still insists on our right to *lead it,* on the humanity his own talking represents.

This is because there is no truth with which our lives are congruent, only the truths of our individual perspectives, the truth that belongs to our viewpoints and relates to our lives. This is also why he maintains that we cannot understand each other—stand in another's place—and must settle for "tuning" and "translating." He names our difficulty—and our desire to confirm "humanness"—the "count of monte cristo paradigm." Our truths, moreover, are never wholly reliable, no more reliable than memory, are as various as our selves. Pragmatic, not correspondential, they do not fit "reality." Our stories are *our* stories. This humbles us.

Antin is a critic of the mind and its limited instruments, as anyone who would open poetry must be. He is only one of a number of poets who question the career of literalism. When I think of the matter of freedom in respect to societies and history, I think especially of Dorn because *Recollections of Gran Apachería* rehearses the conflict of literal and oral cultures. See the cartoon cover drawing where the American male consumer astride a cow seeks guidance in the desert landscape with a roadmap. In Dorn's account of the destruction of the Apaches, the "primitive" (which Antin replaces with "oral") is overwhelmed by the "civilized," by a way of thought the Apaches cannot *understand.* The mything way of mind is overcome by the predictive mind. Dorn notes its work of "frag mentation," its rejections and constraints. And its political bearing:

> They were by Mind overcome,
> I have a mind
> is the highest mutation of force

There is a great deal at stake in all this talk and reason enough
for some people to feel threatened by it. Antin's talks are as
functional as arrows, and sincere arrows, he notes, get right to
the point. But even so, and even though he, too, roadtests the
language and engages in the poetry of thought (*dianoia*), he is
not Dorn. For the good reason that he stands within not outside the society he criticizes and never forgets the playfulness
of utterance. His mode is comic, in Kenneth Burke's sense: inclusive (both/and), tolerant, ameliorative, communal. The
comedy, moreover, is often at his own expense.

Though his intent is often pedagogical (and this, as Olson
would have it, may also define the epical nature of his work),
when he talks we do not become sick and tired, as Whitman
said on hearing the learn'd astronomer, nor do we wish to
wander off alone into the mystical moist night air.

Gertrude Stein says in *Narration*: "You are always listening to
some one to something and you are always telling something
to some one or to any one. That is life the way it is lived."

I thought I was done when I left for the woods, but the first
letter of the season, from George [Butterick], prompts me to
write this entry. In an earlier letter, George had defended
the omission of Antin from the revised edition of *The New
American Poetry* he is editing with Donald Allen. Now, as always helpful in forwarding my work, he sends me an Antin
talk poem and adds another paragraph to our argument:

> He sure is on the right track: the primacy of story. I
> mean the guy's irrepressible. Imagine him in the CCNY
> cafeteria, circa 1952. But: Is it Poetry? Need it be called
> such? Can't we reserve the term for something more
> formal (says the exponent of polymorphism!)?

I don't want the last word and this isn't the last, by any means. *Is it Poetry?* It is *poetry*, lowercase *p*, and less *formal*, or form-ridden, than the privileged uppercase variety. How hard it is to come into the open, to cling to the advance, as Williams said. How much talk is still needed at the boundaries!

Ever since Emerson, whose lectures on all accounts are his *poetry*, American poetry has tried to get beyond fixity and determinism, to destroy arbitrary boundaries, in order to release the energy and impulse of creation and restore the self's place *in* the world. It has questioned both the sovereignty of mind and the closure of the universe, demanded an ever-greater inclusivity ("the common and low"), and favored an art of individual experience, witness, and truth. It has sometimes been performative. It has respected speech. I can imagine Emerson, whose trial as a poet was so severe, listening appreciatively to Antin in the CCNY cafeteria, gladdened again by the advent of another New York poet.

From David Antin
25 June 1981

> Certainly I have never underestimated my work. But valuing it—taking it as seriously (and lightly) as I do— I still do not expect anyone to give it the kind of attention that it probably rewards, if it does not require, mainly because it seems that circumstances of contemporary criticism do not encourage this kind of attention to the living. On the other hand, I don't really feel specially neglected either, or perhaps I just don't feel alone in critical neglect. Who of us in the real world is not neglected by the critics who write in most of the journals? And would I want to be attended to by the critics passionately concerned with John Hollander, James Merrill or Louise Gluck. I am not surprised to be ignored by that world, which I ignore in turn. But I am a little surprised by George Butterick and Donald Allen.

I would have supposed that they might have overcome
the habits of their own taste in the interest of the
boldness that they are usually attracted to. I suppose
I am not really anthologizeable—not easy to select
pieces from—. Charles Altieri, doing a piece on the
contemporary poetry scene . . . explained that he
couldn't deal with me because I was so difficult to ex-
cerpt. But then the poets he succeeds in excerpting are
not the poets I would want to be seen with in public.
. . . Still, I am not Louis Zukofsky, and I will not, like
him, complain of how Oscar Williams, an old school
friend of his from Columbia days, kept promising to
put him in one of those dreadful little anthologies, perhaps next to William Carlos Williams' *Yachts*, those
dismal little books of the 50's relieved only by the wonderful schoolgirl picture of Emily Dickinson and the
furry bearded Walt. After all, no one remembers the
poets who filled those awful collections, and Zukofsky,
read by Creeley, Ginsberg, Levertov and Duncan, is
available from the University of California Press for
anyone who needs him. I suppose one shouldn't under-
estimate the value of the miserable distribution system
that determines the mythology of literary history found
in the schools and the textbooks and the *N.Y. Times
Book Review*. It is probably the only large-scale distribution system there is, but it can only distribute whatever is sufficiently banal or scaled down to fit easily
within its openings. You can't send a grand piano
through the postal system. And I figure I take my
chances being the kind of poet I am. If I'm a guerrilla
leader I can hardly expect a repressive government to
appoint me to a ministry.
    In detail—some things come to mind. I've always
been embarrassed by a typographical error in *Vort* in
the letter to Michael Davidson, where I am speaking
of my rejection of Kant. What the letter really said was:

> I reject Kant out of hand as the victim of the language genre
> of analysis and I am gunning for a dialectic of knowledge of
> human reality through poetry.

You ask, perhaps rhetorically, if I was ever considered a "political poet" in the 60's. And the answer is a qualified yes, if you take account of the readings of the time—that is, the political performance arena of the time. Some people surely thought of me that way. Walter Lowenfels for one. He was to have included "trip through a landscape" in a political anthology he was producing, but I wouldn't let him cut the third section, which was truly and deliberately too long. "Code of Flag Behavior" was read at readings within the context of the debate about "flag burning" around 1965, and on several occasions—specifically political ones—nearly produced a riot. "the black plague" and "code of flag behavior" were also performed at readings in a political context—one in particular the "three penny poets—reading against the war" in the old Fillmore East. After I read them, a great bear of a man in a double breasted suit rushed up on the stage to embrace me. He was, he said, the correspondent from *Pravda* and would translate them into Russian if I would give him a copy. Somewhere in Russia, perhaps in the library of a Siberian jail, or in somebody's attic, there is an old copy of *Definitions*. If I had the time I could under the Freedom of Information Act write to find out if the FBI had records of my appearance in *Pravda*. I've often thought of adding it to my curriculum vitae, if in fact I was there. Who knows. If it appeared in *Pravda*, it might have been reprinted in Belgrade, Bratislava, Cracow. I might have to have a whole East European file for my early poems. But most importantly, I'd love to read myself in Russian and Polish. I can hardly imagine how I would translate. By now I'm used to my sound in French. But the Slavic languages defy my imagination. —In all seriousness, or as much as is decent, you are right that my way of being a political poet is somewhat different from Ginsberg's or Dorn's or Baraka's. It is more thoroughly interwoven with the everyday fabric of human experience. Which doesn't make me any less serious about my position as a social or political poet. And I have recently had cause to be deeply irritated to see the political context drained from my work by critics coming too late to the arena to know the necessary background. In *The Rhetoric of the Contemporary Lyric*, there is a glib account of "code of flag behavior" as a pleasant little "found poem", the main interest of which is its presentation of prose material as simulated verse. Makes me sound like Ron Gross (remember him—the advertising man's pop poet). While I don't expect anything of people who write for the *Georgia Review*, I was really irritated by the piece.

I very much enjoyed your reading of "novel poem," which usually doesn't get looked at too closely by friends or foes. Incidentally, the little poem with the "Hemingway tone" was derived from an immense Ayn Rand novel *Atlas Shrugged*—you see what may be concealed by continuity. And W. S. Male was taken from a sociological case history. In view of the involvement of some of our social scientists with the military community, I think your comment about the intelligence report is close to the mark.

Probably the only things I don't really understand—an odd word as we know—are your takes on "how long is the present" and your reading of Marjorie Perloff's *New Republic* review. About "how long is the present"—I surely don't require everyone to share my feelings about all my pieces, but for me it is an important piece. The book fair was, to be sure, an alienated place, but peppered with friends. And it seemed somehow symptomatically strange for me—an oral poet—to talk at a book fair among "authors." To represent at a house of text the possibility of poetry as talking, going there to make it happen then. The setting was for me provocative, the audience an unknown. And I came in just in time to hear Michael Davidson read a poem addressed to me about the ambiguities of writing and talking in the two careers of Plato and Socrates, whose work we only know in Plato's text. And I realized then that I may have created, inadvertently, for many poets a kind of anxiety, as if by the possibility of my success—the success of my project—talking poetry—I was pre-empting their ground, obliging them to give up writing for some kind of talking. So I, who am never a simple moralist, wanted to try to clarify to my friends how personal my requirement was to find the present in my work. How long I have been haunted by a desire for the present, how writing seemed to keep me from it. And I began to explore the ambiguous, somewhat absurd and perhaps painful requirements of presentness. Maybe this piece is too long, maybe tortuous, but it is something of an analog for the frustrations involved in trying to find the point of the present. And here I wanted to address the present on its own terms—the point of conscious attention to the here and now. And it turns out to be this ludicrously painful thing, intermittently absorbing and elusive, continually slipping away, in spite of all attempts to focus on it, into past and future. If the piece doesn't feel that way, it may not work, but somehow for me it is important, and I am, I guess, stuck with it.

The other question I had was about your reading of the Perloff review. I see where you have different interests and approaches. She tends to move toward how the pieces fit together rather than what they do. And this is a real difference I wouldn't minimize. But I think sometimes you may be mistaking what are merely tactics on her part for her point of view. Tactics that can be explained by the context of her writing. For example, I don't think she agrees for a moment with Robert Kroetsch's assessment of the works as boring or lacking form. I think she merely entertains the notion to answer such criticism on its own terms—that there are principles of selection, that there is an organization imposed by the mind . . . etc. . . . For myself, I am not very much concerned with defending the propriety of formal organization in my work. I have a functionalist view of organization in part—the efficiency of the arrow. And a representational view of it in part. That is, style framed as a marking of values, social categories, modes . . . in this sense it is "representational" rather than "an extension of content," and I suppose it is my background in "pop art," that analytical bracketing

art that suggests this allusive use of it. I could cite
Duchamp here too. —But there is also the use of
framed styles to mark categories in a shorthand kind
of way. To cite "techno talk" "folksiness" "Romanism"
"old World" "new York" "black rap" etc. I thought my
treatment of walking in "sociology of art" was addressed to that. That's not "form as the extension of
content" it's form as "representation," as I see it.

From Marjorie Perloff
23 July 1981

I think we really do agree largely on David Antin. . . .
I think you somewhat misunderstand my essays on
David. If I took a formalist position, it's not at all because I agree with Robert Kroetsch, but because I feel,
practically speaking, that I have to defend David on the
grounds others are attacking. You have no idea what
hostility he arouses. When I gave a talk . . . at the
Folger Symposium on Contemporary Poetry last year,
Harold Bloom, Richard Howard, John Hollander, and
Donald Davie were dismayed at my even having the
nerve to talk about someone as awful as Antin. The
conference organizer, a former student of mine named
Liam Rector, phoned me a few weeks later and said,
"Well, after all, Marjorie, that stuff just isn't poetry!"
And he's a bright young guy who writes good poetry
himself. And has read a lot.

When I defended Antin in the *PN Review* . . . the
editors have repeatedly used Antin as their whipping
boy and made sarcastic remarks about this silly talk
etc. etc.

For a long time I couldn't understand why Antin
made people so mad. After all, he's a very genial fellow
and, even if they weren't crazy about him—why the anger? I think it is largely caused by two things (1) the refusal to write standard free verse; and (2) the absence of
"emotion" in any confessional sense. . . . People find
him cold, too "intellectual," too abstract. And I mean
people who may well love, say, Olson.

So it has been my sense to try to stay with the form problem precisely because ultimately that's what others are objecting to—no form.

From David Antin
14 October 1981

About Cid's [Cid Corman's] take on "oral poetry," I'm not really in a very good position to enlighten you. I know I had been moving toward my talk pieces around 1968 or so. When I came out here that Spring, I had sort of promised the Institute of Contemporary Art in Boston, where I had worked as a curator the year before, that I would do a series of "sort-of lectures" that they could put on cassette machines for the enlightenment and amusement of visitors to their galleries. They ran out of money around that time, however, and it happened, at just about the same time, I got a call from Dan Graham, the conceptual artist, that he was putting together an "information theory issue" for *Aspen* magazine. He asked me for something and I promised a piece, having in mind what I had been sketching out for the ICA "lectures." The work I sent him turned out to be *3 musics for 2 voices*—the controlled improvisation for me and Eleanor on experiment structure in science and the problems of discovery. *Aspen*, as usual, was delayed in coming out, but finally appeared with my piece printed as a microminiature pamphlet designed by maniacal Fluxus friend George Maciunas, and was reprinted in my Kulchur book *Talking*, that didn't come out till fall, 1972. I went on that same year—1968—to do another controlled improvisation with Eleanor—*the london march*, and both tapes were performed (played) for an audience at St. Marks in the Bowerie in I think late 1968 or early 1969. So you can see that basically my conception of oral poetry—which I didn't call oral poetry or anything else at the time, had much more to do with the talking, with discourse and a kind of lecture-like framework. I then moved into the pieces built on obligatory word lists—to offer some kind of

obstacle to the flow of my talk—that resulted in the
poems published in "meditations." This work was completed by the fall of 1969 but publication by Black Sparrow (as usual) was delayed a whole year, and the book
appeared in 1971.

As I see it the first really clear talk poem came in late
1970, when I was invited by Dore Ashton to be part of
a series of speculative lectures to be given at Cooper
Union and subsequently published under the title Cri-
tiques. For this "lecture" I prepared a set of notes on in-
dex cards dealing with medical diagnosis of diabetes,
the development of molecular theory, the course of Im-
pressionist Painting and avant garde sculpture. When I
got there I never referred to these notes; I simply talked
the piece—called "The Metaphysics of Expectation or
the Real Meaning of Genre." The piece was so long—
over two hours in talking—that I never finished preparing it—and I missed Dore's publication date. So the
piece sat and sits as a resource drawn from and can-
nibalized conceptually in other works I have done since
then. But it was "talking at pomona," the talk piece I
did in early 1971—around April, I think, that was the
first piece I knew was a talk "poem," or rather I found it
out from Ely, as the two of us listened to it together on
the drive back from Pomona to Solana Beach. It was, I
believe, shortly after this that Cid came to UCSD as Re-
gents Lecturer that Spring. While he was here he gave a
couple of readings, which I attended. In the course of
some conversation he mentioned doing these tape recorder poems some years ago in Paris. He had had an
old wire recorder and he wanted to try composing directly on it. So late at night in his small room that was
not much bigger than a broom closet, when there was
no noise to interfere with the recording, he had read—
or spoken—in a hushed voice lyrical passages onto the
machine. I was interested to hear what they were like
and asked if he could play them for us. Apparently he
had transferred the older recordings to conventional
reel to reel, and he played them for us at a subsequent
reading. As I remember they were quite odd, the hushed

voice, the insistent lyricism, the conscious awareness
that this was an utterance for no present audience, created a very strained performance that I believe most of
the audience found somewhat embarrassing, though
some were strongly impressed by the lyricism. Myself,
I was mainly interested in the peculiar dislocation of
speech from its occasion—from the situation of speech.
I found the lyricism unpleasant, but attributed the un-
pleasantness to the dislocated situation, and I was willing to regard its lyrical awkwardness as an outcome of
the situation rather than a reflection on Cid's capabili-
ties. The awkwardness seemed to me to result from a
profound lack of judgment of the dramatics of the situation he had accidentally created. I never really dis-
cussed any of this with him, and I'm sure he had no
idea what aspect of the work interested me; but it must
have been quite clear to him that I was interested in
what he had done. . . . The performance of those isolated, strained, improvised lyrical pieces did mean
something to me—in the way they confirmed my interest in the necessity of discourse for poetry. So—coming
the long way round—yes, Cid affected me, but not in
the way he seems to think.

Photo by Becky Cohen

II. Founding

JEROME ROTHENBERG

Husk and kernel. It begins here, with *White Sun Black Sun*   1 September
(1960). The seed-book.   1981

The title gives us the contraries. Primary terms, not either/or,
but both/and, their boundaries blurred, dialectical, toward the
unity of experience, "into inter-everything." Primary terms
of creation:

> I form the light & create darkness
> I make peace & create evil
> I Yahveh do all these things
>   (epigraph, *A Big Jewish Book*)

Poesis is Creation.

Such a black book! Its signature might be Harry Crosby's
"Photoheliograph," that concrete poem, a square of heavy
black *black*(s) enclosing an equally black *SUN*. (Rothenberg
reprints it in *America a Prophecy* and *Revolution of the Word*.)
How little relieved by joy and brightness; limited, too, in respect to fullness or inclusivity, since there is no bawdy, no
comedy, no presence of Coyote. These limitations indicate the
direction of Rothenberg's growth, toward "joy bright with
sexuality."

A young man's book. He has been to postwar Germany, courtesy of the army; has translated, in *New Young German Poets*,

the poems of the poets of "the generation that's come of age over the ruins of Hitler's psychotic Reich" and who, having survived to sing, are "quick to sense the darkness." Like the young men in Creeley's poem, he knows "the darkness sur / rounds us," knows the weather of our age. This bitter book of translations establishes the large context of Rothenberg's politics.

And much besides. See Antin's review in *Chelsea*, where he places these poets over against the established older poets, the Beats, and "Black Mountain's desert saints" and defines what is central by calling Paul Celan a poet of the deep image. His expert scrutiny of prosodic elements explains the reason (along with the "dark tone") why he considers Rothenberg "an American Celan, who is harder, clearer and more musical than the German."

The landscape of *White Sun Black Sun*, even where New York City is suggested, belongs to no place. If it did, it would be Europe more than America. The vision of these poems is one of threat by soldiers and atom bomb. The sense of loss, of the precariousness and transience of the humanly precious, of powerlessness in the face of ever-present death arises from the extremity of the political situation. From the start, Rothenberg is concerned with the revolution of the word as a revolutionary word that will deliver us from this darkness.

His political animus? There is, for example, "Seeing Leni Riefenstahl's TRIUMPH OF THE WILL," which names Hitler and does not, I think, bear out Hans Magnus Enzensberger's belief that to do so violates poetry—though I understand the loathing that prompts him to say it does, and his need to keep poetry undefiled (though not unpolitical) as a means of resistance. Rothenberg, in other poems, speaks of "the president"

but doesn't name him, not out of respect for Enzensberger's
stricture but because of his concern for the deep image. He
says that he had Eisenhower in mind.

In this poem the fact, told imagistically in other poems ("The
moon was a spider"), is told without deep images because the
actuality of Riefenstahl's images, projected on the screen, belong to the order of phantasmagoria (history is nightmare) and
are coextensive with dream. The prosody of the poem is cine-
matic, a series of takes. But the film itself is a retake: "Again
the curtained armies start out again the barriers shudder."
This is to say that it is now history and, as the inconclusive
poem reminds us, history that continues, thereby involving
us, compelling identification.

> HITLER IST DEUTSCHLAND I am the child
> in the furnace the rotting feet of the
> German soldier cry out with my pain
> the tanks roll blindly through Russia
> And the eye of some Jew my mother's
> brother and son glares without end
> in the whiteness covering Poland

The enormity of our time—Isaac Rosenfeld called it *an age of
enormity,* the time of terror, when the concentration camp
becomes the model institution and good and evil are no longer
adequate moral terms—finds its focus in that glaring eye and
in the transvaluation of whiteness. That eye awakens guilt
as vast as the frozen landscape. That icy waste figures the absence of love as much as in Crane's "North Labrador."

This line ends but doesn't close the poem. What it asks of us
is the political *and* poetical burden of Rothenberg's work.

Of what, after all, would a shaman heal us? I think of Buber: 2 September
"If man had simply to live in the good, then there would be no   1981

work of man. That work is: to make the broken world whole."
I think of Enzensberger's great poem "Sommergedict," where
he cites Lao-tse: "was noch nicht da ist / auf das muss man
wirken" (one should work upon that which does not yet exist).

The real work, as Gary Snyder says. I think of him because
Rothenberg does. Not then, but now, in the first issue of *New
Wilderness Letter.* In the editorial statement he joins Antin
and Snyder, using Breton as a link. From Antin, he takes a definition of *poesis:* "those linguistic acts of invention & discovery through which the mind explores the transformational
powers of language & discovers & invents the world & itself."
This fundamental work of mind is "sacred action" (Breton),
what Snyder, himself so much an explorer of consciousness,
defines as "the real work of modern man: to uncover the inner
structure & actual boundaries of the mind."

Rothenberg recalls that Duncan, having read the poem on the
Riefenstahl film, suggested to him that he turn to and not away
from his Jewish identity. Why? Was his essential autobiography as well as the essential myth of our time to be found
there? This "Jewish poem," as Rothenberg now considers it,
already proposes *Poland/1931.*

Politics is black, where love is white, as in another poem of this
time, "A Bodhisattva Undoes Hell": "the white sun / carries
love / into the world." But in this book, love is powerless,
though the book itself may not be ("Write the poem / The
image / unlocks Hell"). The deep image of greatest moment is
that of the spider-moon in "The Moon Was a Spider," a political poem preceding the Riefenstahl poem. In conjunction
with earlier poems of cosmic abandonment, this may account
for "The Madman on the Roof," a madman who is easily
placed in the world of *Howl* but, here, is angry not antic, pro-

voked by cosmic absurdity and lack of cosmic generativity
(the sea-egg and the sun). He protests the lack of creativity in
a time of death.

Cosmic abandonment. The initial poem, "'A Little Boy
Lost,'" takes its title and substance from Blake: "The night
was dark, no father was there." And there isn't, as with Blake,
a companion poem, "The Little Boy Found," where the little
boy, led by God-the-Father, is found by his mother. More than
any other poem, this one names and polarizes white sun and
black sun in terms of good and evil. Perhaps because a child
tells it, and tells of innocence violated (which is also the case
of the flowers in "Invincible Flowers"). The child has been
taken from the white sun and left in the black sun. This image gathers his experience of homelessness, horror, and dread.
An extreme experience like Crane's in "The Tunnel"; more
extreme than Ginsberg's in "A Meaningless Institution"; more
like Mandelstam's, in the poem in *A Big Jewish Book*, where,
on the death of his mother, the poet says, "I woke in my
cradle, / lit by the glow of a black sun." The *child* speaks for
the poet's primary self and the initial estrangement of life, for
an inalienable sense of things subsequent events awaken and
nothing will wholly redeem. He also speaks for the depth and
naturalness of apprehension in images. In this poem we enter
the world of deep images with the simplest, the most natural
and common, recalling how images whose resonances we may
have forgotten were once adequate to express our psyches. As
much as abandonment, this addresses the lost child in all of
us. We are lost because we've overlooked (sight and insight are
in question) the depth of our images.

I think he begins with this poem because, as he says of the
dream with which he begins *A Big Jewish Book*, it is "central
to my life, an event & mystery that dogged me from the start."

Black and white, danger and death, figure in both, tallied in
the latter instance by the lines from the Aztec Florentine
Codex he had cited in *some/thing:*

> It is deep—a difficult, a dangerous
> place, a deathly place. It is dark, it
> is light. It is an abyss.

The dominant sense in his first book is of a "dark traveler"
who journeys from "darkness to darkness" and shares the fate
he ascribes to all of us when he says, "We love and we die
in dark rooms." Yet in his dream the darkness is beyond the
room and he is compelled to name it (*naming* is a primary
creative act) in order to open and enter it. He names it *Creation*, which, in fact, is what *White Sun Black Sun* names.
Though the book is dark, the darkness is also creative ground
(hence possibility), and in writing the book, Rothenberg has
made good such possibility—*answered to it.* So the darkness
that surrounds us is also what Antin, in "The First Black," a
deep image poem he wrote at this time, considered the origin.
"The sun and moon," he says, "are the signs of its clemency."

3 September   One of the black suns in the cover drawing has a white center
1981   to remind us not only of contraries (Buber: "According to the
logical conception of truth only one of two contraries can be
true, but in the reality of life as one lives it they are inseparable") but of the Kabbalistic-Hasidic notion, central to Buber,
of husk and kernel, which variously figures the hidden life
deep images reveal, the sparks of divinity to be discovered and
gathered, the union of God and the Shekinah, and the seed of
creation.

Death sharpens his sense of life. As in "When I Think We Will
All Be Dead," this is often associated with his wife and the
desperate need expressed by "The bull cries out in the sea."

His sense of life is also associated with the flower-principle he treats in "Invincible Flowers." Here the cut flowers in a florist shop, humanized after the fashion of Ginsberg's sunflower, no longer grow "red overnight in the sudden anguish of spring." Yet this is what happens to him when he forgets things better forgotten:

> I hear (at first in the distance) the sound of a great
>   Flower
> crying out loud in the sun.
> And the thought of something I would not betray grows
>   wild in my heart.
> The light is enclosed on each side by the darkness of
>   flowers.

If he has forgotten things better forgotten, the great Flower is probably not, as Williams has it in "Asphodel," the exploding atom bomb, though it is hard to exclude this meaning and not necessary to do so. The image may be one of all organic life— "a great Flower," in Bachelardian terms, is a cosmitized image, an image that insists on extending its meanings to the entire cosmos. Here it cries out the anguish of spring, the very thing the poet would not betray: the life-out-of-death he elects to serve. There are many reasons for Rothenberg's allegiance to Whitman, among them, this profound sense of the cosmos and the poet's agency in it and his recognition of death as a beginning.

When associated with the sexual significance of flowers, darkness is good. The line "The light is enclosed on each side by the darkness of flowers" is apposite to what precedes it and is a true contrary. It tells of redemptive experience even as it figures the notion of husk and kernel. (In the subsequent poem "A Country Dark Without Ghosts," he asks: "Does the shadow have nothing behind it?" and this prompts us to answer that where there's a husk, there's a kernel.)

The country of "A Country Dark Without Ghosts" is forsaken, marked by absence. It reminds us of the work named by *Alcheringa* and something else he would not betray, the eternal spirits of the (ever-present) dream time, ancestral presences. The landscape of this poem is, finally, spiritual: "Where no one has been [out there, where the door opens] but our dreams." The exterior is the most interior—the deep image privileges a poetry of the deepest interiority. This door is the door of his central dream, and this landscape accounts for his interest in surrealism and the deep image. Nothing in his work is comparable to a poem like "From Gloucester Out," where *out* names a movement outwards to the entire cosmos. For him, the farthest out is the farthest in. The poems in which he, unlike Dorn, would feel closest to Olson would be "The Librarian" and "As the Dead Prey Upon Us," just as the poem by Creeley he happily endorses at this time is "The Door."

Doors. I recall James Hillman, *The Dream and the Underworld:* "The underworld perspective begins at the gates of entry, where entry signifies initiation." Is this book, then, a rite of passage?

Rothenberg proposes that we explore the dream time and include it, make it coextensive with our "reality." We do this by means of the deep image, which, Hillman would say, gives us the poetry of the soul by permitting us to enter the underworld. *Nekyia.* "Our depth psychology [psychology of images] begins with the perspective of death."

"I believe in the future resolution of these two states, dream and reality, which are seemingly so contradictory, into a kind of absolute reality, a surreality" (André Breton, "Manifesto of Surrealism" [1924]).

The boundary between dream and "reality" is nullified by the
deep image. The deep image is the first instance of the *poesis*
that opens the door.

In *The Maximus Poems* (I, 150), Olson is dismayed by the fact   4 September
that we no longer have a sense of mythological presences.   1981
This feeds the anger he feels at the betrayal of America. Perhaps the equivalent in Rothenberg's book is "The Real Revolution is Tragic," a poem whose central statement is explicit
enough:

>   (voice
> of the graveyard pressing my skull,
> this graveyard of voices):
>   oh listen,
> we're dying again in
> America, dying
> the deaths of our highways and houses,
> and love's the gaud least attained.

I cite this undistinguished verse—its imagery is not deep but
commonplace—because it speaks for a generation of poets.
The lost America of love. "I and my love and [my secret] America." Is "America," the *she* of so many poets, the Shekinah,
exiled, lost? Is *America a Prophecy* a local instance of the desire to repossess her?

There are intervals in the darkness when the presence of   5 September
death diminishes, when the sensuousness of summer drugs   1981
him. "A Poem for the Weather," for example, where everything springs into life (in response to the summons of growth
first spoken in "Invincible Flowers"—these poems, incidentally, are placed side by side, to advantage, in *Poems for the
Game of Silence*); when the transformative power of life is so
great "Roses grew tigers," evoking the fierce creativity spoken
by Blake, and even the voice of the president belongs in the

nursery where the cow jumps over the moon. The final lines, set off, are the vision: "under the oranges, / summer sat without moths." Which is why I said summer drugs him.

Are the vision because the poem fulfills the most important declarations of Program One in *Poems for the Game of Silence,* the manifesto of the deep image Rothenberg worked out in his correspondence with Creeley and first published in *Poems from the Floating World* in 1961.

> The poem is the record of a movement from perception to vision.
> Poetic form is the pattern of that movement through space and time.
> The deep image is the content of vision emerging in the poem.

Copying this, I now see that the deep image is the entire poem, not just the last two lines, even though they are the most brilliant and arresting; and I find another reason, besides the incantation it sometimes makes possible, for what Rothenberg, in contradistinction to Creeley's "hesitant" line, calls his "cumulative" line. He insists on movement ("The vehicle of movement is imagination") as much as Olson does, and in the section of *America a Prophecy* that deals with renewals and images, he says that the concern with image making is implicit in "Projective Verse" and the proceeding is given in "ONE PERCEPTION MUST IMMEDIATELY AND DIRECTLY LEAD TO A FURTHER PERCEPTION." Recalling another Olson (Creeley) dictum ("FORM IS NEVER MORE THAN AN EXTENSION OF CONTENT"), we can easily see how the form of the poem constitutes the deep image.

The sensuous interval is not enough. Rothenberg's deepest reliance is Diane, to whom, in a prefatory poem, he dedicates this book. "For Diane" stands outside the book, is also set in italics. Diane is his Muse, to be associated with Diana and, more to the purpose, with the Shekinah. (Saying this has sent me searching for the following quotations: "ladies do mean more to me than God," to be considered with the fact that "poetry, as a faith, [is] more central to me than religion," and the further fact, as he notes a Hasidic rabbi saying of prayer, that "poetry is copulation with the Shekinah.") Diane is the redemptive agent he needs in his exile, who in her exile accompanies him on the "journey from darkness to darkness." She is also the darkness. She appears here in her double nature, associated, as the Shekinah is, with the moon and its dark forbidding side. She is not evoked in the spirit of romantic love, after, say, Arnold's fashion in "Dover Beach." Rothenberg has opened a door ("To find the keys that will open the doors," Gershom Scholem says, "is the great and arduous task"). This permits him to return to the Great Mother, and this is what, at times, privileges darkness. So, in "The Counter-Dances of Darkness," dedicated to Duncan and playing off "Often I am Permitted to Return to a Meadow," he says: "you woke to it under the moon, but in darkness— / in darkness it had begun—in darkness, in darkness it will be ended."

This is the place to think of Creeley's "The Door," the wanderer in search of the lady. But "Three Landscapes" initially brought Creeley to mind because of the sexual distress in the face of the persistent other's denial and because Rothenberg does not tell it in Creeley's way, even though such statements of Creeley's as "The moon is / locked in itself" is the most natural of deep images. According to Rothenberg, Creeley's hesitant line accords with thinking-out-loud, with a discursive rather than imagistic proceeding. But perhaps a more

6 September 1981

profound difference is that Creeley never situates love where Rothenberg does—"the place of our love is a rest between dyings." Here, *dyings,* given significance by the entire book, speaks not only for private psychic deaths but for social and political dying, *that* death of love in our time. As much as anything, this accounts for the programmatic insistence on the deep image and the other insistences—among them, the communal work of vision and its agency in liberation and change.

When Rothenberg and Quasha composed *America a Prophecy* (1973), the discussion of deep image was modestly placed in a historical perspective of renewals going back to the oldest (earliest) poetries. Even when Rothenberg was writing to Creeley, pressing the claims of the deep image, he remarked that "our tradition . . . is great enough to hold whatever new approaches we bring to it" and noted that in a forthcoming issue of *Poems from the Floating World,* he would include some "ancient" texts. His sense of tradition is both capacious and continuous.

In *America a Prophecy,* the comment on deep image follows one on projective verse, as in point of time this poetics did. What is notable about it is that it reminds us that the newer generation of poets was coming from a direction that differed from Olson's.

> DEEP IMAGE: Late fifties, early sixties: one response to the re-opening of American poetry at this time was a new consideration of "image" as a power latent in all poetry and thought. Attention to "deep image" (derived from Spanish and French surrealism, archaic and primitive poetry, etc.) centered in magazines like *Trobar* (ed. Robert Kelly and George Economou) and *Poems from the Floating World* (ed. Jerome Rothenberg), while re-

lated concerns with "image" informed Robert Bly's *Fif-
ties* and *Sixties*. Kelly's concern with a synthesis of
"deep image" and "projective verse" . . . marks one difference between the former and latter publications.

The program introducing a selection of poems from *White
Sun Black Sun* in *Poems for the Game of Silence* reminds
us that Rothenberg deliberately featured the deep image and
rallied to it, characteristically, all of his resources, a magazine
and a press. *Poems from the Floating World* (1959–63), the
first of Rothenberg's magazines, was issued by his Hawk's Well
Press. So were his first book and the first books by Robert
Kelly, Diane Wakoski, Armand Schwerner, and Rochelle
Owens—and a book by Buber. Hawk's Well tells the auspices:
Yeats, whose play *At the Hawk's Well* opens with "I call to
the eye of the mind / A well long choked and dry." *Eye of the
mind* calls up Blake's admonition to see not only with but
through the eye: it tells us that vision may be visionary. So
does an epigraph from Rimbaud. And such images as "In the
eye of my needle / everything sprang into life" and "The dark
bull quartered in my eye" tell us that Rothenberg is "focusing
within on things," practicing "inner sight." He hasn't lost
sight of things, but seeks a "subjective exteriority" that he
feels is "closer to a basic poetic experience." What he cites
from Williams in *Poems from the Floating World* is "Only the
imagination is real!" He wishes, as he says in *Revolution of
the Word*, "to return to the ever present origins of poetry
within the human mind" (my italics). Poet, he insists, is better defined as creator than as maker.

Like Emerson, Rothenberg recalls us to vision and initiates "a   8 September
silent revolution of thought." Emerson, as much an *Augen-*   1981
mensch as Rothenberg, is concerned with "subjective exteri-

ority" in his doctrine of correspondence, a doctrine liberating the imagination. This doctrine also informs Stieglitz's notion of *equivalents*, those images (a photographer speaks of images rather than symbols) of the encounter of self-and-world, inner-and-outer, that are at the very heart of the poetics of the "American Moment." Williams owes much to this poetics and so does projective verse, where projective, as Creeley explains in his early letters, involves the attempt to project one's inner concerns by means of the materials of the external world, that is, to go *in* by going *out*, so that the famous dictum on form might read, "Form is an extension of *that* content."

The *poesis* of the deep image is what Williams and Olson share. Williams speaks for it in *Kora in Hell*, an inward exploration in which he seeks to turn the mind inside out, and in *A Voyage to Pagany*, where, at impasse, he descends into the mother-stuff darkness of the self in order to breed with himself. Olson speaks for it in *Poetry and Truth*, where he tries to understand the deepest nature of his being, the unknown that is the "self's insides," the place of blackness where the sun of being is finally to be found and where the signal task is "to *light that dark.*"

The epigraphs in the five issues of *Poems from the Floating World* instruct us in the significance of the deep image, and the contents variously, with catholicity yet concern for the work of a new generation of poets, demonstrate its uses. The name of the magazine is as much to the point as *Alcheringa* later on. The following epigraph from Lorca exemplifies the deep image even as it explains the title: "Our eyes remain on the surface, like water flowers, behind which we hide, our trembling bodies floating in an unseen world." The deep image is of such depths; it belongs to an oceanic existence, and the poet employs it because otherwise "the darkness rises up to drown him."

What most rouses Rothenberg comes at the end of the fourth issue. Here he appends an essay, "The Deep Image Is The Threatened Image," in which he says that "the 'deep image' is the poetic image struggling with the darkness . . . the image rescued from the lie of the unthreatened." To apprehend a deep image, then, is to experience this sense of threat and struggle, to realize the extremity of creation and vision, and that this is the truth of things. The deep image renews creation and requires "heroes of the word," the "real poets" who refuse to be daunted by the "unfathomed darkness." This great refusal is the foundation of his work.

> The world as it existed for the first man still exists. It taunts us & breaks into our dreams. The poet dares to face it without hope & to create from pure desire, from pure love. The world as it existed before man. The primal world, not yet hardened into the mold of law. . . . A return to the beginning. A struggle to shape the world through the power of the creative moment, the flash of light that overthrows the darkness & is itself a greater darkness. Creation struggling with death.

Creation struggling with death. No reason to cite all the poets this enlists, but, among Rothenberg's friends, the Antin of *Definitions.*

The best explanations of "deep image" at this time are to be found in Rothenberg's letters to Creeley and in his essay "Why *Deep* Image?" in *Trobar* (1960). In the latter he says that "the direction of seeing in this kind of image is into a man rather than outside him: not a habit of the eye so much as a penetration of the self to refocus the world through the eyes-of-feeling." A description that covers more comes later, in one of those incredibly wide-referring notes in *America a Prophecy*, this one taking off from Freud's notion of "the antithetical sense of primal words" and N. O. Brown's concern with the "dialectal imagination." It especially impresses me because Bachelard is mentioned, and what Bachelard says about the necessary ambivalence of primary images and the conjunction of contraries in the "poetic moment" are exemplified in Rothenberg's first book. So, for that matter, is what Rothenberg says of Gabon Pygmy song in *Technicians of the Sacred:* "Characteristic of *all* poetry where sensitivity to the shifting polarities of light & darkness, etc. becomes a matter of cognition &, perhaps, of tragedy."

9 September 1981

How is it this poetics is omitted from *The Poetics of The New American Poetry?* Though it recovers aspects of symbolism, it does not aestheticize, divorce art and life. It subscribes to process, not to Idealism.

Also: *Poems from the Floating World* is not the *Kenyon Review.* Robert Kelly says, in an interview at this time, that "this revival had to come, this awakening to the fullness of poetry, after the dry wit and tricks of words that marred so much of the poetry of the 50's." And speaking of tricks—both Kelly and Rothenberg distinguish the deep image from surrealism, the latter, as Kelly claims, a technique with the former as essentially a mode of vision.

Depth is the measure of vision. If one sees deeply enough, one lets in the light. The poet is a seer or, better, a shaman, defined by the Copper Eskimo as "the one who has eyes." So " 'Deep image' (if it was more than a gimmick) carried the hope, like poetry in general, of 'finding the center,' which is an activity the ancestors in the old myths of founding engaged in at the start & that we have to learn to do again." *Finding* is *founding.* Rothenberg's immediate reference is to Dennis Tedlock's total translations of Zuni narrative poetry, *Finding the Center,* which exemplify "the freeing of the 'sparks' or 'germs' in language & consciousness, the possibilities of finding meaning in a situation in which there's no longer a recognizable center." From the start, his concern is with what, in *A Seneca Journal,* he calls "ethology [of] visions":

> the speakers of deep tongues point
> a route this generation
> will be privileged to assume
> a universal speech
> in which the kingdoms of the world
> are one

The deep image belongs to this universal speech.

The Seven Hells of the Jigoku Zoshi, published by *Trobar* in 1962, belongs to Program One. It is a long poem, long but not serial because it is formally closed. Rothenberg does not turn to Japanese scrolls, as Snyder does, for the possibilities of open form. He is not interested in the pictures but in the titles of the several hells: "I was working off those seven titles . . . that and the *concept* of a scroll of hells . . . keep the poems together" (my italics). The blurb on the back cover says that he "orders the fragments of the contemporary world." 16 September 1981

These poems comprise a visionary journey. Like Dante, Rothenberg is in the middle of the journey of his life and has entered the *selva oscura,* the dark wood of world and self where, as the dedicatory statement says, all of us "struggle with demons." In cold hell, in thicket, he needs the succor of a Shekinah-Beatrice ("light of my eyes"). Unlike Dante, he is not righteous and often identifies with sinners. When vindictive, he recognizes his own evil.

Every time Rothenberg reprints these poems something is lost, essential epigraphs, a prefatory poem. Of most importance are the lines from Whitman's "This Compost":

> Now I am terrified of the earth, it is
>   that calm and patient,
> It grows such sweet things out of such
>   corruption
> . . .
> It gives such divine materials to men,
>   and accepts such leavings from
>   them at last.

These lines speak for radical transformation, for Whitman's wonder, to cite the original title, at the resurrection of the wheat. Death and life, decay and growth, dark and light, are inextricably related, contraries not opposites. Their correlative in *The Seven Hells* is the fact that below (Hell) and above (Earth) are experientially continuous kingdoms, both places of pain and suffering, hell, in fact, a replication of earth. There is also the fascination with meat in the butcher shop of "The Fifth Hell," which derives as much from Whitman as from Rothenberg's contemporaries—from Whitman's "foul liquid and meat."

The prefatory poem is also connected with "This Compost." The poet speaks of interment in the earth, of the initial sorrow and pain of being confined and shut away from life, and of the yielding (decomposition?) by which, it seems, he enters the still creative cosmos and feels "this strange joy." The experience recounted in this poem permits him to enter hell.

Isn't this a variant of the dream that figures his essential autobiography, tells his secret mythology? Consider these notations of dreams in *A Seneca Journal:*

looked into the other room
the black hole
where I could feel creation going on
& said it was
CREATION

                    *   *   *

a dream word
speaks to me
—Creation—
came in a dream about
the dead

The Seven Hells is a dream about the dead, a necessary night-
journey and initiation, from which Rothenberg emerges in "A
Bodhisattva Undoes Hell" to take up his creative task. A vision quest certifying his shamanistic role.

Considerable formal experiment. Each poem is different, and
the differences, however modest, are compounded by juxtaposition. There is the deep unity of deep image. The imagery
clusters, as Burke would say, and the sequence might be said
to be dominated by blue—the color, incidentally, that the
Seneca associate with ghosts. Most impressive is the lyric-
dramatic power Schwerner notes: the remarkable lament of
"The Second Hell" ("The thieves the thieves the lovely thieves
are no more"); the use of anaphora, parallelism, and refrain
("They have left her") in the quatrains of "The Sixth Hell,"
where the long line and the flow of the verse are skillfully
managed in ways recalling both Whitman and Ginsberg; the
interior rhymes of "The Seventh Hell" and the reiterated
"pity" the poem enjoins in its incantation—incantation here
and elsewhere in the sequence now a conspicuous feature of
Rothenberg's work.

17
September
1981

The hells are not necessarily progressively deeper. What is progressive is the deepening identification, the growing horror, the extremity. The hells he explores are both of his own psyche and the death-ridden civilization to which it belongs. He is one with what he observes: psyche is civilization. The poem, accordingly, is epic.

The important thing is the psychic course of the sequence. The first poem, spoken by a swindler in hell, ends with a verse opening into the rest of the work:

> The white eye watches
> through the window
> Where we live is where
> we always lived
> The sea of death

In the second poem, the poet himself speaks out of his sense that with the removal of the thieves to hell, a "door" has been opened "for the sea" and that he needs to be comforted ("stay with me light of my eyes"). In the third, he speaks his revulsion at the pederasts with a power equal to Lorca's in "Ode to Walt Whitman"—though by the end, he knows that what moves here, if not love, is still a hunger for love. In the fourth, he expresses the cruelty born of madness that binds him to the cruel ones who "wait forever at those windows / watching me" and account for the fact that "My eye bursts, the green / pulp trembles from the socket." In the fifth, where the sexuality already suggests *Poland/1931*, he reflects on the butcher shop. In the sixth, he speaks the terrible desecration of woman and his loss ("There is no one nothing I can hold . . . / They have left her"). In the seventh, he asks us to pity all those in a world afire, a waste land, as the echo of Eliot tells us: "The shadow of the fire-raisers lost in the smoke / The shadow of the smoke where the hot sand is falling"—to pity because the fire is interior as well as exterior, and, as the concluding, apposite lines explain, "The mind of man is on fire / & where will his eye find rest."

The coda, "A Bodhisattva Undoes Hell," answers this question. This quiet narrative poem tells of the advent of Jizo, who is said to have descended to the world because "he was moved to pity." Pity, or, better, compassion, is the requisite emotion, and this essential democratic humanity is what the poet acquires on his journey.

When Antin reviewed Rothenberg's work in *Caterpillar #7*, he considered *The Seven Hells* solely in terms of linguistic experiment and measured it against *Sightings*, the work of this time that most closely approximates his own. He considers *The Seven Hells* a continuous long poem and *Sightings* a discontinuous long poem, and he prefers the latter because it "corrects" the literary format and loss of striking power of the former. "Rothenberg," he says, "was in the predicament of wanting to cover more ground [than he had in the small poems of *White Sun Black Sun*] and still wanting to make it possible to attend the individual images. . . . [So] he provided rhetorical settings for his images . . . [and] managed to take in more ground by giving up the idea of striking power." I can see the justice of Antin's remark that *The Seven Hells* is a "step backward in order to move forward," and I concur in what needs to be said, that Rothenberg is an experimental poet who follows the dialectic of experiment and wishes to be interesting on that account. But I don't agree that Rothenberg's eloquence—Antin is referring to "The Seventh Hell"— "renders it absolutely powerless." I think Schwerner hears more in these poems than Antin does.

18 September 1981

22
September
1981

Though published separately, *The Seven Hells* has a more inclusive context in *Between: Poems 1960–1963* (1967). There
the sequence stands between other significantly titled groups
of poems: "The Counter-Dances of Darkness" and "Ghost-
light/Ghostsong." The concluding dramatic fragment, "The
Black Flower," tells us where the poet now is in his perpetual
journey through (to?) darkness. Designated a hero, he says,

> My heart has sought always
> for the dark thing, but the black
> flower eluded me.

Now black and flower are joined; the invincible flower also
grows down, or is to be found in the depths. It is death *and*
love, in keeping with the Whitmanian resonances of the book;
it is source, as in Olson's Black Chrysanthemum, from which
"everything issues" and which, "imbued with the light of
heaven . . . grows down." Fruitful ground, of self and culture.
"The earth under our feet," as Williams, a poet of descent,
says in "To Elsie," that we (the too pure products of America)
have wrongly considered "an excrement of some sky."

> I would like to know death
> not as this fear
> but as my hand touched form

The poems fully acknowledge this fear and recognize death
in all its horror, yet would transfigure it. When one accepts
death, death becomes home, the end of exile, the completion
figured in the round dance and sexual embrace.

Between. The title is glossed by the commentary to "The
Counter-Dances of Darkness": "There is no light or darkness
that, in itself, can orient us to *where we become*, but only a
constant shift of planes *between* the two—light & darkness,
life & death, speech & silence, sight & blindness" (my italics).
I also hear Buber, reminded of the "narrow rocky ridge be-

tween the gulfs where there is no sureness of expressible knowledge but the certainty of meeting what remains undisclosed." And James Hillman, who once proposed as the title of *The Dream and the Underworld* the more exact "The Dream Between World and Underworld," a signpost, he says, for a vesperal movement "into the dark."

So "The Counter-Dances of Darkness," a major sequence in prose and verse, responds explicitly to Duncan's belief that "all life is oriented to the light from which life comes," but also responds to, and challenges, *The Opening of the Field*, a book celebrating dance and the return to the meadow the poet is sometimes permitted: "Could light teach us the whole dance without the counter-dance of darkness?" Here Rothenberg addresses the dialectic that brings Duncan to *Roots and Branches*.

Rothenberg speaks to Duncan in terms of Whitman and the Kabbalah. The long lines and their spoken quality and meaning recall Whitman. The sexual metaphor belongs to the Kabbalah. The penis enters the womb of woman as the root enters the earth, both places of darkness, where darkness signifies both life and death, or death-generating-life. *This dance* is a marriage. One *weds* the darkness. And the darkness is the exiled Shekinah, whose exile ends in the act of love, in the dark.

Rothenberg enters the dark out of Orphic necessity. See "Words," where language rises from the earth, "our footsteps / speaking / like a dance," and silence is born from speech, "& silence / footsteps breathing / softly / where we learn to die." In this poem he brings his whole vision to bear on *words*, in words. And he brings his whole vision to "The Journey Between Summers," where he enacts with *her* (the pronoun includes the Shekinah) the wedding of §V of *Song of Myself* and learns the

23
September
1981

lesson of §VI, that "The grass / / swarms with old alphabets." In this poem, dark with death, death itself awaits us in what's nearest—in the voice that he says is "enough" and that, perhaps in Whitman's sense, permits him to "wait." Has he learned, with Whitman, that "a kelson of the creation is love"?

Like many of the poems in this volume, "The Counter-Dances of Darkness" explores the darkness of doubt, the terror and horror of death, *which is also a root*, and, in the sexual sense, provokes the satanic outrage that accounts for her (the Shekinah's) shadow. Doubt and death are the counterparts of exile and lovelessness. He inhabits a world of extremity, is obsessed with isolation and the unavailingness of help and comfort. The signature of this book is: "death is on all sides. . . . I write these words from Hell." Still, the journey of "The Counter-Dances" and some of the other poems takes place in a universe eroticized by the presence or absence of love. I frequently hear echoes in these poems of Whitman, Crane (especially "Voyages"), and Duncan—and Eliot, too, whose shadows and garden scene have analogues here, and whose "What are the roots that clutch, what branches grow" may not be amiss.

The book is modulated by the love poems of "Ghostlight/ Ghostsong," in keeping with Rothenberg's belief that love only intermits the darkness. I hear *goatsong* in *ghostsong*, and wonder at the paradoxical title. Is it to be explained by the fact that love is a deathward yearning for darkness and silence? I am reminded, especially by "A Slower Music," dedicated to Diane, that the *she* of "She is my wonder" is the Shekinah. Rothenberg says in "Whichever Road I Took . . . ," "I will watch you forever / The white darkness / is black in your voice." That dark moves here, with something comparable to the realization Williams expresses in "The Shadow":

Soft as the bed in the earth
where a stone has lain—
so soft, so smooth and so cool
Spring closes me in
with her arms and her hands.

Yes, Kora is goddess of the underworld, a black flower, as in
Spring and All.

Two things to say right off about *Poems 1964–1967.* It's his   1 October
most experimental collection—his collection of experi-   1981
ments—and is rightly dedicated to Antin because it meets
him in point of experiment in a work comparable to *Code of
Flag Behavior,* also published by Black Sparrow in 1968. And
like Antin's book, it is political. Rothenberg places it under
Program Two in *Poems for the Game of Silence,* where the
manifesto, originally proclaimed in Great Bear Pamphlets in
1966, is the personal manifesto with which he now prefaces
all of his pre-faces and manifestos in *Pre-Faces.* No question
of its centrality or of what he's after in declaring, "I will change
your mind." What he says in his four statements is still at the
heart of the "poetics of liberation" he sets out in "Manifesto
& Collage" in 1980.

His poetics of liberation involves a "poetry of changes."

He has what Olson calls "the will to change," which names
the push of postmodernism, the necessity it's under, the exi-
gency of the case. And his work is political because it is experimental: "The tradition I identify with has tended to be
experimental in both poetry & life." This tradition, as he
teaches us, is as old as poetry, though it is more readily located for us by citing Blake and Whitman and the Dada "fathers" or the gathering of twentieth-century American avant-
garde poets in *Revolution of the Word.* Here, incidentally,

Rothenberg begins by placing himself autobiographically, using his experience to explain "how we found our way to new views" (*sightings*), to "a virtual revolution of consciousness."

Poems 1964–1967, which includes *Sightings, Further Sightings, A Steinbook & More, Conversations*, and *The Gorky Poems*, marks Rothenberg's own revolution of the word. Though this work is grounded in the "deep image" and is continuous with the desire to turn the mind upside down, it moves beyond the more readily recognized forms of the previous work into the domain of the frankly experimental.

Continuous with because his experimentation is being pushed by what he is learning in preparing *Technicians of the Sacred*, published at this time. This is the first of the anthologies by which he would also change our minds—or, better, open possibilities. It is remarkable not only for how much it gathers from the remote past and for its extensive commentary, much of it involving the present situation in poetry and the exemplary work of his friends, but for the pre-face in which he schematically presents what he demonstrates throughout, the "intersections & analogies" of the oldest and newest poetries.

The biographical note on the dust jacket of *Between* succinctly puts the continuity of purpose:

> About then (1952) too began to sense "Image" as a power (among several) by which the poem is *sighted* and brought close—a concern that developed quickly after 1958 & later in close workings with Kelly, Antin, Schwerner, Bly, others, readings in Blake, Rimbaud, Neruda, Whitman, New American & German Poets; Ancient Texts of Lost Tribes, Aztecs, Navahos, etc., leading (in a world cut-off from *vision* and thereby incomplete) to reconsideration of the poem's roots in, e.g.,

shamanism and to a growing sense of powers, new and
old, of word and song and image still here as *keys* for
any man who reaches for them to-his-limits and spite
of cautionary schools, etc. But I hope never to have
locked that *door*. (my italics)

Technicians of the Sacred, as the source of the title in Eliade
tells us, is a manual for shamans, for poets intent on recovering vision and interested in its forms, its structures. "Eliade,"
Rothenberg says, "treats shamanism in-the-broader-sense as a
specialized technique of ecstasy. . . . The shaman can be seen
as protopoet, for almost always his technique hinges on the
creation of special linguistic circumstances." Rothenberg
maintains, in "Revolutionary Propositions" (1966), that "a
revolution involves a change in structure; a change of style is
not a revolution" (see Antin's definition of *interesting*) and
that "a change in vision is a change in form. A change in form
is a change of reality" (see Antin on *representations of reality*). In an interview with Kevin Power, he addresses the need
to liberate the mind from fixed or confining structures and
says that what the shamans did to this end modern poets do—
those poets "involved [with] vision & structure (or the break-
ing down & building up of structures)." In fact, modern poetry
enabled him to appreciate the shaman, whose role of vision-
ing and healing (making whole) he in turn appropriates for
modern poets. In the crisis of consciousness that marks our
time, the poet has again taken on the necessary work of *turning the mind upside down.*

Which is, in Rothenberg's explanation of this Iroquoian term,
a concern with depth, with vision, with seeing. With *sightings.* Like the shaman, the poet has a fundamental concern
with "the thing seen," and *seeing* is "at the heart of the [mod-
ern poetic] enterprise."

3 October
1981

Sighting. An obsessive word, naming the primary work of the poet. In Rothenberg's case it is primary, or first. "So the deep image," he tells Creeley, "remains for me the primary arbiter, *at least as* first thing sighted."

Creation is seeing and sighting, what the verbal action of the poem brings to light. Is this verbal action cosmogonal, as with Duncan? What is notable in the initial section "Origins & Namings" in *Technicians of the Sacred* is the concern with light, with cosmogonal genesis. *Sightings = lightings.* Sightings enable us to see that universe. Then the songs called *Sightings* are, as he says of shaman songs, "the keys to unlock" the "obstacles" [doors] on our journey in the cosmos?

The best glosses on *sighting* (and *Sightings*) are the commentaries in *Technicians of the Sacred,* among them, those selected for *Pre-Faces.* The commentary on images involves two "primitive," single-line poems:

> something has been sighted & stated & set apart . . .
> fixed, held fast in all this vanishing experience. It is
> this double sense of sighted/sited that represents the
> basic poetic function (a setting-apart-by-the-creation-of-
> special circumstances that the editor calls "sacralism")
> from which the rest follows—toward the building of
> more complicated structures & visions. . . . There is
> nothing naive or minimal about the "sightings," save
> their clarity & the sense that, starting now, the plot (as
> Cage would say) is-going-to-thicken.

He is speaking of his own work.

5 October
1981

Sightings. Exercises in indeterminacy. You can put the lines in various/several juxtapositions, and use them to construct several narratives/scenarios. You don't read them; you sound them, meditate on them. Try/pry the individual lines. Exercise yourself. They demand participation.

I. Composed of nine lines, with intervening spaces (of silence) of equivalent duration. The sightings are soundings; they emerge from silence as bursts of light from darkness. As Antin says, "The words appear only where the pressure to speech is irresistible." When sounded, they are necessarily serial; on inspection they have other relationships, though the essential one is juxtaposition, the importance of which Rothenberg acknowledged in the first epigraph in *Poems from the Floating World,* cited, significantly, in the commentary on Bantu combinations in *Technicians of the Sacred.*

> The image cannot spring from any
> comparison but from the bringing together
> of two more or less remote realities . . .
> The more distant and legitimate the
> relation between the two realities, the
> stronger the image will be . . . the more
> emotive power and poetic reality it
> will possess.
> —Pierre Reverdy

So, as he says in the commentary, the poem is an "opposition or balance of two or more images," and the more the connection between them is strained, the greater the interest. "Not subtlety," he explains, "but *energy:* the power of word & image. For it is right here that the light breaks through most clearly; not the light of logic & simile, not even the flashing of a single image or name, but what feels 'deeper' . . . and to which . . . the word 'vision' might be said to apply."

There is a speaker, for the poem is spoken. The poem is composed of declarative sentence, question, injunction, sentence fragment, and single word. The initial line—"He hides his heart"—is made up of monosyllabic alliterative words, is verbally interesting in itself as well as in what it tells. I read *heart* here as *feeling, love,* and I imagine situations in which one might act in this defensive way—the "image" is one of defensiveness. The next line—"A precious arrangement of glass & flowers"—I take as apposite to the stated act of the first line, and am also prompted to stress *precious.* Of course, arranging flowers has romantic associations and "connects" with what may be the situation suggested by the first line. But now I hear *precarious* in *precious* and see why *glass* is there. A narrative seems to be unfolding. In the third line, *They* seems to fill out the situation and *covenant* plays off *arrangement,* while the modifying phrase, *the circumstance of being tried,* may "explain" why he hides his heart. But with the fourth line—"Who will signal you?"—the narrative sequence is violated by a question presumably addressed to the reader, unless the speaker previously has been addressing himself in the third person; and after that, the subsequent lines, more tenuous in connections, open into confusion. But this confusion may be ground that prepares for my reception of what I consider *the* deep image of the poem: *A pigeon dreaming of red flowers.* This is lovely in itself and all the more so since it ties back over the greatest distance to the first line. The man who hides his heart is (like) a pigeon dreaming of red flowers, where the *red* answers to *heart* and *flowers* picks up and secures the flowers of the second line. *Pigeon* accounts for his defensiveness in terms of vulnerability: he is defensive because defenseless, a man of spirit. And most wonderful of all, *hiding* isn't selfish but is the equivalent of *dreaming.* Both belong to interiority. Isn't the fable hidden in all this about the soul and the way love makes visionary, deep imagists of us?

II. Already formally different. Most of the poems/parts have two pieces, one has three. The logic, again, is associative. Lovely things, like *witness* → *whiteness.* And in the final line, again *the* deep image:

> A finger growing from a finger:
> Hell in glass.

III. "A male-shaped womb—of darkness before the birth of light." What is a male shape? Shaped like a man? God, as dark, giving birth to light? Or God as female? as God/Goddess? Is the womb dark, or itself the darkness? And turning back to the first line, which seems to be the way of these poems, don't we hear *light* in *lie?* "The lie, beginning, persists with us." Does the lie begin with us? Is *beginning* a lie? Or does the light of beginning persist with us?

IV. Here the points marking the silences are replaced by numbers. The last line, more solemn and biblical, perhaps speaking up for the Shekinah, seems to answer the previous lines?

V. Cosmogonal sexual beginning? *At best an abandonment* is lovely in itself and reminds me of Emerson, in *Circles:* the way is by abandonment. *Salt:* Olson's *Monogene* ("the original unit / survives in the salt"). Then, the terminal *But that which weeps is the mind.* Yes, the *But,* because we have been estranged from the familiar world (Heraclitus) by the mind, and the mind should weep, *salt tears.*

VI. This poem is cited (yes) as an equivalent to the Kunapipi fertility songs published in *Technicians of the Sacred.* These Australian songs are carefully considered in an appendix, filled out with commentary to show us what must be brought to understand the words—though they, I find, convey the central sense without such explanation. What's interesting is that in

6 October
1981

his own rendering of the songs in *Further Sightings* he condenses and visually forms the material to his own ends and the end of sighting. He calls his version "Sightings: Kunapipi," where *Kunapipi* is a referential clue (the songs are narrative) and *Sightings* a formal clue.

His own demonstration in VI, even with the suggestiveness of the first line, is more cryptic, less available. It probably doesn't derive from any specific ritual, and we are under the burden of imagining one. "The earth shudders under the rain." I immediately think—and relevantly—of Crane's "A forest shudders in your hair!" And the entire poem, which works well enough *as it is* without any prying, reminds me of Schwerner's *The Tablets,* from which Rothenberg quotes in *Technicians of the Sacred.* When Schwerner reads them he reads, as part of the poem, those portions visually represented as missing and untranslatable. "Tablet X" contains only two words, *the the,* supplied by the so-called translator. The sequence is called "The Emptying," and one of the things that must be emptied is our expectation of complete "meaning," that set of mind. Rothenberg reminds us in his commentaries that "words *are* music [and] act upon us before their sense is clear or against the possibility of any fixed meaning." Such poems, then, instruct and exercise us in negative capability, the requisite condition of their working and our sighting, where sighting should be read as *sparks* (bursts of energy) and *chance hit.*

I take *chance hit* from another commentary of Rothenberg's which seems to describe the mode of *Sightings.* In the following he remarks on Jung's account of the preference in the *I Ching* for chance hits (configurations) over "causalistic procedures."

Thought of this kind, when applied to the field-of-the
poem, defines that field both in primitive/archaic & in
much modern poetry: that whatever falls within the
same space determines the meaning of that space. What
Jung called "synchronicity" (with the problems it raises
of indeterminacy & the observer's part in structuring
the real) becomes a principle of composition: common
link between such otherwise different modes as chance
poetry, automatic writing, "deep" image, collage, projective verse, etc., & between those & the whole world
of non-sequential & non-causal thought.

Whole world. He would have us realize that our way of thought
is limited to a very small part of the world.

Chance poetry gives me an opportunity to note that Rothenberg doesn't follow chance procedures or free association. The
lines of these poems—each fragment—had initially been put
on cards, to be shuffled and ordered in various ways. But un-
happy with such randomness, he *composed* them in a fixed
order.

His method of composition capitalizes on the fact that one
perception immediately follows another and emphasizes the
"jumps" or interruptions. What Lawrence says of "rotary
image-thought" in *Apocalypse* applies.

Read this book, as he says, for "new ways of structuring"—"I
wanted very deliberate ways of structuring." Not by the breath
phrase, at least not now. Later, in *Poland/1931*?

VII. I begin to see beyond the single poems to the sequence as   7 October
a whole. In what way is each "Sighting" an installment of   1981
something larger? There seem to be filiations between them,
an erotic one, for example, spoken here in "Or find her, let

her nipples swell against my lips" (which owes something to Kunapipi?). And images *cluster* (hand, fingers, horse, sleep, clock, etc.). Notable here is the glass jar that shatters on the floor, which calls up Antin's "Definitions for Mendy."

VIII. Reading this aloud, I notice that the silence between the lines provides space (time) for mulling their relationships. I am pleased here most by a syntactic parallel, which may not be semantically parallel: *disclosing in the light / Exposing in the night.* My pleasure is in words.

IX. Why only nine? Anything Kabbalistic here? *Summoner* and "summer ayre" is nice, and the rhyme of *burn* and *spurn.* But why the caps in *FIre?* Is he scoring the sound? The poem begins with *Shut,* and the penultimate line is *Shut.* Doesn't this make for closure? The final line is certainly closural: "All light we will become, be gathered."

What to note now? These poems have a ritual sound. On one hand, they are minimal (not so much as "Cages" in *Further Sightings,* which he calls "pared-down"—pun on the paired lines?—and "quasi-minimal"); on the other hand, they comprise, as Antin says, "a discontinuous long poem." Like Oppen's *Discrete Series?* Rothenberg describes them best: "*Sightings* . . . was for me an experiment with a particular kind of collage technique: an experiment in the use of fragmented materials basically put into a kind of musical juxtaposition. . . . There was a pick-up also from certain 'primitive' forms: cycles of short poems extended into larger structures." *Sightings I–IX* is a single poem. Collage, in the definition from Antin he cites: "the dramatic juxtaposition of disparate materials without commitment to explicit syntactical relation between elements." The characteristic modern form that makes for inclusivity, that opens the poem to "everything"—'"anything the mind can think."'

It represents the reality of that opening? To a connected and fluid universe? And with it stirrings of eros and process, on-going cosmogonal renewal? Has he hidden his heart only to find it moving at the heart of the universe? Has he had that in-sight?

The more I ponder it, the more it seems to be a cosmogonal poem. Who hides his heart? God does, by hiding His light. "To the God of Fire," included in *Technicians of the Sacred*, begins: "He hides himself . . . in the hidden cave in darkness." It is this light, then, that is gathered at the end. I hear Crane's "unhusks the heart of fright" and, recalling the Kaballah, replace *fright* with *light*.

Further Sightings. Dedicated to Ian Hamilton Finlay, who writes of his concrete poetry: "It is a model, of order, even if set in a space which is full of doubt." Writing to Eugen Gom-ringer, whose work he was translating in 1967, Rothenberg says his interest in concrete poetry is in "the clear light it throws on the nature of *all* poetry": "You speak of constellations, Finlay speaks of corners, I speak . . . of combinations— but always it's a question of making the words cohere in a given space, the poem's force or strength related to the weight & value of the words within it, the way they pull & act on each other." The poem as a high energy-construct, its coherence created by the tension of its elements, formed from within.
8 October 1981

Gomringer says that the constellation is the simplest poetic structure, a "model of verbal play in action," a "play-ground as

a field-of-force" to which he invites us, to play with the poem
in the spirit of play.

Rothenberg's epigraph to *Further Sightings* is the fourth statement of his manifesto: "And if thou wouldst understand that
which is me, know this: all that I have said, I have uttered
playfully—and I was by no means ashamed of it" (Jesus to
his disciples). Duncan also cites this and subscribes to it
when he speaks of the "amusement the muse meant for us"
(*Derivations*, 53). By way of experiment, both move beyond
the unremitting seriousness of their early work.

9 October   Ten poems, some with several sets. All but the first have titles,
1981   and in some the title is repeated as the first line of each of the
             subsequent verses. Most are cued by numbers indicating the
             number of lines in each verse and the number of verses, *e.g.*,
             2 × 7, a *mathematical* cue, and a *structural* cue, like 2 by 4!
             What is curious here is that the cue calls our attention to the
             fact that the first line, also set in italics, is the title of the
             verse or is to be read as in some significant way juxtaposed
             to it. In the first poem, the cue is 2 × 7, but the verse is as
             follows:

> *The Boat*
> will return to water,
> dry.

I read this and the rest of the verses of this poem in the spirit
of "Aztec Definitions." I find on going back to *some/thing*
that installments of *Sightings* and *Further Sightings* were juxtaposed to "Aztec Definitions." I also find that the title of the
verse, which one is inclined to read as the subject of a sentence as much as an object to be defined, is in the early version widely separated from the rest of the verse:

The Boat
will return to water,
dry.

This enforces a pause, not only between the sections or verses,
as a note explains, but within the verse. The selection from
Further Sightings in *Poems for the Game of Silence* restores
this wider spacing. *Game of Silence?* Yes, and not only in the
Chippewa sense of the title of that collection, as an assault on
the reader's mind.

The second poem, "The Old King," is a series of takes on King
Lear (in Hades), its coherence secured by the repetition of the
title, which, as Antin notes of other poems, becomes a refrain,
and by our knowledge of Lear, set in reverberation by each
verse. A poem like this collects its fragments, since all bear on
its subject. This is true of "The Sabbath Queen," even of "Zen
Soup," which is of a more "confusing" Zen character. "Cages"
is another matter for which John Cage may be evoked, in part
because of the fixed nature of the playfulness. This is the
most minimal poem, composed of the reiterated title and ac-
companying single words—fourteen words in all. Rothenberg
cites it in relation to his Kunapipi translations, where single
words deliver themselves so forcefully. But even so, I hear
Cage and find this more interesting. The single word makes
much of silence, and of the dialogic relation with its companion as well as playful relation to other words. When I read

Cages (i)
Wires.

Cages is pitched higher, and *Wires* responds. The sequence of
Moon, Summer, Summermoon, Summerflies is playful. So is
the closure where the thing predicates itself:

Cages (vii)
Cages.

"Hell," in three sets of five numbered parts, is a naming poem. *Hell* is reiterated in each part, and variously addressed, as, for example, in this definition of contraries: "Two bodies struggling—Hell. / A touch deferred—also Hell." "The Names" is also a naming poem, with the title repeated in all ten verses and *name, names,* or *naming* repeated in all but one of the verses, in which, incidentally, a fairly limited number of words are sometimes recombined. "The Witnesses," again in three sets, is of a different kind, since the reiterated *I* is not necessarily the same person and what the various *I*s declare does not compose a coherent narrative—but then, the title is in the plural, and each *I* witnesses, testifies from its own perspective. The Kunapipi poem that follows is the most stunning and the most interesting. The concluding poem, "The Sisters," a 3 × 7 poem formally like some of the others, is inconclusive because it is composed mostly of phrases and sentences from "The Witnesses" and demonstrates how to continue by taking up "old" or previous material in "new" arrangements.

Do these poems form a long poem? If so, a very loose one, and not a "deep" one like *Sightings*. The Kunapipi poem, which seems to me to belong to *Sightings*, is the measure of what is missing (missing? therefore included) in *Further Sightings*.

10 October
1981

"Did Stein do right the way she did write?" Duncan asks this in his Stein imitations in the 1950s, and perhaps what he says there of *a hut of words primitive to our nature* provides a clue to Stein's importance to Rothenberg. She is present most conspicuously not in *Revolution of the Word* but in *Technicians of the Sacred*, where she is the modern instance of much primitive practice, particularly of the repetition/naming that makes things present, the "passion for the names of things," as Rothenberg says, "that Gertrude Stein saw as the basis of all poetry." Citing Stein's prose poem to "poetry really loving the name" in *Lectures in America*, he notes how Stein "points to a material condition of poetry prior to verse or sequence" and how words, having weight and extension, are themselves things that have the magical property of making things present. He values Stein at her own estimation—"the most serious thinking about the nature of literature in the 20th century has been done by a woman"—but he especially values her because her intention, as she says, was to "work in the excitedness of pure being . . . to get that intensity into the language." As much as the *I Ching*, Stein, he claims, is "a handy [*ancient* deleted] manual of [*ancient* restored] poetic process." She is a technician of the sacred.

When Rothenberg is questioned about the presence of Stein in his work, he answers by noting 1) her early influence, at age twelve, and 2) the fact that she offered him new ways of structuring the poem—"deliberate ways"—as an alternative to the breath poetics of projective verse. In the first part of "Three Homages" in *A Steinbook & More*, he says of Stein: "This woman who speaks without breath has opened the ring for me."

The issue here is lineation. You speak these poems, but the line is not necessarily determined by breath. These poems, in Williams' phrase, are "machine[s] made of words," deliberately made, but without, as Williams insists, using the words one hears in speech, "in the speech that he uses." Nevertheless they are, as Charles Morrow says, essentially sound poems. When sounded, they give the most pleasure, the heightened sense of ritual saying. In this respect they belong with *Sightings*.

These exercises open the realm of verbal possibility, where language itself is of most interest, what it does and one can do with it. I especially enjoy the humor and verbal euphoria of "Some Notes For A New Series of Poems to Celebrate the American Revolution (1776–1976)," its last and best section inexplicably omitted in *Poems for the Game of Silence;* the brilliant *naming* of "Red Easy A Color"; and "Three Homages," which explicitly follows Steinesque examples (see her *Bee Time Vine*).

The first of the homages, to Stein herself, is the *Valentine* it declares itself not to be, such is the way of language; it is also the *Valedictory* it says it is. These words are neither etymologically nor logically related. Their relation is syntactical. *Syntactic,* from *syntaktikos,* putting together. Things can be put together in innumerable ways, as these poems demonstrate, if one goes back to the primary meaning of *syntactic,* not the usual meaning of following the rules. Is a *Valentine* a *Valedictory?* Perhaps if you hear in *Valedictory,* as I do, Donne's "A Valediction: Forbidding Mourning," and let that play with the thrice-repeated *morning,* which chimes so clearly in this poem of blessing.

The last of the homages, to I. B. Singer, follows the structure of Stein's "Dates," replacing her words—not always syllable by syllable—with words from Singer's novel, *Satan in Goray*. The interest here, as Rothenberg remarks, is in the tension between Singer's highly charged words and Stein's structure, and in the narrative Singer's words, even in this minimal way, summon. But these are more readily appreciated if one has Stein's poem at hand and has read Singer's novel.

13 October   *Conversations.* Very much after Stein. "He talks I talk & you
1981   talk" (73).

Talk, colloquy, I find, is not the first but the third meaning
of *conversation*. Is such talk necessarily dialogic, a meeting,
as Buber has it, or is it idle talk as in "Conversation Thirteen," talk to no purpose, inconsequential, even talk at cross-
purposes, *converse*? The word contains *verse*, and verse itself
is a turning (line by line, as here) and may be adverse. What's
more to the point, verse can take the form of conversation,
can be composed of two (or more) voices. Or to reverse this, as
Antin might, conversation is a fundamental human genre, *is*
poetry.

The form is stable. All fifteen conversations employ a twofold
give and take, the response to question or statement set off in
parentheses. The visual emphasis strengthens the dramatic aspect, makes the poem, the tensions so expressed, a language
event. Each event is a representation of reality, an image, a
kind of *sighting*. Form follows simply from the fact of the
logic and sequentiality of conversation. But the form, which
may satisfy Rothenberg's desire for deliberate ways of structuring, accommodates an endless diversity of conversations,
though the variations are finally limited but the verbal content—the humanity of the form—isn't. What can be said of
every conversation, however confusing, nonsensical, or inconsequential, is that it is a human event. Talking is human. This
is the chief difference between *Conversations* and Antin's
"Stanzas," both stable forms for endlessly variable content.

But of course the ways in which Antin uses the syllogistic
form are eminently human—he shows the something-less-
than-human of logical thinking. A comparable instance is
"Conversation Five," which takes the form of dialogue between the righteous man and his God:

> On Monday I decided to love those who hated me.
> (I will reward you.)

> On Tuesday I avoided the eye of a needle & started to
>   sing.
> (I will sanctify you.)

The ironies here are at least threefold: in the ritual, running through the days of the week, which seems to be performed for its own sake, as thereby efficacious; in the patently insignificant things confessed to the Lord; and in the Lord's ever-generous response, which, as I sound the poem, is quieter than the declarations, interior, *enclosed* by the parentheses, the confessant's own wish fulfillments. Clearly, Rothenberg doesn't think much of this egoistic way of talking with God.

What sometimes happens in these language events is a reversal of roles, as in "Conversation Twelve." This poem is a ring composition: the first exchange

> The child is young.
> (The house is old.)

becomes the last, reversed

> The house is old.
> (The child is young.)

And so on, with all the incremental value of Steinesque repetition.

Some are metapoems (Six and Seven); some play on expected responses, as in "Conversation Two":

> Forget Jerusalem.
> (He forgot it.)
> Forget Detroit.
> (He forgot it.)

Note the third-person, seemingly authorial response, which perhaps signifies a kind of absent self, a self later present in

the first person. Or "Conversation Three," evoking childhood
for me:

> A penny.
> (Two will get you candy.)

Not a penny for your thoughts?

> I want a rope.
> (I want a pair of bright suspenders.)

The end of this conversation—

> It's good to be a brother.
> (Kiss me.)

—is picked up in the ominous context of "Conversation Ten."

> They will live on the fringe of your cities
> their faces will be like yours & they
> will kiss you like brothers.
> (Then I will rise up & murder them.)

So talk is also fundamentally human for the good reason that
what the talk reveals is. Perhaps because some of the voices
are ancestral, Rothenberg thinks of these conversations as
"conversations for ghosts." I don't find them so, unless *ghosts*
speak for the depth these poems sometimes reach.

The Gorky Poems comes last, and comprises the largest   15 October
group, but the poems were begun before *Sightings* and are said   1981
to be structurally related.

Much in Harold Rosenberg's book on Arshile Gorky (and
in the exhibition catalog and the larger, primary study by
Ethel Schwabacher published in 1957, from which Rothenberg
worked) supports the "convergence" of painter and poet, not
least the biographical aspects that Rothenberg says led him to
identify with Gorky's "particular desperation." He came to

Gorky, a model of restless experimentation, at a critical moment in his own development, but also because Gorky knew the desperation of an immigrant. Rosenberg says that abstract expressionism is *"a newcomers' creation"* to be explained only by a consciousness in which "uneasiness about the past is mixed with a radical sense of possibility." Rothenberg himself observes that he could say more about "the personal identification & old-country matters"—about the germination of *Poland/1931!*—but that Gorky's artistic concerns were more important to him. He refers to these as "abstract surrealist." This names Gorky's importance, as when Rosenberg says, "In Gorky's painting a provincial version of Paris Cubism visibly changes by combination with Surrealist-inspired data into something new."

This change opened the closed parentheses of modern art, opened the field to a deep imagist who deploys images in space as Rothenberg does in silence. Gorky not only has *sightings* of the deepest kind but *sites* them in remarkable ways in space and also *cites* by way of allusion and the titles his poet-friends (Breton among them) gave his paintings. Moreover, he does not follow the surrealist practice of automatism.

17 October
1981

All but two of Rothenberg's Gorky poems take their titles from masterworks of the painter's last, most original, surrealist phase. The epigraph to this section, taken from Gorky's notes to *Garden in Sochi*, prefaces that phase of Gorky's work as well as Rothenberg's poems. Rothenberg omits Gorky's childhood recollection of this garden in Armenia. Yet, when thinking of Gorky, don't we usually recall the *The Artist and His Mother*, where the artist is a sad, dutiful, adoring *boy* and paints in fidelity to a photograph from that time? And isn't this garden of wish fulfillment, said to be his father's, a garden of incredible images, the blue rock, the holy tree, and the women, including his mother, who expose their breasts, to rub them on the rock for fertility? Instead, Rothenberg cites three initial declarative sentences, assertive sentences, and erotic, too, omitting again, a sentence that would enable us to see how much Gorky is moved by the eternal feminine.

The title of Rothenberg's concluding poem "Portrait of Myself With Arshile Gorky & Gertrude Stein" is of course his own, though allusive, calling up not only Gorky's *Portrait of Myself and My Imaginary Wife* but the potraits of his sisters, the *family cycle* (Schwabacher's words) he had begun. So Rothenberg's poem is a family picture. Gorky and Stein are his father and mother. By way of closure he acknowledges the two artists to whom the book is most indebted.

The relation of poems to paintings is problematical, not of the direct kind, say, of Williams' "Pictures from Brueghel." It is as if poem and painting were the juxtaposed terms of a deep image, creating mystery, calling for conjecture. Not correlation but convergence (Rothenberg's term for how he stands to Gorky) is the rule, and this may be, variously, biographical, thematic, or formal. Is the piracy of the "Pirate" poems, for example, a way of speaking for emergence into the fluid world of dreams and for artistic depredation? Or is Rothenberg's interest chiefly formal, in finding (successfully) verbal equivalents for the *tache* and the calligraphic line? There is no obvious relation between Gorky's *The Diary of a Seducer* and Rothenberg's poem of that name, but then the title was originally fortuitous. Maybe the painting, *en grisaille*, appealed to the poet of *White Sun Black Sun*. But the poem itself is a chant, a naming poem indebted to Stein, to be enjoyed for its colorful sound, and its evocation of "Don Roberto" (Kelly?) may substantiate the title. Does the evocation of flesh and blood in "The Water of the Flowery Mill (I)" approximate the "bar-

baric" Kandinsky-like colors of the painting, and the bleeding penis, in this poem for the Rabbis, evoke a rite of initiation? What about the long lines of "The Betrothal" that don't comport with the painting, though their *movement* may be the verbal equivalent of its conspicuous calligraphy? And "Agony," doesn't it belong formally to *Further Sightings*, its order at odds with the violent colors of the painting? It is not itself an agony, though agony is intimated as a consequence of opening to love and roots. And isn't this why the two poems "The Orators" follow, one a ceremonial pointillist poem of small couplets, presumably burying the father; the other a poem both fierce and tender, commanding us *to be* in war and love, and also to *let be?*

22 October 1981

Child of an Idumean Night is the only painting from Gorky's earlier cubist phase. This small canvas is dominated by a geometrical abstraction that suggests a birdlike hieratic head, a "primitive." It is essentially two dimensional, though composed of planes; is of stark contrasts (black and white, like the reproduction?). The most easily recognized form, variously repeated, is the eye; in fact, what I take to be a head may be a very large eye. It is mostly black in contrast to the smaller white head above it; and both are connected not only by the smaller head gazing down on the larger but by a ribbon of white that issues from the powerful phallic vertical over which the dark head is superimposed, its mouth inscribed within the phallic column. The phallic shape rising from the black ground at the bottom of the painting is capped by a circular form not defined by black but to some extent defined by brushstrokes that evoke radiance. It is the rising sun, the cosmogonal creation of light. And eyes are suns, definitely so in the eye that is aloft and almost in line with the phallus. The head of the dark god is connected by a black stalk to the dark

Courtesy of Hirshhorn Museum and Sculpture Garden, Smithsonian Institution

ground. The god is earth-born, night-born: earth is his body, and from it the white phallus of light emerges.

Why have I troubled to describe this painting? Because here is the focus of the poems in this sequence, perhaps in the book; here Gorky and Rothenberg converge, Rothenberg liberated, so to speak, by the paintings he has already studied, stirred to assertive creation. The dead father of the previous poem now gives way to the artist as primordial father.

Surely, in turning to Paul Klee's *Diaries*, Rothenberg paused at #943 and #944:

> In the beginning . . . insertion of
>   energy, sperm. . . .
> Works as form-determining
>   sperm: the primitive
>   male component.
> My drawings belong to the male
>   realm.

This, the longest poem, begins by transforming lines from Klee's *Diaries* (entry #837): "*I, the fat god / I, the good gardener.*" Rothenberg adds the *I,* makes the identification that will be extended in the chant that comprises section two, its long vertical form itself phallic. I am not wholly certain why these lines in their context in Klee's *Diaries* attracted Rothenberg, but *fat* has something to do with it. I think of the Venus of Lespuges, to whom this generative father-mother god may be assimilated, fat, yes, and of "wide hips." Then there is the "Fat. Fat. Fat. Fat. Fat" that opens "The Diary of a Seducer," followed by

> This is the forbidden kingdom.
> This is shape
> That balloons & is a power
> In the light.

The shape is later linked with a "man's penis." In "The Water of the Flowery Mill (I)," one finds:

> Of thy muscle
> fat
> thy armature
> Between the thighs it
> bunches

This has a correlative in the present poem:

> & I reached between my legs
> I grew fat
> I became the father of my race

And in "Satan in Goray," there is the eighth section: "Fat yes fat yes fat yes idol . . . etc."

Rothenberg wishes to become (or become familiar with?) the god evoked by the opening italicized lines. This will enable him to go to war gaily and to be "a singer to Philistia / & carry an American flag / to the border." It will enable him to become "the first architect, be / Father of your race / / & let men fuck your beard."

The title of the poem calls up the cosmogonal activities of the god. Rothenberg himself places the poem by putting it after his commentary "The Chapter of Changing into Ptah" in *Technicians of the Sacred,* and what he says of the Egyptians' concern with the energy of the deity applies. *Energeia.* Ptah is the god of (some) poets because he brings the elements of the universe into being with his tongue (= phallus). He is father by virtue of the spermatic word.

Convergence. Isn't it also in the myths to which Gorky's images open, the myths common to both of them? Isn't it in the fact that the myths so vividly present, recovered by the ec-   23 October 1981 static speech of the poem, summon the primordial powers for which he has been searching? Rothenberg's researches are directed to use. He does not wish merely to acquire the techniques of the oldest poetries, he himself wishes to be a technician of the sacred. The ecstatic in his work vouches for this. And he is after something else: the generativity and generosity of true fatherhood.

My heart
Was with the children
Believing
Their peace, their warm days

What, after all, is the sacred? In a review of Eliade, Rothenberg says it is what we, the profane modern men and women of Eliade's account, experience "through dreams and the unconscious"; it is a realm of "human experience" poets may again open for us. This has been the burden of his work as poet *and* pedagogue, and what has been remarkable about it is that he has avoided the "conflict between the culture of the interpreter and that of the creator" that Eliade resolved for himself by remaining primarily an interpreter.

Both Gorky and Rothenberg are admitted to this deeper realm of experience by their metamorphic method. This method, as Breton points out in an essay on Gorky, depends on the "eye's spring," the imaginative seeing of relation—that is, "the free and limitless play of *analogies.*" When he says that the function of the "eye's spring" is "to provide the *guiding thread* between things of the most dissimilar appearance," I recall Emerson's remark on man-the-analogist: "He is placed in the center of beings, and a ray of relation passes from every other being to him." In looking at Gorky's biomorphic forms, I also recall Emerson's delight in the "occult relation between man

and the vegetable"; in looking at *Child of an Idumean Night,*
Emerson's own transparent (*parent?*) eyeball.

Heraclitus puts it best in Fragments 54 and 123: "Invisible
connection is stronger than visible." "The real constitution of
each thing is accustomed to hide itself."

The multiple identifications in section two and the fluid interpenetrations of the unpunctuated extended utterance(s)
in section three of "Child of an Idumean Night" are good
examples of this method. Another example is "Charred Be-
loved," which has no thematic or formal connection with the
painting. This means that, at this point, Rothenberg had only
to cite any Gorky title to identify their common method—
and, as the poem insists, a method Stein also shared. For the
poem proceeds in the fashion of the previous Stein-exercises:
words and phrases are repeated, sometimes in new contexts, as
the poem, with the introduction of new words, "advances,"
gathers (snakelike?) its verbal length. Every word has a formal value, even the few not repeated, and might be assigned a
color. Both actual color words and other words and phases, by
repetition and syntactic parallelism, visually construct the
web of the poem. One of the most repeated lines ("makes a
place for it") is taken up in the following: "To say to make a
place for it covers me over discovers a leaf no a life not a life
in me." This is an example of the mode of the whole poem.
Nothing halts its fluidity, and verbal elements, like *over,* literally metamorphose in *covers* and *discovers,* as do *leaf* and *life*
by virtue of the vowel change.

26 October
1981

The most spirited poem is the last, "Portrait of Myself
With Arshile Gorky & Gertrude Stein." It derives from the
Steinesque "Conversations," is a composition of voices that

sometimes suggests liturgical responses even as Rothenberg's assertion of artistic maturity and equality is questioned by his for-the-most-part less assertive elders.

The poem is composed of interpenetrating statements. Take Gorky's opening speech: "I do direct the night. / I do. / & walk through it." This characterizes him, the *I do* of his assertiveness in the knowledge of uncertainty, the *night* that is his surreal terrain and his meditative(?) way of moving through it. Against this yet chiming with it is Stein's characterization:

> The sea is cool.
> The boats are dominant.
> The idea of algebra is lost.
> Almost nowhere is worthwhile.

Doesn't *sea* link with *night?* And isn't it *cool* because Stein does not probe it in the way of the surrealists, attends instead to the solid verbal elements on the surface, which she disposes as she wishes, according to no a priori rules? So that this field of play—the *nowhere*—has (almost) a value in itself?

Now Rothenberg: "My own care my trade plied that eases occupations. / Nowhere at ease." *Trade* plays off *occupations,* so one may read him to say that his care as an artist eases his discomfort at not being employed in more gainful ways. *Trade* associates his art with manual skill, and his care, his craft, eases his *preoccupations.* And *eases occupations* in another sense, prompted by *Nowhere at ease,* enables him to place himself, to be at home everywhere in the field, which is how Gorky hears it when he replies, "Not because peace [ease] is with us."

Of course, *Nowhere at ease* may be read in two ways, which is the way in which Stein goes on to treat it, finally deciding the matter with "Nowhere more at ease." This cool easefulness makes Rothenberg querulous. He tells Stein to "Turn turn & beg exceptions. / Scold the sea." This, he claims, is what he does:

> I salvage
> * * *
> I scold the sea.
> I try turning.
> Spurning remembering.

Is he recalling her to her own concerns in "Melanctha"? Later, when she says, "I am ball. / Am I," he grants her godlike shape (see *fat*) but also reproves her by reading *Am I* as a question and *am ball* as *amble:* "Yes & the motion of wanting to be cool."

Wanting to be cool. As they seem to want, in chorus:

> Before law.
> Before water.
> Before water the dove.

Law = Father? Water = Mother? The final line (in these often triadic utterances) says something else, and asks us to read all the lines in a cosmogonal way. Dove = holy spirit?

What was *before law* (order), *water* (chaos)? Before *the dove?* Who knows? So Gorky and Stein petition Rothenberg, "Please warm us," to which he warmly responds. And they send him on *his* way:

> (gs)   Fish warmly.
>
> (ag)   Fish & designs.
> (gs, ag) Desires.

(jr, ag, gs)   Manage an oracle.
                Manage a meal.
                Manage an oarlock.

(jr)   & a preparation to be already drowned.

Yes, he's going a-fishing. Their work has been done; his is still
to be done. *Warmly,* with *designs,* and with *desire.* He will
probably manage because there seems to be equivalence in all
that we manage to do, and because he goes to sea sufficiently
playful (an *oracle* → *an oarlock*) and sufficiently chastened to
know that one must be *already drowned* as well as *ready to
be drowned.*

1 December   Even though I know the answer, the question that keeps com-
1981   ing to mind as I think about *Poland/1931* is: Did he always
              think of himself as an American-Jewish poet? This is the
              question in which we converge, and he himself pondered it be-
              cause of the problems of taking up "material from which a
              separation has occurred." We are no longer Jews without money
              so much as Jews without Jewish culture. And this displace-
              ment, among others, it now seems has, as he says, "a lot to do
              with my work & the questions of loss & separation that run
              through it." This is why he cites Dahlberg.

              Living in our time does not make it any easier to feel *placed.*
              For all of us. Because, as he knows, all of us, not only Jews,
              bear the burden of human history. Exile is not an experience or
              a theme peculiar to Jews—it is, for example, one of the things
              the Amer-indians and Jews of *Poland/1931,* those lost tribes,
              share. Rothenberg is fond of quoting Marina Tsvetayeva's re-
              mark, "All poets are Jews," because, as a non-Jewish poet, she
              learned that poets are not exempt from the kind of experience
              she associates with Jews. Yet such statements would have
              more truth if they were amended to apply to all of us. Because

all of us—isn't this the burden of Rothenberg's work?—have in
his large view of human history been exiled from the tribe to
the state, from the primitive to the civilized, and are still
wandering in search of the primitive (Stanley Diamond names
the project), in search of the communality that will allow us
to be fully human.

This is what Rothenberg has at stake and defends with a vehemence I had not expected even from a maker of manifestos.
I am not thinking now of *Poland/1931*, which emerged in response to personal events (the birth of his son, the questioning of his identity by Paul Celan, etc.) and to a particular historical crisis, but of the article on Harold Bloom that I recently
read in *Sulfur 2*. In fact, I sat down this morning to explain to
myself, if I could, the enormity of his comparing Bloom to the
"exterminating angel" of Auschwitz. This is the only instance
that I recall in which Rothenberg abjures Jesus' "all that I have
said, I have uttered playfully," and it reminds me of Duncan's
"Passages," where political evil awakens deadly outrage. I am
not offended by Duncan's assimilation of contemporary public
figures to Satan because the political evil (as Rothenberg at-
tests in his account of writing *Poland/1931*) is demonstrable.
But I am offended by Rothenberg's assimilation of Bloom to
the *Malakh ha-Mavat* because it is an unworthy act, much
too *ad hominem* (perhaps only as it can be when Jew confronts Jew?), in no way commensurate with Bloom's
"offenses."

Does it really matter that Bloom has written off as second
rate the American-Jewish poets of our century? (See *A Big
Jewish Book* for a partial list.) Of the "American-Jewish poet,"
Rothenberg says, "I'm a particularized version of that entity . . .
have a personal stake in the matter." Does it really matter
that Bloom is a selective tradition-maker, who proposes a

canon as narrow and restrictive as those established earlier by New Critics and New Humanists? It might matter if Bloom had the authority of Babbitt and Eliot, but he doesn't, and he doesn't seem to me to threaten the most substantial and significant work of poets in our time: the "re-visioning," as Rothenberg himself says here, "of the larger human past & present." *Does it really matter?* Everything matters, and I can understand how poets who made their initial push against the poetics and ideology of the New Criticism feel now (Rothenberg notes the "current New Conservative & Moral Majority maneuvers") when confronted again, and in the same place, by critical authority.

I prefer Antin's comic dismissal of Bloom: "I don't think about Harold Bloom." And I would have settled for the fact that *A Big Jewish Book*, with its ironic title, answers Bloom, and, even more, so does the achievement of *Poland/1931*.

8 December   Rothenberg's concern with "primitive & archaic cultures" (I
1981   cite Program Three in *Poems for the Game of Silence*) seems always to have belonged to his interest in poetry, in *poesis*. "From A Shaman's Notebook" opens the fourth issue of *Poems from the Floating World* (1962) and is the title he employs nearly ten years later to group samples of his extensive translations. This preparation enabled him to undertake the search for his ancestral past: "Along with my own search for the primitive, I became more willing to explore my ancestral past"—where *willing* and *explore* express an initial reluctance—"my own origins, from which I had been running for most of my grown life."

So he opened the field. And began his field work in 1968, perhaps earlier, having had the help of Gary Snyder and Stanley

Diamond, and finally took up residence with the Seneca Indians at Salamanca, New York. "Exiled in Salamanca" is how he puts it in *A Seneca Journal*—

> Exiled in Salamanca
> & driven mad by
> Image of the Temple

—concerns, he says, echoing Pound, that he cannot bring together.

Yet didn't the occasion bring these concerns together? Hadn't he chosen exile at Salamanca for the same reason that he undertook *Poland/1931*, to find a way of not being "bounded by the established present," that is, by the "American present" of the Vietnam War? I recall Enzensberger's "man spricht deutsch" in a volume of translations by Rothenberg and Michael Hamburger, published in 1968. And I cite Rothenberg now because we may have forgotten the extent to which the occasion was a crisis, and a crisis of faith in "America."

> If America meant anything to me it was in some nineteenth-century sense, as a meeting place of the nations. What America had developed into as a separate American entity was something that at that point I felt to be repulsive, and I wanted to, in some very violent, for me, sense, dissociate myself from this. And it seemed to me no longer worth very specifically *not* being Jewish or not being what I was ancestrally to have a share in the American present. In other words, it seemed much more interesting and a much better position morally and spiritually to dissociate myself, to take my stand against the American present [but such a different stand than the earlier one of the Southern Agrarians], and in that sense it seems to have been done by others (black and Indian poets, and so on) in other ways. Perhaps it re-establishes a broken American continuity— of the country as a meeting place of nations.

A meeting place of nations. Rothenberg recovers the values of Randolph Bourne's transnational America. But when he speaks of *nations,* he includes the Amer-indians. And to the extent that the nations he includes are "primitive," he makes us aware of the fact that the "detritus of cultures" Bourne despaired of may involve "cultural genocide."

At this time, with Dennis Tedlock, he began *Alcheringa.*

4 January 1982

So Rothenberg begins where we begin, with the fact that we are displaced from the materials of *Poland/1931* just as he is from his "tribal past." He remarks on this in "The Fish": how "we live without associations," yet *nourish* (key word) "incredible polands" by way of artifacts, like the photographs of the mothers. Our remembering is a kind of fantasizing, and what we move toward, as the path of the poems indicates and the last poem of the first section realizes, is the "tender treasure" of the Shekinah. He is like, and we are too, the displaced, fallen-away Jewish businessmen who open stores in Kansas, their Jewishness now recalled by some occasion like a wedding (a primary ritual occasion of these poems), a wedding, however, likened to a game of chess in which the queen is suspended, her power unemployed because of the death of the player.

These poems are in the service of that queen, very much as Henry Adams explains, because "owing to the revival of archaic instincts, he rediscovers the woman." They mark Rothenberg's entrance to her service as well as enabling our entrance into her world. Only by exercising poetic modes that we may find strange if we have not been instructed by him does he reach her, indeed recover the (old) ecstasy that informed her worship.

It is appropriate, then, that the initial poem, one of four structural blocks entitled "Poland/1931," is an invocatory, evocatory *naming* poem, concerned with dreaming and memory, the fantastic and surreal, and turning, as the subtitle has it, on a wedding. It is significant also that it introduces us to one of the normative forms of Rothenberg's verse: an unpunctuated, uncapitalized free verse of great syntactic liberty and fluidity that conveys the interpenetrations of many levels of experience. For Rothenberg, *experience is multiphasic and fluid*, and *impulsive*, moving by the pulses of breath that the lineation scores, and underscores. For the poem is a score, meant to be performed, and is much more efficacious when it is. "The magic," as Malinowski says, "is in the breath, and the breath is the magic." Rothenberg chants the lines, syncopates them by stressing the initial words. He reads the last lines impressively, as appropriate closure; reads exuberantly, making us aware that speech is sensuous and that sensuousness has an important place in what he is doing.

And why shouldn't he sing, since it is his way of participating in what is gone, of recovering the tribal past? Singing is an achievement he records in the dedication—something he recently learned by living with the Seneca Indians—and it accords with the shamanist work of summoning the ghosts of the past, the ancestors, and of healing and making whole.

"The Voice should never be separated from the Utterance" (Zohar).

By virtue of the fact that these are poems to be sounded, they belong to a tribal past, belong to a different world, ask us to attend in a different way. Poems like "The King of the Jews" and "Satan in Goray" are sounding, ritualistic poems, and the latter is reprinted here, not merely to recall an important historical event, but to recall Stein's "primitive" practice, the primitivity of avant-garde practice. "The Key of Solomon" also begins with soundings, with seed-words, as in Duncan's "The Fire," though these, I suspect, are from *The Key of Solomon*, a magical text, and remind us, as the poem does, of magical rites.

5 January 1982

Shamans are magicians, technicians of the sacred, and Eleanor Antin pictures this in the collage facing the title page. Here, Rothenberg, in top hat, with a black cock resting on it, with two white doves(?) fluttering nearby, holds a crystal ball/crescent moon/star in his hands. He surmounts a pyramid composed of cutouts, photographic and painterly, of immigrant women mostly, some mothers with small sons, among them at the apex, just beneath Rothenberg, the naked figure of (presumably) the Shekinah (a classical torso, hence the essence of all women). In another guise, Rothenberg, placed among the women, is reading a prayer book, subduing, it seems, the demon beneath his feet. So, prayer and magic are assimilated to each other.

By placing Rothenberg at the apex, Eleanor Antin may be scoring a fact Rothenberg himself recognizes by enclosing "The Grandmothers" with the word *man* and considers in *The Notebooks* when he observes that the Shekinah may be a creation of "male imagination," a view easily acquired, I think, from Raphael Patai's *The Hebrew Goddess*.

Eleanor Antin's *collage* is the analogue of the poems, of the book, which in part and whole is a collage composition of the real and the fantastic, of different times, different places, different modes, materials, and forms. With this difference: the movement from poem to poem is kaleidoscopic.

And the ball Rothenberg holds? "Properly, we shd. read for power. Man reading shd. be man intensely alive. The book shd. be a ball of light in one's hands." Pound, cited in *America a Prophecy*. Emerson: read for lustres.

An analogue? A key. The poems in this installment unhusk the kernel, increasingly bring forward the Shekinah, whose presence in some degree informs them, is hidden there. The Kabbalah provides the major key—the key being the fact of keys, of the need to read for hidden meanings. Which is to say that words are magical. "The Key of Solomon," by way of naming a book of magic, links religion with the occult; but my own fumbling with the key to this key introduces the *seal* of Solomon, itself a magical sign, numerically magical, even calling up the name of God. And a significant sign, signifying, as its interlocking triangles do, the union of contraries: light and dark, spirit and flesh, male and female, heaven and earth.

Shamans, magicians, tricksters. The poem insists on the oldest ways of *poesis* even as it employs avant-garde means. The antic is a conspicuous element of the poem, so much so that Rothenberg thinks of *Poland/1931* as "yiddish surrealist vaudeville." I think of Barbara Tedlock's fine essay, "The Clown's Way," because what she says of the sacred Indian clowns, of their indecency, of their contrary spirit (they are spirits of the contraries), of the use they make of laughter to open the realms of spirit, readily applies to Rothenberg. Two things, especially, mark Rothenberg's development as a poet and measure his depth: the comic turn his work has taken and its performative nature. He has learned to sing, and in doing so, he has, *as a poet*, not only as translator and anthologist, come into a tribal past.

The trickster is the sign of this because he is contrary, the primordial "mental rebel" as it were, "a model for the Great Refusal to the lie of Church & State"—the *order* and *constraints*
of civilization. The trickster denies Plato, is the outlaw poet
who refuses to be outlawed. This, Rothenberg insists, now defines the essential burden of the poet, the work of "'liberation
from spiritual & political oppression,'" and his own work is
now more conspicuously political than before. Both *Shaking
the Pumpkin* (1972) and *A Big Jewish Book* (1978) are explicitly political in commentary and pre-face. They align themselves with the political directive of Stanley Diamond's *In
Search of the Primitive*, the search, that is, for what constitutes our primary, fullest sense of what it means to be human.
This searching of our tribal past brings forward the excluded
elements of the Great Subculture, and in doing so, in speaking
for inclusiveness, speaks for a profound will to change. *Makes
new.* Rothenberg prefaces *A Big Jewish Book* with a Talmudic
saying that defines the *fixed* as whatever *blocks the will to
make it new*—a Talmudic context for Pound's modernist
slogan, and a kindly jibe. The work of anthropologists like
Diamond and Tedlock and of poets like Rothenberg and Olson,
and Snyder and Antin focuses its political meaning and makes
us realize that we may make new by renewing the old, repossessing what we have needlessly, thoughtlessly, and at peril
put behind us.

6 January
1982

Where does the trickster appear here? In the presentation of
the sensual, sexual, scatological; in the insistent vulgarity; in
the assault on cleanliness; in the concern with "mystics,
thieves, & madmen"; in the redefinition of the Jew as fully
human, something also proposed in *A Big Jewish Book*. The
"humanizing redemptive gusto" Duncan praises in this book
recovers what Diamond, remembering Marx, calls the human
possibilities of our "species being." Also in the forms: another

normative verse form, in "The Mothers," "The Grandmothers," "The Fathers," recalls the sonnet. In the mixed (impure) diction and verbal play: the "hijacked innocence," say, in the hymn to the Shekinah, herself addressed as "o Hole o Holy Mother."

Though there is another naming poem, "The Beards" (to the Patriarchs and Elders), this book is anything but patriarchal, subverting the Rabbis and the rule of Law. Think of it as a book of the mothers, the Great Mother of "The Grandmothers," a term inclusive of Indian culture also; a book whose ambivalence directs us to the issue of cleanliness, the primordial strife of order and chaos. Marduk and Tiamat, as Harris Lenowitz, one of Rothenberg's collaborators in *A Big Jewish Book*, spells out the *mikvah* in the article "The Blood." The milk and the blood—the purity and the sensual impurity—of *Poland/1931* are not kept separate, and they are united and legitimated in marriage, which is also ritually recalled on the Sabbath when sexual union again figures the reunion of God and the Shekinah. As Lenowitz says, "The overall thrust in *Poland/1931* is toward acceptance of fluidity, sex, violence, etc., with all its felt dangers." The service of the Shekinah is a *trickster's*, but as the Shekinah in her exile reminds us, this service would bring an end to our exile from much that makes us human.

Exile. Emphasized in the program of *A Big Jewish Book*:

> •a sense of exile both as cosmic principle (exile of God from God, etc.) & as the Jewish fate, experienced as the alienation of group & individual, so that the myth (gnostic or orthodox) is never only symbol but history, experience, as well;
>
> •from which there comes a distancing from Nature & from God (infinite, ineffable), but countered in turn by a *poesis* older than the Jews, still based on namings, on an imaging of faces, bodies, powers, a working out of

possibilities (but, principally, the female side of God—
Shekinah—as Herself in exile) evaded by orthodoxy,
now returning to astound us;

•or, projected into language, a sense (in Jabès's phrase)
of being "exiled in the word."

All of this underwrites the mental rebel—rebellion against
exile, alienation, division.

7 January
1982

This installment closes with a poem celebrating the Shekinah,
a hymn, a catalog of attributes, in its way like Duncan's treatment of Venus in *The Venice Poem* or, more to the point since
Rothenberg notes it in *A Big Jewish Book*, "The Maiden,"
which begins, "we consider / precedent to that Shekinah."
The poem comes with a kind of suddenness, as if to compen-
sate for the previous poem, addressed to fallen-away Jews. Its
ecstatic pitch also lifts it above all that precedes it. And ecstasy is the point of *poesis,* and works here to recreate a past
feeling, makes it present, not in the same way but to the same
end as the movement in many poems between a narrator and a
first-person speaker, where identification *presents* a past experience, makes it new.

The rhythm of the work—and what I feel as suddenness—
comes from what is resisted by Rothenberg as he moves forward. The story he has to tell is one of displacement and falling away, of forgetting, where his own movement is one of
return and remembering. The poems turn on home, on leaving
and returning. He is returning and so moves in a contrary direction, and the difficulty can be felt in the resistance of his
materials.

The exile and displacement figure our own, especially as, in
light of the Shekinah, they concern male and female. To have
lost the religious sense is to have lost the full understanding

of woman, the "mystery" that respects all of her attributes.
Rothenberg refuses the genteel/gentile code, stated in "The
Fathers": be a friend, be a brother to your wife. A far cry from
what is summoned and lost:

> some were in love & grew
> beautifully in the half darkness of the home
> for which they lit candles

This poem is a fitting closure. The revelation, the disclosure
at the heart of the faith, an emblem of exile and homecoming.
For the poem itself ends in a vision of homecoming, of an
end to exile by coming to America; translates the dream of
"America" into Hasidic-Kabbalist terms, making "America"
serve an even greater vision. *America a Prophecy.*

Rothenberg recalls Blake, to good purpose. Perhaps the most
important thing these poems bear witness to is Rothenberg's
belief that the Shekinah's "reappearance among us is an event
of contemporary *poesis, not* religion."

In the beginning, at least, *The Book of Testimony* represents a
subsidence from the previous installment. It is a book of representative characters, a book of the *beards*, of males, anyway, a kind of *Spoon River Anthology* out of *Satan in Goray.*
A book, too, almost exclusively concerned with Poland, with
the orthodox world represented in the photograph of a woman
helping Rothenberg put on phylacteries. Women don't do this:
the daily prayer begins with thanks to God for not having
been made a woman. So maybe prefigured here is the defilement that constitutes the theme of this installment. There are
five testimonies, two in quatrains, three (the more notable,
longer ones) in a triadic form, where the lines step down from
right to left—just the reverse of Williams' triads. This is a curious formal means because the movement is resisted by the

8 January
1982

eye. Rothenberg employs it to suggest the right-to-left reading of Hebrew; he uses it elsewhere to translate early Hebrew texts. Yet in his hands it remains fluid—lines often divide within themselves and run over—and helps him syncopate the narratives, spoken by the characters and sometimes by himself as narrator. It is not a form for meditation like Williams', but for the vertiginous motion of simultaneity, as in "The Slaughterer's Testimony." It is appropriate to the mad, fantastic, visionary, con-fused world presented here.

The poems answer to the need for density, for the palpable as well as visionary world of Polish Jewry. And, notably, we enter that world in terms of defilement. This is the book of blood, meat, sensual hunger, and sexual license. Rothenberg enjoys sexual evocation as a healthy sign of humanity and because sexuality, even when it possesses the student in the form of a demon, stirs one to vision. The reason the initial subsidence doesn't last is that "The Slaughterer's Testimony" and "The Student's Testimony" reach a visionary pitch in which the profane employs sacred imagery. The latter, incidentally, ends with a coda on restored spirituality and reminds us of the Shekinah in the first installment.

9 January 1982 | *A Book of Writings,* of the order of the postal card facing the title page. News from the homeland; an artifact of the Poland to which this section returns, a deeper culture even than that in the previous section. There is a kind of anthropological interest here; the density of particulars; and the section itself is a grab bag (or so it seems at first) in which there is some sorting and progression.

Four ancestral scenes provide a way in. Not Poland/1931 but Poland/1910. All are interiors evocative of a life in which the

old ways persist but are about to be lost. Electricity, introduced before World War I, is a nice image of this, the broken
light bulb reminding us of the Shekinah, the "Dazzler." The
poems carry over Rothenberg's insistence on sensuality/
vulgarity versus the Law, and here their diverse forms, as with
other groups of poems, remind us that there are no formal re-
strictions. The first poem, and the collage aspects of others, is
a clue to the composition of the section, and *four* is a number
of Kabbalistic significance.

The *Amulets* and *Polish Anecdotes* are further ways into a
world of folk-oral forms, perhaps antiphonic here because
there is much in this Polish world to guard against. They are
followed by two poems of "neolithic" bearing addressed to
contemporary poets: Gary Snyder, whose shamanism and
politics conflate with the vision and boldness of Rabbi
Nachman's Hasidic meditative practice, and Nathaniel Tarn,
whose *Lyrics for the Bride of God* brings forward the vision of
the Shekinah. In this way, and subsequently in his own use of
archaic forms, Rothenberg insists on the currency of "old"
ideas and *poesis*. So we go deeper, farther back, and to poems
like "A Poem from the Saint's Life," an extravagant fantasy of
the "folk" mind, and "Amulet" (p. 63), a concrete, sounding
poem composed of four sets of two words, the initial word the
Hebrew name of one of the four rivers of Paradise, the second
word the first spelled backward. We have entered deeply the
world of sacred letters and numbers.

At the center of the section, and its pivot, are ten (*ten*) poems
under the title "From *The Code of Jewish Law.*" All are pro-
hibitions, in what we would now consider excessive patho-
logical detail, that for the most part involve food ("blood in
milk") and sex. They enable us to read back into earlier in-

stallments, and their presence here demonstrates how the Law, not without its superstitions, exists with other kinds of spiritual lore.

Another "Amulet" (p. 71) is composed of four columns, each made up of single words, except for "22," which refers to the number of letters in the Hebrew alphabet. These tell of the practice of the "master / of / dreams" and the ecstasy of song and dance that leads to vision. We've entered the Kabbalists' world. A found poem proves it: "Tree Spirit Events (Zohar)," also printed in *A Big Jewish Book.* Subsequent alphabet, word, and book events ask us to participate in the sacred magic of letters and numbers. Rothenberg himself becomes a master of dreams; the past is present here, in these "happenings" happening again; universal events, in fact, because, as he has shown us elsewhere, they have counterparts in other cultures (see the Australian "Lily Event").

Tedlock: "to tell these words is *to happen* the beginning again."

These events play off woman's events which involve defilement and purification and matters of a sexual and generative nature. Men, it seems, deal with letters and numbers; women have a different magic (though soon enough there will be a Mme. Shekinah who reads cards—ten of them—tells fortunes).

Finally, two poems on numbers, on four and seven, the very long one relating a satisfactory union of man and woman. This is followed by "She," a naming poem in praise of the Shekinah, who is herself Lilith, and by a closing "Amulet" in Hebrew (so we finally come face to face with the original), which contains the names of Lilith used to ward against her. As in the previous sections the closure culminates in poems summoning the presence of the Shekinah.

The fourth section, "Galician Nights, or a Novel in Progress," is comic, a kind of Jewish soap opera. The advertisement sets this up: Esther K. as Mme. Shekinah, fortune-teller, healer, spiritualist. Mme. Sosostris. The design of the advertisement is amusing in the way misspellings used to be—there is much here to give the greenhorn away, yet much to show (characteristic of Esther) that she is resilient, quick to catch on, exploit the occasion. K to the contrary, she is not exclusively a Kafka character, but, as the con of the advertisement indicates, a female trickster, the Shekinah as Lilith. Williams would call her a "modern replica."

Esther = Aster = A star. See Rothenberg's "Death Poem" inside the back cover of *Vort*, modeled on the Greek "Epitaph" in *A Big Jewish Book* (pp. 446–47). Esther = a star. So why not Astarte? Great Goddess?

Fragmented narrative, prosy; no linear story. "I have brought you these circumstances toward a tale of Esther K." We are to piece them together and fill out the glimpses we get of Esther and Leo Levy, to whom, it seems, she was married and who wrote to invite her to China. Esther has had a career as picaresque and *outlandish* as his, has been, among other things, the paramour of the governor of Poland, has "tasted of the Gentile's honey." This explains her exile, why she can have "no reunion in her father's tent."

Leo, with his glass eye, is also a trickster, who, enamoured of his wife, writes a good letter. And she, in one of her "melodies," says that she "will follow his motorcycle / up the Great Wall of China."

Closure? Again, the Shekinah, by way of Isaac Luria's "Hymn to Shekinah For The Feast of The Sabbath," which (again) richly figures the union of God and the Shekinah. In *A Big Jewish Book*, where Rothenberg reprints his working of this Kabbalist poet's hymn, he explains, citing Raphael Patai, that the Shekinah is an independent feminine divinity and the heir of ancient Hebrew goddesses of Canaanite origin like Asherah and Anath. He also notes her counterpart in Lilith. Mrs. Leo Levy. L.L. = *Lilith*.

The fifth part is (so far) the most accomplished. Is this why Rothenberg chose to publish it separately in the handsome performance edition by the Unicorn Press? The title, *Esther K. Comes to America*, tells very little about it, unless the poem of that name is intended to suggest the thematic thread: the something-less-than-perfection of immigration, the dream of a fantastic life reduced to small rations: tea and onion rolls in a cafeteria (called The Wilderness); bitter almonds and sour lemons. (Leo's sign is a lemon.)

All of the poems except the last, which in any case doesn't read differently, are in Rothenberg's normative free verse. All are narrative, descriptive, richly detailed, composed of images that, like the lines, are fluid, easily con-fused; that form a montage presenting a delirium of experience, the world-in-consciousness. One of the possibilities Leo Levy entertains is "to remake '1931' as a talking movie." This is what Rothenberg may be said to do in this especially filmic section of the book. In an interview with Spanos, where a portion of the title poem serves as an example, Rothenberg explains this normative verse as a collage that forms a single structure, that is, whose fragments are not kept apart but join.

Poland/1931 has a complex, well-joined structure. Its fragmentary nature and openness are deliberate. Rothenberg's concern with collage compositions that tightly fit represents his

sense of reality and the work of inclusive form, to bring the
diverse into unity.

The concluding poem of this section also calls attention to
the epical aspect of the work. Here he recalls for the first time
his own experience and family history, but denies autobiography (or is it confessional verse?), insisting, as he had by citing
Cézanne in his earliest magazine, that "we are all one man."
He shares Olson's belief that

> The only interesting thing
> is if one can be
> an image
> of man
>   (*Maximus*, III, 101)

"*Poland* is the self as much as possible in terms of ethnos."
The voice is communal. What we hear, as Michael Bernstein
says of epic verse, is "the voice of the community's heritage
'telling itself.'" The tale of the tribe.

Isn't the fact of familiarity for those who have heard these
tales, heard these voices, part of the pleasure and the power?
This tale is especially telling because the tone throughout is
fitting: bittersweet/sad, the accepting tone of recollection, of
tribal memory, which, in giving us the past, gives us the un-
alterable. And immigration—the never-ending diaspora—is
anything but happy. Whether they end up in shoe factories or
as gangsters, the immigrants are all like Charlie Chaplin,
their representative here of "the sweet soul in exile."

13 January
1982

Incidentally, Rothenberg's poem on Chaplin bears comparison
with Crane's and with Mandelstam's reprinted in *A Big Jewish
Book*. It is composed of clips from his films, and Chaplin is
the clown/trickster to whom Rothenberg, with his derby and
pack, likens himself. He concurs in Mandelstam's view of

Chaplin as one of us: "as all of us live poorly— / strangers, strangers."

Exile from what? Oppression? There is oppression in America. From love? Very much so, and from other sensual satisfactions. Rothenberg catches the Jew in troubled transition, entering the secular world and still wearing earlocks. See the closing poem of *A Seneca Journal*. What is history in the section entitled *A Book of Histories?* An anthology. A collage of stories; things repeated, as the Steinesque writing of the facing mandala reminds us (is history circular, Viconian?). The diverse materials, prose mostly, often fragmentary, need not have been gathered into *seven* poems, but that is *the* number of this book, and there is a progression, from Polish materials to those of America, in number six. These collages are filmic, and in many instances the verbal record could be read aloud and accompanied by images projected on a screen—as in a Carolee Schneemann performance. Representations of reality? Yes, the mix/simultaneity of elements of Jewish life, secular and religious (though always a Jewish way of life), ridiculous ("hernia/hemorrhoids") and sublime (Rabbi Shimeon's praise of the supernal beard): the "fantastic life."

The seventh history returns to Poland. It plays off the previous history (its last entry, following one on the Mafia, about a play called *Demented America*). With its entry on Kabbalistic vision, the seventh sets up the concluding poems on Cokboy.

14 January 1982

Cokboy. The grand finale. One of Rothenberg's finest poems, inimitably his, in form, mode, content. A set piece, of high comedy. Could be vaudeville, even a script for Lenny Bruce. The Jew as Cowboy, and the Baal Shem, no less! As rich in its way as *Gunslinger*, taking up, among other things, elements

of the six-gun mystique. *A jew among / the indians.** Outlandish, yes; but there were Jews in China; there are Jews (almost) everywhere. And lost tribes, in exile, dispossessed of
vision, might as well find each other. *The* tale of the tribe*s*.

Pace Pound, whose representation of Yiddish speech Rothenberg reproves with his own comic use of it. The Yiddish speech
is in the present, of stunning immediacy, and plays off the past
tense of Cokboy's narrative ("saddlesore I came"), which in
turn is made present by Rothenberg-as-narrator in his asides,
"(he says)." This is not unlike what Rothenberg notes of the
Cuna Indians, who are mentioned in the poem: their "narrative mode . . . shifts the perspective from third to first person, both to make historical time immediate & to freely in-
teriorize some of the objective material."

Actually the poem is in the present of what Rothenberg speaks
of as "kabbalistic time"—and Kabbalistic space. It belongs to
a visionary present in which all persons, places, and things
may be read synchronically. So the Jew in the Wilderness is at
once Moses, our Puritan forebears, and any number of sheriffs
with a mission to bring the Law (and order) to this godfor-
saken place. Kabbalistic time—and the Kabbalistic way of
reading—"brings all men together": Buffalo Bill, Custer, lonely
riders, Senator Goldwater, the Baal Shem (searching for "my
brother Esau among these redmen"). In Kabbalistic time,
one conflates history and myth—the myth, in this instance,
of the terrible mother, whose *vagina dentata* Rothenberg,
with folk humor extravagance, replaces with chainsaws. And

*David Marc reminds me that the movie *The Frisco Kid* (1979)
treats this theme. Did Rothenberg's poem inspire it?

Kabbalistic space? The Baal Shem, who makes a medicine bundle of Jewish things, travels the "Wyoming steppes."

Kabbala. The letters. Not just Cokboy's grandfather, one of the men-of-letters, humorously linked with the pony express, but, more disturbingly,

> the letters going backwards
> (he says) so who can read the signboards
> to the desert

Displace is maybe crazy (displace: so is displacement). "*Demented America*—his final play" (p. 136), and the take on Williams' "The pure products of America / go crazy" (p. 151).

The Baal Shem comes to America to "feed them visions." He is a shaman, like the Cuna *nele;* like Rothenberg, who is writing/singing, in the ecstasy of his materials, a visionary poem of visions and visionaries. The Baal Shem has two visions: of the disappearance of a man and a city (I recall Leslie Silko's *Ceremony*) and of a city of glass, elevators, brown-skinned people (itself approximating a Cuna vision). Is this a vision of the promised land? of liberated slaves?

Then the Baal Shem/"old jew" undertakes a vision quest and meets an eagle, which translates into the history of manifest destiny, the exploitation of the continent; actually a continuing present event that he is powerless to stop. The eagle also "lifts him / / to a safe place above the sunrise" and gives him a song, which Rothenberg records in both Indian and Yiddish nonsense syllables. Finally, having become a bona fide Indian shaman, the Baal Shem joins his Indian confrere in a comic routine that prefaces a story of creation.

Part Two opens with a scatological creation myth, in which 15 January 1982 the continent, likened to the human body, gives birth to a female beaver. We are in the world of *A Seneca Journal*. The myth is comic, overlaid by another delivery that suggests the uterine journey of the Cuna Indians, both in turn assimilated to Moses and the Egyptian princess (the Shekinah). The point: "so hard America is born."

The Baal Shem—a correspondent of William Blake's—dreams of America's birth. In the company of his Indian friend, he tells of this in terms of his own birth as a beaver from the plastic, despoiled, no longer terrible mother of the continent. He finds himself "a beaver among the rushes" (his mission Moses', to be "the Great Deliverer"). He finds himself in "the female swamp," and, discovering his penis ("like great cock of the primal beings"), he becomes the veritable CO[C]KBOY, a creator-god, say, like Atum, and asserts his patriarchal authority by shows of sexual prowess taken directly from accounts of Coyote, the trickster. And since we are in Kabbalistic time, Coyote's fucking the Indian princess *is* "The Marriage of America," *is*, for the Baal Shem, the union of God and the Shekinah, inspiring him to ecstatic praise of God and his own marriage to an Indian girl—all this coexisting with Custer's last stand and with the moon, now "a silver dollar over Barstow." (There is also the phrase "his train has reached Topeka," which for those who know Dorn's *Recollections of Gran Apachería* has an ominous resonance.)

The Indians are not pleased with the Baal Shem's marriage because, in Kabbalistic time, it is one with the historical spoliation of the West by those "bringers of civilization heros heros" the Baal Shem himself deplores ("I will fight my way past you who guard the sacred border"). But he never crosses the border;

like Moses, he is denied "true entry to the west true paradise." And when he "stares at California" it is not the promised land, as the lost leaders of Steinbeck's story discovered,
only as the chant has it

> America disaster
> America disaster
> America disaster
> America disaster
> Where he can watch the sun go down
> in desert

The exile isn't over, the redemption hasn't come. We witness
instead the decline of the West. We stare westward into death.
Like the Baal Shem and "his grandfather's / ghost of Ishi," the
last of the Yana, we look to the west in silence, speechless.

Poland/1931 supports the old saying, "It's hard to be a Jew." It
gainsays the optimism Rothenberg may have had when, at the
end of *Shaking the Pumpkin,* he endorsed Snyder's belief that
the ghost of the Indian "will claim the next generation as its
own." The primary reason, as the Baal Shem and the ghost
of Ishi know in looking west, is the Vietnam War of the
"bringers of civilization."

16 January   Kevin Power, who has written so well on Rothenberg, speaks
1982   of *Poland/1931* as a "transcultural and open-ended epic."
Transcultural, yes; but open-ended? It is no more open-ended
than *Gunslinger* and for the same reason: it closes with a
vision of closure, and with an end to speech—"guess I got
nothing left to say [no period]." It also has the completeness
of its *seven* sections. If we feel otherwise, it may be because
here, as in *A Big Jewish Book,* where there is much to dismay
us—the "Book of the Wars of Yahveh," of exile, speaks for itself, the only commentary a footnote telling us that here is "a
record of *poesis* (vision, voice) as the struggle for human sur-

vival in a world of mind-forged manacles & racial bondage"—
it may be because Rothenberg demonstrates the gener-
ative/creative force of language that informs so much of the
lore the poem assimilates and hence the fact that "the ecstasy
& the [visionary] journey do persist . . . & the impulse to
poesis survives the disappearance of the shamans." *Poesis:* the
"basic poetic process, in which the recognition of contraries
conditions & is conditioned by a pressure toward their
reconciliation."

Are *history* and *vision* among the contraries Rothenberg
reconciles? Vision in this poem involves a journey in history
in which the past is not transcended but made present—
brought into presence by virtue of the intensity, the incandes-
cence of the poet's seeing. He has a *vision of history.* This accords with what he cites from Stanley Diamond:

> Human consciousness is historical; in order to under-
> stand ourselves, to heal ourselves, in this age of abstract
> horror, we must regain the sense of the totality and the
> immediacy of human experience. In order to determine
> where we are, we must learn, syllable by syllable, where
> we have been. The sense of history is, for society in cri-
> sis, what relentless self-searching, psychoanalytic or
> otherwise, is for the individual in crisis, that is, it can
> be releasing and enriching, cathartic and creative; it
> may be the only thing that can save our lives.

Who can read this and not recall H.D. writing in praise of
Freud's recovery of the dream, the "dream of everyone, everywhere" that, understood, would "save mankind"? Or the opening line of Duncan's "Rites of Participation" in *The H.D.
Book:* "The drama of our time is the coming of all men [and
women] into one fate, 'the dream of everyone, everywhere'"?
In this chapter, rich in the lore Rothenberg has made his own,
we learn that like the Australian aborigine with his tjurunga
and the Kabbalist with his Shekinah, "we, too, in a hostile en-

vironment, [must take] our faith and home in our exile, live in creative crisis."

By remembering. Mnemosyne is the mother of the Muses, and epic poems such as *Poland/1931* turn to her because, as Hannah Arendt says, "memory and depth are the same, or rather, depth cannot be reached by man except through remembrance."

2 February 1982

The tribal book, his shaman's notebook: *A Seneca Journal* (1978). Named in the title, located. "It was a very special *place*," he tells Spanos, "& I was turned on to that also: the first time that not just 'people' or 'ethnos' but 'place' & 'city' got into my work. I mean by that the *actual* place & the *actual* people, who aren't simply story-book romantic Indians." He recovers the community a shaman-poet needs—what elsewhere performance may help him gather. And he gets turned on to animals, the mystic animals, which permits him to enter the Society of Shamans. Had, he says, "a sense of identification with all of life, as in the animal and biological poems and the mysteries of the hidden, universal language."

A book to be considered with Dorn's *The Shoshoneans* and *Recollections of Gran Apacheria* and Snyder's *Myths & Texts* and *Turtle Island.*

The book, appropriately, is in four parts.

The prefatory poem, "Salamanca A Prophecy," substitutes *Salamanca* for *America* in the title of the revisionist account of American literature, *America a Prophecy*, published in the same year. Comparable to Snyder's use of Turtle Island, the turtle, here, in Rothenberg's poem: "a city on / a turtle's back." Though he conflates this with Jerusalem, and so speaks of the

tribes he would bring together, the resonances, I find, are
more telling. The city whose location waits on the second line
is the Puritan city upon a hill and Pound's Dioce, which in
turn carries all the longing for the Wagadu in the African
story of Gassire's Lute. Pound is the presence here, echoed
again in "impossible to bring it all / together," and when you
turn the page to the prose preface to *Beavers,* Pound is present
again, his notion of epic and history linked with Olson's notion
of history as the "new localism." Which defines this poem
of the local as an epic? And isn't the initial poem, "A Poem of
Beavers," Poundian? an ideogrammic, constellating bringing-
it-all-together?

The Baal Shem was born a beaver and so was Rothenberg: "I
became a beaver in 1968. Richard Johnny John was my father.
The ceremony took place in the longhouse."

Seneca Journal 1 ("A Poem of Beavers") has five parts. The
first part is formally the most interesting because it puts in
juxtaposition a found poem (Harry Watt's story of his dream of
beavers); Rothenberg's recognition of the story as a memory of
his "grandfathers," the ancestors in Poland (this set out in an
almost Antin-like score); and his poetic statement of the "logical" conclusion. This part of the poem concerns vision and
speech, and its logic involves the actual dream/vision of Harry
Watt's communication/communion with beavers, the Baal
Shem's acquisition of animal speech and "biological fellow-
hood," and Rothenberg's own shamanist vision of the shamanist inheritance. Thematically, this is of the greatest importance not only for this book but all of Rothenberg's work:

> ethology the visions
> of McClure & Chomsky all
> the speakers of deep tongues point
> a route this generation

will be privileged to assume
a universal speech
in which the kingdoms of the world
are one

Impossible to bring it all together? Doesn't he bring it all together when he repeats, declaratively, "the kingdoms of the
world are one"?

3 February   To become a beaver, one meditates on beavers, on the world of
1982   water, the "fluid world," and the *animal* one is, the generative
sexual being one has. So

the Baal Shem leaves the light of Torah
& becomes   [full stress]
any old animal inside
the sacred wood

—where the wood is sacred but not exactly in Eliot's sense.

The verse in this part and those that follow is normative, a
spoken free verse, sometimes personal in the way of *The
Notebooks:*

what is it to be a beaver truly
when I think of it I think
                *   *   *
& I am now living in
a place called Bucktooth once

The parts are divided by a line, in the manner in which he
chose to divide Oppen's *Discrete Series* in *Revolution of the
Word.* This is the only poem divided in this way, which is
why I think of an ideogram. Numbers, employed elsewhere,
insist on seriality.

The parts of this poem are lovely, a good Creeley word I use
now, as I haven't so far in talking of Rothenberg's work, be-

cause of the personal meditative lyricism I find so attractive in
The Notebooks. How otherwise to speak of what he says of
Bucktooth, a place named after a small Indian with a single
tooth (he cites the documents; he is doing his research in the
poem as Olson does it in *Maximus*)? This pygmy or lepre-
chaun, he thinks, might better be called "Old Beaver Tooth,"
which leads him into considering his initiation as a beaver
and the significance, in this context, of his new identity:

> if I could make my face a mask
>   [such as he's seen]
> I'd be Old Bucktooth
> Beaver once again old founder
> of a town we can all live in hoping
> that no other
> Duke of Salamanca comes
>   [the reservation is at Salamanca]
> to sponsor a new railroad

Like Olson/Maximus, he, too, would found a *polis*; "The initiation / of another kind of nation" (Olson, at the end of *Maximus*). Like Olson's, his epic concerns foundation.

To be a beaver truly is to be a "power," he says in the next
part, where the longer lines, somewhat elevated, treat in a visionary way the *deep* mysteries of life and death. And life
and death enclose the subsequent part, only now the mode is
folkish, like a Coyote story, and the tale a wholly natural one
of sensual "animal" satisfaction. A beaver's life (and death) is
never far from his nurturing "mudder" (picking up on *udder*),
though to survive he has, sometimes, as the concluding part
tells us, to fight otter, chew off his balls.

Each of the four parts of *A Seneca Journal* has the unity of its
title. Part One, about beavers, is composed of four installments of "Seneca Journal," interspersed with songs and other
kinds of poems, in *keeping*, as we say. The first is "Old Man

4 February
1982

Beaver's Blessing Song," a chant repeating two lines, one of
meaningless sounds, set up on the page as a concrete poem.
The second "Seneca Journal" is an Indian story of a boy who,
following his dreams (his vision), kills the Great White Beaver,
thereby outraging the witch, the terrible mother, who subsequently dies in a sweathouse. So we enter the primordial
world.

And the cosmogonal world of "Song #2," where the beaver
dives for mud with which to make the world, followed by an
ecological poem, "The Cycles," about the aboriginal popula-
tion of beavers, whose work "maintained" it. I recall Edmund
Wilson's *Apologies to the Iroquois* (1960), where he considers
Salamanca and the proposal for the Kinzua Dam—Wilson,
who erroneously compared the Corps of Engineers to beavers!

The third "Seneca Journal" concerns the Baal Shem, who did
indeed go to the woods to pray, and "The Speech of Animals"
is a more comic narrative poem, jived, interwoven past un-
weaving. The "'Beavers, an Idyll'" that follows also joins animal and human, four legs and two legs. It is ironic ("American
/ idyll," where *idyll* puns on *idle*), the vantage being that of a
blissful beaver overhearing the "ridiculous musick" of slaves
(tame beavers).

Olson's *musick*, muse-sick; *pejorocracy*.

In "Poems from the Beaver Notebooks," brief notations under
headings that cover the beaver's world and life, animal and
human life again intertwine, though the narrative thread concerns the hunt of the beaver—the extermination of the beavers
by 1640, told in the concluding "Seneca Journal." Here the
verses correspond to the "Alpha & Omega" of the subtitle and
tell not only of beginning and end but of separation, the di-

vorce from the cosmogony in which the beaver was "father master / builder god / / . . . progenitor of tribes."

And the Baal Shem had a beaver hat!

Part Two, *Midwinter*, is a sheaf of minimal poems, none over six lines, with plenty of white space to tell us it's winter— winter, as one poem says, "when I cough." The poems are almost wholly Indian, ancestral materials, with neither the presence nor the perspective of a narrator. The epigraph, a few lines about a man-crow who asks essential existential questions, establishes the context. Then, songs, riddles, events, etc., which, if read through and sounded, are themselves a winter ritual. "Conclusion" provides a closure.

In Part Three, *Serpent*, the book moves literally into cosmogonal depths, not just those of the Indians, but, as Charles Doria points out, those of Mediterranean peoples, including the Naasenes, a Jewish Gnostic sect of snake worshippers. *The dream of everyone, everywhere.* There is more history and story now, more evidence of Rothenberg's immediate personal occasion. Here, it seems to me, he conspicuously joins Olson in the richness of materials and their disposition, and in theme. He, too, is a partisan of the serpent, associated with water and women and the primacy of matriarchy. Like Olson, he sides with Typhon in his battle with the Thunderer(s)—at Salamanca he translated "Of Typhon & the Gods a Narrative after Apollodorus."

We enter this part with a story about the curative power of the snake, though I suspect displacement, the snake increasing rather than reducing the girl's "swelling." Then, in "Seneca Journal 5," we learn that the Thunderers (whose lightning is sometimes taken for the wavy/jagged/shaky water sign) hate especially the sexual aspect of the snake: "snakeskin or prepuce / was the gift of love / remembered in the Dark Dance." And hate the generative nurturing power of woman, mother earth, as "snake island lament" so nicely puts it:

"her hair became trees & grass
"her flesh the clay
"her bones the rock
"her blood the springs of water.

Snake Island = Turtle Island = the continent = despoiled America, where "The Xtian lady" considers the Indians, who imitate reptiles in their dance, "freaks." So we come to "Three Landscapes," recalling perhaps the poem of that name in *White Sun Black Sun:* landscapes here documented not deep imagist, telling of spoliation, the railway, as Crane said, raping the land. Yet, at the same time, there is the atavism of another cokboy, this one a scout whose diary shows him to have "opened his tongue to / other tastes." Finally, following an interval of stories and personal entries in prose and some notations in verse (very Olson-like), and the shortest of entries on the serpent becoming a whale (Olson-inspired?), "Seneca Journal 6" called "The Witness."

5 February 1982

This masterful poem in four parts begins in the present ("as day by day new separations / obliterate all peace") and moves into the witness, or vision, of an Indian boy who has seen in the propitious relation of black snake and white woman "snake of foundation / & a prophecy." This vision, in turn, is assimilated by Rothenberg, who relates his own visionary encounter with the snake lady of Snake Island, a present-day encounter in the bar of the Hotel Dudley that ends with the reenactment of the sexual intercourse of snake and woman—an equivalent, in its way, of the union of God and the Shekinah. The verse is nicely humorous, and I hear in it the confrontation of She and Paterson in Williams' poem, with just a touch of Faulkner, enough to remind me that what we have here countervails the biblical account of American history in *The Bear.* And aren't "the old people" of the subsequent prayer the old people, say, of *Go Down, Moses,* dreaming of the ancestors? They are keepers of the dream, where it all still is. The mind, "she" tells him, is "an entry to all thought there ever was!" So politics, which certainly concerns Rothenberg, yields to concern with "the dimensions of the mind" (the brain, "the dragon head," according to the Naasene cosmology), and this *finale* opens into the last part, *Dreams.*

By *gematria,* serpent = messiah.

Why should he, "Exiled in Salamanca," be "driven mad by / Image of the Temple"? Is it because the Shekinah was exiled when the Temple fell, the Temple in which God lived in connubium with His Shekinah? Is it because "exile" from the Godhead explains the husks that conceal the sparks?

Isn't this related to *Dreams* and the initial poem, "Seneca Journal 7," subtitled "The Dreamers"? In this poem he remembers the last of the Seneca diviners, or shamans, one who still had the primary gift of *poesis,* the ability to summon the "powers," the gods who inhabited these sacred woods:

> they would appear in words
> our language hides them
> even now
> the action of the poem brings them to light

The ambiguity of these lines belongs to *even now,* which may be read with either the precedent or antecedent line. If read with the former, we are still in exile; if read with the latter, exile is over by virtue of the *poesis* of this book. And though both are to be entertained, I think the latter is to be preferred because it is in keeping with what follows. This poem

is addressed to David Antin, who does not himself follow
Rothenberg's visionary practice. It tries to win him not only
by the ingratiation of "as David sounds like deva / means be-
loved" but by meeting him on his own ground of concern with
fundamental language acts such as asking a question. So it is
asking, in this instance the question pondered in *Beavers*, that
summons the poetic power:

> asking
> "who is Beaver?"
> forces them out of the one mind
> in mything
> mouthing the grains of language

Which accounts for the subsequent dream poem on creation
and the poem for Olson called "The Art of Poetry."

Deva also calls up *devil*. The perspective of the meditative
narrative of the poem's second part is that of a Jesuit who reports a shaman's death with an anthropologist's superior objec-
tivity and yet not without awe for the fact that " 'all their
cabins they have filled with dreams.' "

Like the moon dream/vision of the next part, linked here to
the ancestral world of *Poland/1931* and to the lost world of
humankind ("that old woman / once lighted up our minds").
The Iroquois woman's dream which enables her to become
Red Lady—the Indian Shekinah—is presented directly, with
an intensity that recalls the Mayan myth of Moon and Sun that
Olson tells at the end of "Human Universe"—his evidence of a
human universe and of the fact, not lost on Rothenberg, that
these Indians "were hot for the world they lived in." He ends
"The Dreamers," " 'hot with conception / the presence of their
world,' " and the poem to Olson, "in hot pursuit."

Olson's Mayan myth is reprinted in *Shaking the Pumpkin*,
where the cited lines are reserved for the commentary, a brief
paragraph that puts Olson in the context of Stanley Diamond's
search for the primitive. This paragraph, part of which follows, takes up Olson's own writing to the end of making the
political point of the collection:

> The "hotness" in Olson's description parallels Paul
> Radin's cry of recognition at presentation of a Pima nar-
> rative: *This is a reality at white heat,* & he [the reader]
> may consider both against the diminution of said inten-
> sity factor among the rulers-of-our-own lives today &
> may ponder if the triumph of the American republic
> didn't in fact accomplish the rub-out of the tribal poets
> Plato had proposed for all republics, *The way it was—*
> *The way it is, my fellow citizens!* [The last italicized
> words are Olson's.]

Elsewhere, in *Shaking the Pumpkin,* he defines poets as
"people hot in their seizing of reality through language." And
this involves dreams, what he speaks of in the poem as the
mind "turned upside down." (He glosses this in *Vort:* "an old
[Iroquoian] ritual that involves the guessing & acting out of
dreams.") So we have a cosmogonal vision of renewal, the
woman in the poem acting out the vision she has of "a new
world," becoming "red with a new promise / [as] the world-
child takes root in her."

"The Dreamers" is especially interesting because it includes
the personal and problematical as no other poem has. The
texts of documents within the poem are responded to by
Rothenberg in the dialogic fashion of *The Notebooks.* He says
in the coda:

8 February
1982

> I didn't see the red woman
> but wrote of her
> the poem breaks free from the mind
> it's crazy

Yes, it's turned upside down, which is why

> it's crazy
> that I can still turn to a friend & say
> "I wish they'd stop with this religion"

And then as he would dismiss the sacred it overtakes the poem, which in terms of several kindred myths of creation enacts what it says:

> "in dreaming
> "the images can cross
> "each other
> "become a single image
> "cross of light

Reality, here, is at white heat. And not only poems like "Dream Poem," but some, like "THE OTHERS   HUNTERS IN THE NORTH   THE CREE," are dreams. His.

The dream world contains the eternal ones, the ancestors, the windigo, ghosts with blue lights, and they are invited to "Dead Feasts," as told in "Seneca Journal 8." Indeed, the dream of the dead is the signal dream:

> a dream word
> speaks to me
> —Creation—
> came in a dream about
> the dead

And to a large extent because of the dead, vision remains alive in the persistence of "superstition," the remarkable providences, it might be said, of Indian culture, related in prose in "METAMORPHOSES, & OTHER STORIES." These, in turn, prepare for "A HISTORY OF SURREALISM IN CATTARAUGUS COUNTY," which is framed by the carving of a deer he sees above the local milk factory and by the dream of Thelma (Thelma Ledsome, his wife's tribal sister) which enters his, fills out the "good omen" he feels he has seen. The wonder of these dreams and ghosts is the renewal they promise, their prefigurement "of ripe days to come," when the tribe will again flourish, preserved by the "angels Metatron & Beaver" (a nice example of Rothenberg's con-fusion).

Much as I am stirred by this, much as I would like to believe in the Ghost Dance song, "We shall live again," and in Rothenberg's patent fable of the ascendancy of the Great Subculture, I find myself on reading the concluding lines ("a gift of whiteness / the pale-grey masters of our snow") recalling his early poem on the Leni Riefenstahl film. I do not dismiss this association because in the next poem on the Kinzua Dam, the juxtaposition of "DAM[N] / CIVILIZATION" speaks a hope the very dam forecloses. As before it the extermination of beavers had, and the coming of the railroad.

How does Rothenberg close this long poem, make it good? In the penultimate poem, "A SONG OF QUAVERING," we return to the beaver's frog-inhabited marsh, to primordial sexuality, and, in "Seneca Journal 9," to the Jew, who has not yet been wholly defeated, who has lived as long as the Indian with visions, and who instructs his American tribal counterparts with a fable of his experience. This poem is subtitled "The Pearl," another name for the Shekinah, and it begins with the story of a noble youth who can only "inherit . . . our Kingdom" by recovering the Pearl.

> "when thou has gone to Egypt
> "has brought the one Pearl from
> "middle of the sea the roaring serpent
> " 's wrapped around

Now the Shekinah, by way of the Canaanite Asherah (Lady Asherah of the Sea: Olson's Our Lady of Good Voyage!), is linked with the sea. But so is Lilith, who resides in the Red

10 February 1982

Sea and is wedded to Samael, the satan/serpent. Rothenberg
has conflated this and also reminded us of the serpent in the
second section of the book. Reminded us that redemption is
as deep and conflictful as creation itself.

In any case, the sections that follow tell of exile and return, of
a young Jew's journey to America and the fading of the "images of the ancient life"—and what could be worse than a Jew
in a strange land, brideless and so bereft of all that's meant by
Jewish life? This young man, in keeping with what we have
been told of ghosts, receives a letter from his dead father, who
now inhabits the muddy tunnel world of Beaver and has
learned its "upside down" wisdom:

> "did we not shun beasts in the old days?
> "o avoidance always avoidance
> . . . .
> "only the Baal Shem could punch his way thru

Beaver corroborates this when he says:

> "I am the beaver god the animal
> "spirit shall never die
> "I live in the remarkable Old Brain
> "yas yas I write mah poems there"

Beaver also considers the exile in terms of "denied flesh," and
calls up Whitman when he says, "sweet body may also be divine." But it seems that he leads the young man astray, or perhaps only because he has already been led astray by Lilith, the
Warsaw prostitutes, and his faith in the almighty dollar. This
contributes to the sensualism he enjoys. And to his death,
when urged on by Beaver he dances naked and is attacked by a
dog (dog = God spelled backward). Is this sacrificial dance a
dreadfully comic version of "The Dance" in The Bridge? It
ends with a delirious vision of consummation ("The Cafeteria
is mating with an Aeon") and, we are told, brings an end to
exile: "my eyes close / happily / I'm sailing home."

Death and return are eminently closural. But has he embarked
after Olson's fashion, in "The Art of Poetry": "'I set out now /
in a box upon the sea'"? He may be happy but I'm not happy
with this closure. Doesn't the Jew figure the present displacement and historical impasse? How could any long poem with
"America" for its theme now end in the optative mood? Yet
perhaps the difference between the first and last "Seneca Journal" poems measures more than the defeat of hope. Maybe the
conspicuous dadaism of the last poem proposes the hopeful
prospect of destructive chaos. Maybe it renews the push of
modernism, the great work of "mental rebels," to prepare
chaos, as Rothenberg said in *some/thing*, "for the birth of
something real."

Just as *Poland/1931* ends with the Indian, *A Seneca Journal*
ends with the Jew. These remarkable long poems constitute a
single vision. It is, finally, to use the title of Mark Schorer's
book on Blake, a politics of vision. As shaman-poet, Rothenberg has only the power of vision, without which the people
perish, because then there is no *poesis*, no creation.

Vienna Blood & Other Poems (1980). Interim work. Interest-   14 February
ing for the ways in which Rothenberg, with two distinguished   1982
long poems behind him, continues and extends his work.

The title took me by surprise. It also names the first section
and its concluding poem. This, with the initial poem, "At the
Castle," frames the section. The castle is Burg Wartenstein,
where Rothenberg performed in the summer of 1977, and for
all I know may be the castle in which I lived for a week when
I lectured to gymnasium teachers twenty-four years ago. It belongs to the world of Kafka and, even more, of Nerval, whose
"stricken tower" in "El Desdichado" plays off "tower. / broken.
/ every castle has." This recalls *The Waste Land* and evokes

a world, as does the *Wienerblut* of Strauss, that has long been ghost-ridden, its inheritance its own disinherited life. Rothenberg himself spells out the allusion:

> I play the prince
> in Nerval's tower
> reading my poems in the heart of
> empty Europe

And when I go back to read Nerval's poem of irretrievable loss and desolation, of what well may be for Rothenberg the absence of the Shekinah and resonant, too, of Crane's "The Broken Tower"—when I read in Duncan's translation, "Bears the black *sun* of the *Melancolia*"—I reenter the world of *White Sun Black Sun*, which, I suspect, was also present to Rothenberg.

Vienna Blood tells of a curious return, a "sailing home," as the last words of *A Seneca Journal* have it, that denies the value associated with return. Though this book doesn't bring him to the icy whiteness of wartime Poland, it brings him nevertheless to an *empty* Europe and to Vienna, a city, he says with stunning accuracy, "imperial but strangely voided." This may be only the way in which a Jew sees it, "the town / where Hitler walked," the now "jewless / hauptstadt" where the music is rock but the "innocence is [still] brutal." Vienna *blood*. Not exactly the blood of the *mikvah* or the earth color of the Indian world. No wonder Rainer Maria Gerhardt, recognizing his inheritance, could not find himself in the new open American poetry he so bravely published in *Fragmente*.

The empty heart of Europe. I am sure that we were meant to recall F. O. Matthiessen's *From the Heart of Europe* (1948), with its testimony of hope, among the evidences the fact that for the first time, Americans in Europe have come there to in-

struct Europeans. Rothenberg measures that hope with *empty.*
Yet here he is "hoping   like Artaud / 'to break through language / 'in order to touch life.'" Here he is, teaching what he
has learned in his twenty-year search for the primitive, how to
renew life by means of "events" that enable us to enter sacred
time and space.

The Indian and the Jew so conspicuous in this section are
carry-overs from *Poland/1931* and *A Seneca Journal,* the sur-
plus, as it were, of their generative energy, indicating the way
in which these poems may be said to remain open. Both the
Indian and the Jew are pragmatic heroes, with Coyote's power
of transformation and survival. This is what they have to
teach us. * Also the necessity of madness.   15 February
1982

They serve the grandmother/Shekinah who has gone to the
wilderness, which now belongs to the vertical ("the new geography is up & down"), and who can only be reached by descent ("from air / to earth"). The patriarchal, in which "everything is charted from the sky," is no longer the way. We must
go "down / & down"—the descent beckons—descent into the
wilderness of ourselves, the "wildness we rouse / inside us."
This ground is the ground of poetry, and ground enough for a
Begründer. Recall Kerényi, who purposely chose this rich German word to nominate the "mythological 'fundamentalist' . . .
who, by immersion in the self, dives down to his own founda-
tions, founds his world." The *Begründer* is a shaman, no longer
heaven-bound, still at the primary work of origination, creation. So Rothenberg, confronted by so much that is empty and
hopeless in Europe and America, will "practice our wild system / —of talk & song— / that makes us poets." Language, he

---

*Maurice Kenny says that Rothenberg is preparing an anthol-
ogy on the Trickster.

insists, "is the ground / we grow from—wild— / who has to look outside / to find it?"

True enough, but desperate. As desperate as Tzara, a major presence in this book, who is cited as saying, "There is a great negative work of destruction to be done. . . . Those strong in words or in strength will survive, for they are quick to defend themselves." Which reminds me of what may also have been in Tzara's mind, the prayer that ends *A Great Jewish Book* ("strong strong we make ourselves strong")—the prayer Edmund Wilson recited daily in Hebrew and I wanted to use to close *Repossessing and Renewing*.

This book, as well as "Notes for a New Wilderness" from which I quoted earlier, is the poetic accompaniment to *New Wilderness Letter*, which Rothenberg, moving on from *Alcheringa*, started in 1977. This development gives me pleasure because it brings me back to Thoreau, conspicuous here because of his absence. Certainly Thoreau's "*In wildness is the preservation of the world*" is the proper motto for this magazine because the wilderness it addresses is a condition of the psyche. "It is not the part of a true culture," Thoreau said, "to tame tigers." Life, moreover, "consists with wildness": "The most alive is the wildest." So, as Jean Pierre Faye suggests, *New Wilderness* might better be *New Wildness*. This is in keeping with Rothenberg's editor's note: "*New Wilderness Letter* again explores the wilderness of language & mind, time & space." Which is to say, with Dada in mind, that life may consist of wildness in language. Yes, as Artaud says. Faye quotes Rothenberg: "We have had to break the mental *set* of our culture."

Rothenberg's etymological consideration of *wilderness* in "Indians & Wilderness" recalls my own in *Here/Now* (5 May

1980): "*World,* from OE, *woruld,* human existence. *Wild, world,* from OE. . . . *Wood,* too. . . . OE, *widu, wudu,* wood, tree; and *wōd,* insane, etc." What's most important to Rothenberg is "madness" as "wildness of the mind," as a movement "beyond the boundaries" into the domain where vision is possible. The sacred wood is a sacred *wōd.*

And as Ken Friedman reminds us in his comic drawings (*New Wilderness Letter* #8), this is the *New Wild Earnest Letter.* If anything, Rothenberg is pushing harder now than ever before, is wildly earnest and earnest about the wild.

Still the interest of this book is not in formal experiment. There is little of that: the use of prose explanation in "Coyote Night Poem," which may derive from Williams' *Kora in Hell;* the Steinesque poems in *The Cards,* written in response to postal cards that Rothenberg received; the acrostics, *gematria,* and number poems of *Letters & Numbers.* Instead the interest resides in the degree to which the poems are personal, both in answering to specific occasions and in summoning deep personal recollections. On first working through the book, I thought it might be a book of cities—Vienna and Chicago, San Diego and the Bronx—and a book whose personal element accompanied a journey. The personal here does not depend on place or travel. It arises most often from other occasions, like the birthday of his wife, which evokes his first poem on the Shekinah, and the bar mitzvah of his son, which stirs memories of his own childhood. Or the death of Michel Benamou and the imprisonment of Breyten Breytenbach, the first turning on an awareness of nurture and death (as in Whitman), the second on madness and death and the political aspect of a poetry that is so deeply personal, that is, of the very self:

16 February 1982

revolution makes us what we are
o poets
minds whose minds turned upside down
revive the oldest maddest dream
a word called freedom

Much here, to cite a line from "The Chicago Poem," looks
"back upon the future of." Much, in the card poems, for example, involves the Shekinah, confirming the declaration in
the poem to Breytenbach: "o poets poets / we are all split for
love of woman   of the world." And isn't it in recognition of all
of this—the profound issues he had pondered in making *A Big
Jewish Book*—that he chose to include those poems of *The
Notebooks* that are responses to friends and deeply cherished
writers and chose to place them with the other poems notable
for what I've called "personal"? The selections are addressed
to Nathaniel Tarn, David Meltzer, Wallace Berman, Armand
Schwerner, Paul Celan, and Franz Kafka.

17 February
1982

The concluding section of the book is the most ambitious, a
long poem in three parts called *Abulafia's Circles*. It brings
together many of the insistences and places already mentioned
and allows Rothenberg to complete the unfinished work of
Poland/1931 and *A Big Jewish Book* ("I was left with after-
images of largely unresolved messianic figures"). Allows him
to resolve what may have been his own messianic feelings by
beginning and ending with Tzara, of whom he writes in the
endnote: "His own path went through poetry & communism
[lowercase], & he made no messianic claims."

Abulafia's Circles (1979) is testamentary, a poem like the remarkable poems that conclude *Poland/1931* and *A Seneca
Journal*. Rothenberg gives over the meditative personal mode
for that of enactment—performance. The materials of the
book show us that if this poem were in four rather than three

parts, the fourth part would belong to him. Abraham Abulafia, Jacob Frank, Tristan Tzara—all are Kabbalists of the generative word: "Our sperm draws letters on / the belly of the bride." All belong to the heart of Europe that fostered Kabbalism, and Frank and Tzara contributed to its spread, the former to the movement, Harris Lenowitz says in the preface to Frank's *Sayings*, that "freed man" and promoted the French and American revolutions. And all are madmen, whose minds are turned upside down, and who thereby enter on the fantastic life.

Or put it this way: all are Dadaists. And the three portraits that call to mind those Stein did in a cubist manner are Dadaist compositions, incantatory works of great excitement. They turn our minds upside down with their juxtapositions of Abulafia and Hitler, Jacob Frank and Juan Perón, Tzara and Lenin and Mandelstam, the last permitting us to savor his poem to Stalin and take the measure of words—permitting Rothenberg to perpetuate a notable act of defiance, a poet challenging the State.

In the poem on Tzara, Rothenberg says,

> You lead me to my future
> making poems together
> flames & tongues we write
> like idiots
> ballets of sperm

This is true. I heard him perform his poem for Hugo Ball and have read "A Merz Sonata." I can well imagine what the performance of *Mine Yiddisher Dada: Homage à Tristan Tzara & Hugo Ball* was like.

"Messiahs are passé / there is no greater savior / than this": than Dada. The Dadaists are the fathers. He has, as the closing

words suggest, mounted the old horse/lost Dada and rushed
after Tzara "exuding light."* *Light.*

He has done this because he recognizes in such wildness/
madness the source of "the power of the shaman-poets." Con-
sult the prefatory note on visions in *America a Prophecy* and
the endnote after the selection from Melville. It concludes:
"the poet's meditations on the extremes of his own mind may
in fact be a process by which a poetry of endless changes can
be written." Yes, a *poetry of changes,* as we find it in the last
section of a book that offers us the chance to see America
with new eyes.

From Jerome Rothenberg
31 July 1983

> The request for some commentary catches me, oddly, in
> a kind of retrospective season: a sometimes edgy busi-
> ness since it goes against that other impulse to keep
> things moving forward (at least in one's own work).
> Most of the daylight, then, is taken up with the revi-
> sion of *Technicians of the Sacred,* an advance in part
> that also gives me a possibly clearer sense of what I'm
> about as an anthologizer-assemblist & again relates it
> to the poetry. This comes a couple of years after *Pre-
> Faces* & on the heels of *Symposium of the Whole* (which
> has its retrospective side too, at least for the ethno-
> poetics), & is accompanied by a reissue of *Shaking the
> Pumpkin* (projected), in which the revisions will be
> minor but still, for me, a pullback into earlier work—to
> try to set it "straight" again or to show that it will

----

*His most recent book is *That Dada Strain* (1983). It evokes the
terror first acknowledged in *White Sun Black Sun* and renews "that
Dada strain" in order "'to free the forces of poesis from / 'the gods of
power,'" not only the generals but Harold Bloom. It is notable, like
Dada, for the direct sense of the world that comes of opening cracks in
reality.

never be that, the whole enterprise too vast for this individual talent to bring it to a straightness or a closure.
And another project that keeps me busy & happy is
work with Bertram Turetzky on studio versions of
poems from *Poland & That Dada Strain* set for poet's
voice, bass, percussion, & electronic flimflam. A transformation &/or expansion of earlier material in the act
of performing it.

What you've written, then, allows me (along with
all that) to (re)view my work over time & to see how
it changes, & how it doesn't, in ways (some of them)
that hadn't been clear to me before. I'm struck, as a
starter, by how often what comes before propels toward
future meetings for which I would never have imagined
a groundwork had been laid. Take the image of the
"door," say, that you make so much of; I'm suddenly
aware, as I don't think I was earlier, that it would lead
as well to the "between"-ness of that 1960s work (as
book & dream) & would in turn await the meeting with
Victor Turner & ideas of "liminality" in the late 1970s.
"Between" as a title, I should point out, followed David
Antin's suggestion—either because he sensed already
that the work was in transition or on the assumption
we shared that if the work was always changing, it was
always in-between. Still it fit in, clearly, with my own
concerns & continued to do so through *Vienna Blood*,
in which the title poem at least is informed by my
struggle to come to terms with Turner's sense of betweenness—more specifically the side of it that shows
what, in relation to my own work, you're calling the
"optative mood." (But maybe I can come back to that
later.)

Delayed appearances, then, or the failure to predict
what lies ahead. In the same way, my discovery in late
adolescence of Indian poetry buried in ethnographic
bulletins waited ten or fifteen years to come to surface.
The "invincible flowers" of the late 1950s were a presence still in the work around *Technicians* (played off
there against a world of "flower children," "flower
power," & all that), & then reentered, more surprisingly

for me, in the observation, last year/this year, of an actual Yaqui Indian poetics that names a "flower world"
from which the mythic beings & the songs come. Nor
would I have known (in spite of Duncan's urging) that
the "triumph of the will" poem (circa 1960)—or another failed poem admired by Eshleman—prefigured
the way I was to go in *Poland*. Again, where you say
that "the *poesis* of the deep image is what Williams and
Olson share," I wouldn't have acknowledged, even de-
sired, such sharing until the time (roughly) of *America
a Prophecy* & *A Seneca Journal*. But by then, also, my
thrust was deliberately to synthesize or, as you might
say again, con-fuse things greatly.

I don't know if it's clear in the work, but there must
have been some point at which I realized that in so far
as what we do makes a stab at real poesis (not just at
proving one's own worth), others engaged in it become
our most immediate, most valued resource. The problem of course is that we're also working off our private
visions (or think we are) & the idea that mind stops at
the limits of the skull. For myself, anyway, the re-view
of the work indicates how much dialoging there has
been with others—both contemporaries & fathers/
mothers—& how much the work has been advanced by
even oppositional responses. I don't mean, by saying
this, to present myself as either a saint or a pushover,
but the experience of the thing (which has by now sufficiently accumulated) is that usefulness & value are too
unpredictable to reject anyone out of hand.

The most consistent interchange for me has undoubt-
edly been with Antin—& the friendship is by now so
long (&, I would guess, durable) that I think we assume
a measure of agreement that isn't always there. Certainly there was a period—& you spot it—when our
work (at least on surface) was very close, but for now
it's more like a series of issues in common & a sense
(on my part at least) that David provokes me to clar-
ifications (of both of our positions) to which I might
not otherwise come. (Like the "Dreamers" poem—an
opposition which feels at times like genuine agreement.)

And others too, to whom I can think of myself as in some way responding over the years: Kelly, in particular during the early 1960s, but even later, after what I took as an embittered separation; Blackburn, who was my direct link to Black Mountain ideas of verse & line with which I was never truly at ease; Schwerner, whose breakthrough to *The Tablets* corresponded with my own; Rochelle Owens, whose ferocious, even antic, language (especially when she attacked me in an early piece) I had to learn to (somehow) emulate; Wakoski, whose misreadings of me showed me strange ways that I could change; & MacLow, who baffled me at first & from whom I later learned the farthest possibilities of form & meaning. Those & some others—Economou & Eshleman, Tyson & Morrow, Quasha with *America a Prophecy*—were the immediate people while I was in New York; & Eshleman has since become a close friend & a sometimes irritant & goad.

But the poets "from outside," so to speak, were equally important. I've never truly understood the relation with Duncan—often supportive & sometimes strangely distanced—& most of my responses, like "The Counter-Dances of Darkness," come at a remove from what provokes them. With Snyder the dialoging is obvious (or so it seems to me), as it is with Meltzer or Jabès or, earlier, Celan—though in Celan's case I didn't correspond with him & only met him once, the real contact coming (one-sided) through translation, as with other poets out-of-reach. (There is also here an affirmation—now even stronger—of my European side.) Ian Finlay too—as Scottish correspondent—led me to concrete poetry—to have to deal with *that*—& the break with him, when it came, was pointless & painful: not connected to the poetry or serving that in any sense. And maybe, today, I look to some of the "language" poets in the same way—probably end up myself with a greater stake in a kind of primal language-centeredness (as with Maria Sabina & so on) than most of them would tolerate.

This is explicit in the anthologies & in the increasing

number of my poems, I guess, directly addressed to other poets. It is part of my argument too with Bloom's "anxiety of influence," which I find more of a block to "strong" poetry than an enhancement. I feel confident enough by now of my own ability to influence, to be able to think in terms of dialoging (endlessly) even with the dead. Stein & the Dada fathers without question— &, then, those fantastic shamans & madmen to whom I have to respond poem-for-poem. The configuration is my own—& not more or less original for the multiplicity of sources. No, more original if anything: more into "origin" & a sense of whence it issues.

I would say something too about Bloom, though here the opposition is—or is it?—of another order. While I understand perfectly well your objection to my essay, I don't see it, for all of that, as entirely without playfulness; or if it is, it's not the *only* instance I can think of— e.g., publicly against Sorrentino circa 1962 & against Vendler at the time of *America a Prophecy*. (I'm embarrassed at how few of these things there have been.) The *Malakh ha-Mavat* image—without which you would not have thought this such an "enormity"—I felt to have been raised by Bloom & not by me. Clearly, once I've articulated it, I dismiss it myself as, in any literal sense, a "hyperbole" & "absurdity"; but clearly too the dealing out of "life" & "death" is a hyperbolic presumption on Bloom's part. I can't imagine either that he wouldn't have known of the Auschwitz myth that cast Mengele in precisely the role of the exterminating angel—a very corny version of which I used in translating *The Deputy*. And without question I wanted to hit hard & to smoke Bloom out—& while there were indirect & private rumblings in response, in any public way I failed to do so.

The attack, as you rightly suggest, goes back in part to simmering feelings "against the poetics & ideology of the New Criticism" & its canonical survivals into the present. Until three or four years ago, Bloom was someone I also didn't think about much—in the sense, that is, that Antin says he doesn't "think about" him

(but notice that Antin is now writing up a talk piece in
attack that he delivered a couple of years ago in Iowa).
My only encounter with Bloom before this was a letter
he wrote me in 1979 or 1980, which was so weirdly excessive in its attention to my work, that it both gave me
permission (later) to feel that I was not simply responding as one judged second-rate by him *and* gave the lie to
his central proposition—because if he meant what he
was telling me in private, then he was pursuing his
proscriptions against Jewish poets after Auschwitz on
grounds that I still have no way of comprehending. All
of this I could not say in the *Sulfur* piece & hesitate to
say here, but if you want a sense of what was in my mind
then, here is Bloom's letter, after the self-introductory &
sometimes personal opening:

> I have followed your work for a long time, back to *White
> Sun Black Sun*, and I still have an unfinished letter I wanted
> to send you five years ago when I read & was broken by *Po-
> land/1931*. As I suppose my *Flight to Lucifer* shows (if you
> have seen it) or my increasingly Jewish Gnostic criticism,
> we are in much the same stance & place, except for (to me)
> "mere" stylistics. Pound & Olson are not my poets; Stevens
> & Hart Crane are. But your vision & mine are *very* close. It
> is a puzzle to me—I read Ashbery & Rothenberg—his lan-
> guage ravishes me more (though yours is, to me, the strong-
> est in your tradition) but your substance & drive are where I
> find myself. Reluctantly, because I had the full Orthodox &
> normative education, & am still upset to find myself among
> the *Minim*.
> But—salutations & homage—Harold Bloom

My response then was what I thought was a very
friendly letter, in which I may have called attention to
his earlier piece on American Jewish poets that seemed
so much the contrary of this, & may have mentioned
other poets of interest to me (Duncan, Kelly) whose
work drew from gnostic sources. When Bloom's *Times*
piece appeared a while later, I thought it would be appropriate for me to respond (& strongly), & it was only
then that I began to read him extensively & to find myself put off still further by the repressive thrust of his

entire enterprise: no Mengele *obviously* but someone
even so that I thought it worth speaking out against . . .
& from a situation close enough to his own (as he wrote
of it) that he would less likely treat it with indifference.

Yet I don't think of myself, blindly, as a critic-baiter
or as some kind of kneejerk anti-"academic." Antin
once wrote about me, that what most interested me in
poetry wasn't "timeless formal patterns" but "the recur-
rence of good sense, of energy, wherever people address
themselves through language to the things that make
them human"; & I quote this to indicate that something like that is of course more how I think of people
in general than through those pseudo-professional
categories. *Symposium of the Whole* is dedicated to
Michel Benamou, who was a critic, a serious teacher of
French, & a very energetic man who ran the Center for
Twentieth-Century Studies in Milwaukee & helped set
up that first ethnopoetics conference; & Diane & I say
of him there: "Through his presence we were able to believe that a genuine collaboration between artists and
scholars was both possible and necessary for that 'liberation of the creative forces from the tutelage of the ad-
vocates of power' described by the Dada poet Richard
Huelsenbeck in the legendary days of the Cabaret
Voltaire." My life in fact has thrived on such collabora-
tions (including, centrally, that with Diane), & I suppose I point to that here because I imagine, somehow,
Bloom & Company now wanting to brush that piece
aside as another cheap shot at the "academy." But my
abiding allegiance—as I declare it in the poem in *That
Dada Strain* directed at "B. among the *minim*"—is
to the ACADEMY OF DADA, wherever & whenever I
find it.

Your own readings—of Olson, Duncan, Creeley,
etc.—have been of real value in forwarding the discourse in & around the work. In my own case, the reading has allowed me to see all that I've spoken of above,
plus numerous other things I can't even start to get
into. I think also that the invitation to respond is part
of the larger possibility of reading—as long as we're

around to do it. I mean, the most depressing side of
even friendly "criticism" is that it absents the poet—as
if all writing on poetry is about the dead or silent. What
I can do now in some immediately useful way is to send
you a few separate notes on some items in the poems
that may have escaped you, & maybe, for the rest of
this, give some exceptions of my own to certain of your
assumptions about the later work (though it seems
to me that *That Dada Strain*, say, may already have
done that).

It feels to me that your reading gets more tentative
from *A Seneca Journal* on—with work, in other words,
that you've had less time to be with. I'm in perfect
agreement with you that *Poland/1931* & *A Seneca
Journal* constitute a single vision, which I think continues into *That Dada Strain*, where the greatest confusion of all (Jewish, Indian, & Dada) comes in the
poem called "Yaqui 1982." So, I don't see *A Seneca Journal* as in any sense conclusive but as an installment of
the longer poem, the part that runs from 1972 to 1974
in Salamanca. As far as I've now taken that longer poem
in print, it breaks off with the ending of *That Dada
Strain* & the meeting with Maria Sabina, where even
the shaman's *velada* is up for sale & the spirit of Language wanders, lonely & lost, through America:

> the ghost of Juarez
> speaking English
> like my own voice
> at your doorway
> shaking this sad rattle
> singing
> without the hope of god
> or clocks
> with no word between us
> veladas that cost
> a thousand pesos
> this vigil for your book
> & mine
> for any languages
> still left to sell

I'm a little surprised, then, although I can see how it happens, that you take the "patent fable of the ascendancy of the Great Subculture" in *A Seneca Journal* as something one might be asked or (better) expected to believe in. This surprise is compounded by your reading of "The Pearl"—& therefore the book—as ending in the "optative mood" in which "a delirious vision of consummation . . . brings an end to exile." My own sense is that what I've given here is a hallucinated, literally *delirious*, version of my own father's death in America, where death itself is the only escape from "exile" or from the present disaster.

Aside from that, *A Seneca Journal* is patently a poem of the early 1970s, when the "ascendancy" of the Great Subculture (& not merely its surfacing) was an ongoing theme all around me. (Thus Gary Snyder is as crucial to the dialoging in these poems as Pound & Olson.) "A Poem of Beavers," I think, takes it the most seriously—the first of the Seneca poems & the one against which the rest of the book plays off. But even here the fable isn't so much of "ascendancy" as survival ("I survives" at the end of the poem, where the grammar is Rimbaud's)—the survival of a remnant group whose strength rests in its (re)cognition of the consanguinity of life & its gift of ("deep") tongues. Thereafter, on the down side of the book (& this doesn't imply, I hope, that I'm being programmatic about the "up" & "down" of it), I would point out the references to Indian failure & culpability (the killing of the beavers in "Alpha & Omega," the killing of the harmless snake by Richard Johnny John, etc.); the occasional irritation with pretensions to new "religions;" the change from Turtle Island to Snake Island (a more ambiguous renaming of America than Gary Snyder's); &, most importantly, the refusal on my part to claim shamanship while keeping at some distance those who do, e.g., the prayer that ends "The Witness":

the old people will dream
ghosts will arise anew
in phantom cities

they will drive caravan across the land
bare chested   gods
of neither morning
shaman   serpent in thy final kingdom   leave
my house in peace

In other words, while there are parts of the poem in which I indulge an optimism toward *survival*, I think even that is hard to maintain & that the fable of *ascendancy* is no easier for me than for you. In *Vienna Blood*, which is much less informed by the talk of the '60s, I think you sense some of what I feel in your brief remark about "reentering[ing] the world of *White Sun Black Sun*" & your observation that the return (to Europe) "denies the value associated with return." (That would also include the Hebrew *aliyah*.) The key to the chronology of all this is "The Chicago Poem" addressed to Ted Berrigan, in which I point to the re-emergence, circa 1975, of political & personal despair:

> the economics of disaster Ted
> depressions of the spirit
> so unlike the bright promise of
> the early years
> gloss of the young life easing death
> atop a hill in Lawrence Kansas

: a memory ten years later of a "be-in" shared with him amid the "dreams & gauze / of intervening 1960s." But the greatest distress is in the vision of Vienna itself ("Vienna Blood"), whose imperial & Nazi past—& funky present—raise questions in my mind about the optative side of Turner's liminality—that it can issue in some hopeful or radiant "communitas"; hence the three lines dedicated to him:

> communitas
> (I meant to tell you)
> is holy terror

· · · · · · ·

By saying which, I don't mean to deny any good accrued over the years or to sound the note of despair as itself a kind of (ugly) closure. The poems—since *Poland* at least—have been written on the run, & the mood swings up & down. In other words, we do what we can from day to day & can sometimes look back & see the crooked trail (the pattern of our work) behind us. Where you say that you see me out to "renew life," I would never want to reject that so as to seem more fashionably despairing, but I don't want to gloss over the sense of terror either, or of final failure, that "events" (even those that "enable us to enter [the] sacred") continually force on us. I know that you know this too & that it's likely redundant for me to say it here. But I want to acknowledge what your words allow me to say & be— something at which my own words may be only hinting. The "hope" that comes in the "descent" was prefigured in that first book of Kelly's, which I published years ago; & it was Kelly too who suggested that I change the injunction in "A Bodhisattva Undoes Hell" from "keep the old / among you" to "keep the mad / among you." That comes back around also—which I hadn't remembered until this moment, looking at what you write about *Begründer* & shamans. Again I would say: "survival" & "renewal"; or speak the prayer we share between us, to keep that much of it alive.

Emendations and Comments by Jerome Rothenberg

Page 81 (4 September 1981): Re Shekinah & America a Prophecy, see "The America as Woman" section (p. 123).

Page 88 (9 September 1981): Good question concerning omission of this kind of poetics from Poetics of The NAP. Do you have any insights?

Page 102 (5 October 1981): (Re discussion of line "a pigeon dreaming of red flowers") I remember Denise Levertov was very down on this line, on something like pathetic fallacy basis.

Page 104 (6 October 1981): I started SIGHTINGS VI with "the earth shudders under the rain" after someone (Levertov? Sorrentino?) had presented it as a made-up example of an image that shdn't be used in poetry. (Again pathetic fallacy?)

Page 109 (9 October 1981): Re "Cages"—This was written for Ian Hamilton Finlay who asked for one-line poems for Poor.Old.Tired.Horse. I decided to try one-word poems, tho I cheat a little.

Page 110 (9 October 1981): Re discussion of reiterated "I," another example is "Praises of the Bantu Kings" in GAME OF SILENCE—in part a translation.

Page 115 (13 October 1981): In retrospect I don't know either what I had in mind with "conversations for ghosts." Probably that when I read back over them they sounded "ghostly" to me: disembodied voices.

Page 127 (1 December 1981): Re Diamond: he recently sent me an interesting essay on the Jews & the primitive, etc.; tells me it just appeared in THE NATION (sometime in July).

Page 132 (5 January 1982): The crystal ball is actually a beach ball, but intended to look like a globe or crystal ball . . . ; the "immigrant women" were collaged from a LIFE photo article on Russia, while another figure is (I think) Clara Bow; "male imagination" is a quote from a letter to me from Clayton Eshleman, identified as "our old friend Clayton."

Page 139 (9 January 1982): (On Snyder & Nachman) The poem follows a conversation with Gary at Navajo Community College, where I tell him I've been writing "Jewish poems" & he seems puzzled, amused, etc. in (I suppose) a 1960s/70s ecological context. On return I read the anecdote of Nachman & the young trees.

Page 141 (12 January 1982): In the "advertisement" for "Galician Nights," the photo of Esther K. is that of my mother—same as on p. 100. And her name of course was Esther. (Also, the text of the ad itself is from a gypsy handout on the NY subway.)

Page 141 (12 January 1982): Ishtar/star turns up in the "Lady" poem in "The Cards." Similarly addressing Esther K. as "thou my Easter excellence" (i.e. Easter named for German goddess with related name).

Page 141 (12 January 1982): Esther K is not only "paramour of the governor of Poland" but tied to that Estherke (Esther K) who was wife of the early Polish emperor Casimir. (I didn't know about that correspondence of names until after the first Esther K. poem.)

Page 143 (12 January 1982): (Re denial of autobiography) Confessional verse was certainly in mind but also the old lyrical mode in general, at least in favor of a poetry that tried to include the other & the larger epic possibilities of tribe & nation etc.

Page 144 (13 January 1982): "These collages are filmic . . . & cd be read aloud and accompanied by images projected on a screen"—I was in fact doing this in the early 1970s, assisted by folk singer, klezmer band, taped sound collage, clips from Chaplin's IMMIGRANT, slides of old photos & posed stills like those in Esther K.

Page 146 (14 January 1982): "Approximating a Cuna vision"— yes, with some degree of quoting.

Page 148 (15 January 1982): Concerning Ishi, that's of course the Yana Indian survivor, written of by Theodora Kroeber, who couldn't disclose his real name, so was called ISHI = human being (in Yana)—an extraordinary homonym with Hebrew ISH.

Page 150 (2 February 1982): Regarding what you say about shamanism, there was no way I could have entered the Society of Shamans, nor would I have expected to.

Page 154 (4 February 1982): "Beavers, an Idyll" is a separate poem from the one on the following page beginning "ridiculous musick"—the latter shd have been set differently.

Page 158 (5 February 1982): In the line "all their cabins they have filld with dreams" is it clear that these are the objects dreamt about & then supplied as a form of dream gratification? (Or, come to think of it, it's obviously more suggestive if decontextualized.)

Page 161 (10 February 1982): Opening of "The Pearl" is an adaptation of the narrative poem from the same gnostic work (Hymn of the Pearl) that I quote at beginning of CONVERSATIONS.

Page 163 (14 February 1982): Burg Wartenstein—used to be

owned by the Wenner-Gren Foundation & used for anthropological conferences.

Page 165 (15 February 1982): I don't know exactly what he [Kenny] has in mind, though it sounds like a lovely idea.

Page 167 (16 February 1982): Re "The Cards": there was an actual "game" involved in setting this up with nine other poets & artists; i.e., the poems weren't just written casually, etc. (There's a note on this with the poems.)

Page 168 (17 February 1982): I'm not sure what "his own messianic feelings" means. Feelings about messiah would be okay but not, I hope, feelings that one is Messiah.

III. Arbeiten und Lieben

GARY SNYDER

Another time, another perspective.

Rereading Kerouac's *The Dharma Bums*, dedicated to Han-shan, which is to say to Snyder, the coda-hero Kerouac wishes to emulate. When Kerouac first visits Snyder (should I be saying Japhy Ryder?), he finds him in a shack about the size of Thoreau's hut, at work translating poems from *Cold Mountain.* Snyder reads some, and the refrain ("that sounds like you") fixes the identification. Even more binding are a later remark to Ginsberg ("I think he'll end up like Han Shan living alone in the mountains and writing poems on the walls of cliffs") and the dream he has on Snyder's departure for Japan, in which Snyder disappears in China, having, as it were, become Han-shan; a dream of loss, overcome when Kerouac's ascent of Desolation Mountain is rewarded by a vision of Han-shan/Snyder, "that . . . little Chinese bum."

Kerouac's interest in Han-shan was prompted by Snyder's demonstration of the possibility of becoming the *bhikku* Kerouac wished to be. Snyder's appreciation of Han-shan as "a man of solitude who could take off by himself and live purely and true to himself" confirmed it and, of greater consequence, proposed a "rucksack revolution." Snyder's translation of the *Cold Mountain Poems* and Kerouac's *The Dharma Bums* belong to the same history: both provide scenarios for a generation alienated from and seeking to disaffiliate itself from middle-class America. Such scenarios are not unusual, and that is why they move me. Aren't they versions of "what being a male human being involves"? I cite John Updike in last week's New York *Times*. His fictive heroes, he says, "oscillate in their moods between an enjoyment of the comforts of domesticity and the familial life, and a sense that their essential identity is a solitary one—to be found in flight and loneliness and even in adversity."

Kerouac's account of Snyder and Snyder's own early work justify the prophecy of Kerouac's remark to Ginsberg. Yet what merits attention is the fact that Snyder's life doesn't bear it out. The tension that is said to be lacking in his work has been there from the start, in the opposition of ascent and descent, mountain and lowland (river, valley), male and female. Snyder is a poet of this vertical axis. He lives now in the mountains, but with his family, in community. The journey there has been as arduous as Han-shan's, repudiating, as it does, the kind of striving of which this early scenario is representative.

9 October
1982

Snyder published his translations of *Cold Mountain* in the *Evergreen Review* in 1958, the year in which *The Dharma Bums* appeared. His most substantial work so far, nothing was more appropriate, considering Kerouac's portrait of a scholarly Orientalist, Zennist, and mountain climber on his way to Japan to continue his studies. Almost all the early anthologizing of his work, his own remarks on poetics and biographical notes, the NET video tape (1965), and the photographs on the covers of his books insist on this distinction.

Snyder was twenty-five years old, studying Oriental languages at Berkeley, when he translated Han-shan. This work was an exercise subject to the approval of his teachers, who, Snyder believed, would accept neither *high as a junky* (for what became *high on mountains*), though they accepted other colloquialisms, nor the abrupt five-word line that Kerouac thought would render the five Chinese characters in each line. (Kerouac's example, "Long gorge choke avalanche boulders," recalls such economical and evocative lines in *Howl* as "winter midnight streetlight smalltown rain.") The exercise, in any case, was a lesson in riprap. The line in *Riprap* was influenced, Snyder says, "by the five- and seven-character line Chinese poems . . . which work like sharp blows on the mind." And the exercise was riprap ("Poetry a riprap on the slick rock of metaphysics") because his translation of this T'ang poet involved both careful selection and placement of words and of verses, the latter providing him a way for—the way of—an aspiring life.

If you read the translations by Arthur Waley that appeared in *Encounter* in 1954, and those by Burton Watson published in 1962, you see that Snyder's art is a matter not solely of re-visualizing the poems but of selecting those that propose the journey he has already begun. Translating them confirmed him in the way and enabled him, as he says of Han-shan, to talk about "himself, his home, his state of mind." I know of nothing that would inconspicuously represent him (present him) so well.

Of the 313 collected poems, Snyder translates only 24. Like Waley, who did 27, he unifies them by creating a sequence; and Waley, who admirably sets out the drama of Han-shan's entire life, probably provided the model of spiritual autobiography Snyder follows. But Snyder's sequence is wholly devoted to Han-shan's Cold Mountain experience. Because of this, Herbert Fackler considers Snyder's work superior to Waley's and Watson's, "truly a significant work of poetic art." *Structure* is the measure here, the fact that the work is "tightly organized and carefully unified." I find this recognition valuable not because I appreciate structure quite so much but because it is a hallmark of Snyder's work, even *Mountains and Rivers Without End*, the most open in intent. The discipline that Ginsberg and Kerouac found remarkable on meeting Snyder—that made him so attractive and "heroic"—manifests itself in orderliness and tidiness. The compliment in craft is Snyder's preference for revision rather than for either Kerouac's or Olson's spontaneous practice.

Fackler notes that Snyder chooses poems that "deal with . . . reaching for the ideal." Cold Mountain, he says, is a "Zen Walden Pond, to which Han-shan has retreated for his soul's profit." Doesn't *reaching for the ideal* render a Western disposition? In any case, I underscore *retreated*. Both Waley and Watson suggest this interpretation or, at least, that Han-shan's choice was not without misgivings.

Snyder's introductory comments echo Waley's but omit the remark on Han-shan's early life: "He and his brothers worked a farm . . . but he fell out with them, parted from his wife and family, and wandered from place to place [until he settled as a recluse at Cold Mountain]." What Snyder adds bears on his own present life, that of the dharma bums of Kerouac's chronicle: "you sometimes run on to them [Han-shan and Shih-te] today in the skidrows, orchards, hobo jungles, and logging camps of America." What he omits bears on a subsequent course he has chosen to follow.

We meet Snyder where Kerouac did, with a considerable portion of his life and an apprenticeship to poetry behind him. He is not, like Kerouac, a great rememberer, though the past makes itself felt in his desire to turn from it. Nothing of this time tells as much about his family history as *The Dharma Bums*, especially about Snyder's grief over the loss of Alison Gass (married in 1950, divorced in 1952) and his mother's abandonment. Kerouac, who is usually accurate and always alert to sorrow, reports that Snyder's mother was "living [alone] in a rooming house in the north" and that "Japhy didn't like to talk about her" because—the suggestion is unmistakable—in pursuing the way he defers taking care of her.

Like the others, Snyder translates #49, a poem about Han-shan's visit to his friends and family after thirty years' absence, but uses it to show Han-shan's humanity and concern with death, not misgiving over reclusivity. This descent is immediately followed by the compelling and preferable ascent to enlightenment and is taken up in the overall striving of the sequence.

Not ascent and descent so much as withdrawal and return recall Thoreau's inner exploration and vocation of purity. Yes, and conscious endeavor and Han-shan's brag, his confidence, anyway. The poems might be titled "Where I Lived, and What I Lived For." Thoreau's presence is notable, confirmed by Kerouac in *The Dharma Bums* when he evokes the excursion to Saddleback Mountain, where Thoreau had a vision like his own.

The release from the world that Kerouac enjoys is associated with childhood. *The Dharma Bums* is an idyll of boyhood; its purity of feeling, its innocence are genuine. I think of Huck Finn and Tom Sawyer, and Hemingway: men (boys) without women. But Kerouac's determination to do without them sets off Snyder's determination to do with them. Kerouac both admires and admonishes Snyder's sexual prowess (he cites a

11 October 1982

forester who recalls that Snyder "shore was a grange-jumper
with the women"). In Kerouac's account, Snyder climbs mountains with the agility of a goat—and Snyder's version of #28 is
graphic because he uses *clambering,* where Waley says, "I
make my way," and Watson says, "I climb." Isn't Snyder's relation to women, which makes up a good part of the book, that
of a lovely satyr? Snyder initiates Kerouac into mountain
climbing and yab-yum, both rituals of enlightenment. But in
spite of Tantric justification, yab-yum never wholly wins
Kerouac's approval, and not because he realizes, as Rothenberg
does in respect to the mythos of the Shekinah, that Tantra is
the work of men. The Princess, it seems, may not be deeply
moved by Tantric concerns—happier, too, with a ritual less
rigorous than the prescribed one. Slightly shift perspective
and yab-yum becomes an orgy, *balling* in the sense evoked
here of clustering around a queen bee. Even though the victim
is willing, women might consider it gang rape, and there is an
element of put-down in the fact that Tantrists prefer the
queen to be of lower caste. Is what we learn later pointless,
that the Princess is the wife of a graduate student of English?

No question of orgy in regard to Japhy's farewell party; that
Snyder and Kerouac run off to climb Mount Tamalpais underscores it and reminds me of this poem of Han-shan's:

> In my first thirty years of life
> I roamed hundreds and thousands of miles.
> Walked by rivers through deep green grass
> Entered cities of boiling red dust.
> Tried drugs
>
> .   .   .   .   .
> Today I'm back at Cold Mountain.

What counts is the polarity, the uncompromising aspect of
these landscapes of being: one is *purified* in the mountains.
So, when Psyche comes aboard ship to give Snyder the love

she had earlier refused him, he has to put her overboard. "It wasn't exactly in keeping with the diamond cutter of mercy," Kerouac says. But, then, "he wanted to get to that other shore and get on to his business. His business was with the Dharma." *His business*, indeed.

Psyche is a well-chosen name and asks us to think of Snyder as Eros: "Everybody loved Japhy, the girls Polly and Princess and even married Christine were madly in love with him and were all secretly jealous of Japhy's favorite doll Psyche." It asks us to forget that of the two transformations in the story of Psyche and Eros, Psyche's, of the soul, is more important. It evokes an Eros with a macho swagger who gets girls drunk to have his way. True as it undoubtedly is, Kerouac's account of "pretty broads coming up the hill [to Japhy's shack] every weekend and even on week nights" is the wish fulfillment of men who only sometimes would be without women. As late as 1969, in the *Berkeley Barb* interview entitled "The Return of Japhy Ryder" and featuring photographs of Snyder's wife Masa and their son Kai, Snyder still uses the word *chick*.

Don't forget the poems.   12 October
                                                           1982

It pleases me when an Orientalist of such authority as David Hawkes approves Snyder's translations, though, in typically British fashion, his praise is back-of-the-hand. What does he mean when he says that Snyder's "translations read like poetry," since Waley's and Watson's read like poetry? Does he mean *Chinese* poetry, or, more specifically, *the* poetry of Hanshan? How is it Hawkes overlooks Snyder's fidelity to Chinese poetry, the use of Chinese grammatical and metrical patterns, the caesura, for example, after the second character in the five-character line, the matched couplet or parallel sentences, the omission of the subject of a sentence—elements, Ling

Chung points out, that constitute a greater technical achievement than Pound's? Snyder says that Han-shan's poems are written in "T'ang colloquial: rough and fresh," and his versions bring over the T'ang colloquial even as he interfuses it with the tang of Beat jargon. Not only the scenario but the texture of the poems make them a text of the times.

The poems are readily available perhaps because the scenario makes much that we need to know sufficiently clear. Yet I find that the more I know about such poetry and its sources, the deeper it becomes and, in that sense, the better it is. Snyder himself has not really faced up to the need for notes in learned poetry such as his. Having been studied by Bob Steuding, Peter Barry Chowka, and William Jungels, perhaps he no longer needs to. Nevertheless, being expert in neither Chinese nor Buddhist lore, I agree with Hawkes that "many things will be missed by a Western reader which a brief comment could have given him." For example, the explicit Buddhist meanings. Wu-Chi-Yu provides a table of Buddhist terms that derive, he says, from two sutras and give the poems something of the character of a Buddhist manual.

13 October 1982   *Cold Mountain Poems* begins with Han-shan's withdrawal already accomplished, but with enlightenment, a more difficult attainment than finding "the path to Han-shan's place," still to be achieved. *Path* calls up *Way*, and the poem tells us that on Cold Mountain—the rugged terrain of the Sierras is present in the jagged lines—it is as easy to lose the one as the other, even though the point, I think, is Thoreau's, that "not till we are lost, in other words, not till we have lost the world, do we begin to find ourselves, and realize where we are and the infinite extent of our relations."

Thoreau is especially prominent in the second verse, in which
Han-shan's place is set off against the "silverware and cars,"
the "noise and money" of worldly life. Snyder's images insist
on *bourgeois,* and convey his revulsion. Later, in #16: "I've
got no use for the kulak / With his big barn and pasture— /
He just sets up a prison for himself." Not exactly bourgeois but
exactly Thoreau's sentiments. And "What's beyond the yard?"
echoes the conclusion to "Solitude" in *Walden:* "No yard! but
unfenced Nature . . . no path to the civilized world." Wu's
translation—"What is left in the courtyard?"—misses this.

So, in #3, in being *here,* he is indeed "high on mountains,"
which isn't to say he's reached his spiritual goal but has *placed*
himself so as to reach it. The juxtaposition of the desolate
landscape of #4 makes this clear. This landscape "sinks [his]
spirit," and Han-shan is in haste to leave "the wrecked town,"
a city of the dead, of those who have not attained Immortality.
This juxtaposition establishes the essential vertical axis, in
terms of which insistent words like *place* are valorized. "I
wanted a good place to settle," Han-shan says in #5—*settle,*
not *rest,* as Watson has it, already conveying Snyder's notion
of *inhabiting.* This gains force from the fact that his life in
the lowlands is characterized by restless travel, *roaming*
rather than *drifting.*

I find Watson's *ruined city* preferable to *wrecked town* because
it calls up Eliot's *Unreal City,* where spiritual death-in-life
has undone so many. I prefer *sigh* rather than *pity* because
it echoes the "sighs, short and infrequent" of *The Waste
Land* and reminds us that Han-shan's journey is comparable to
Dante's. Verses #3 and #12 evoke Eliot's cityscape, and the
poems in their entirety, like Eliot's, are marked by extremity
and the desire for spiritual attainment.

14 October
1982

The distinction of Snyder's translation is already evident. The sensibility he brings to the poems is not the literary sensibility of Waley and Watson. His experience in the mountains enables him to visualize what Han-shan had seen and therefore translate evocatively. Translation, he says, depends on re-visualization, on projecting "the 'picture' of the poem inside my head, like a movie, to *see* what's happening." This means that he must find a correlative of the poem in his experience. And it accounts for more than *phanopoeia*, for the decisiveness, for example, that results from using the first person in #5.

Watson's version of the beginning and end of this verse:

> If you're looking for a place to rest,
> Cold Mountain is good for a long stay.
> . . . .
> Ten years now he hasn't gone home;
> He's even forgotten the road he came by.

Snyder's version:

> I wanted a good place to settle:
> Cold Mountain would be safe.
> . . . .
> For ten years I haven't gone back home
> I've even forgotten the way by which I came.

This verse reminds me of "Lookout's Journal" in *Earth House Hold* and "Mid-August at Sourdough Mountain Lookout," the initial poem in *Riprap*. They are the correlatives of Han-shan's experience—and the Sourdough Mountain poem is Snyder's most exquisite Chinese poem.

"I've even forgotten" suggests "I cannot remember." But there's more to it than that: he's high on mountains. Elevation frames the poem:

> Down valley a smoke haze
> . . . .
> Looking down for miles
> Through high still air.

The high still air is the clear medium through which he looks, an equivalent perhaps of an empty mind. It accords with his attentiveness, the acuity of his perceptions, and the purity of his simple life. *Valley* belongs to a cluster of values, the un-assertive and "female" yin, associated with Tao. Here it is a place of "smoke haze," an exact image of uncertain content, linked with change of weather and new life. The "swarms of new flies" (you can hear them; they are a disturbance such as Thoreau reports from his lookout) gather meaning from the visual similarity to "smoke haze" and the sibilance of both phrases. The art is careful but he is not composed.

> Down valley a smoke haze
> Three days heat, after five days rain
> Pitch glows on the fir-cones
> Across rocks and meadows
> Swarms of new flies.

The end-stopped, unpunctuated lines convey the flow of per-ception and evoke polarities (heat/rain, far/near), anything but the ostensible calm.

The balancing or complementary verse restores the presence of the perceiver and matches what he sees with what he feels, internalizes the experience, so that even the concluding acts, seemingly selfless, are seen from within his meditative perspective.

> I cannot remember things I once read
> A few friends, but they are in cities.
> Drinking cold snow-water from a tin cup
> Looking down for miles
> Through high still air.

The experience is a quietly troubled one, even though the verse renders the very *looking down* by which he realizes his present being in the palpable *high still air.* He isn't troubled because he can't remember what he once read but because he can't forget the distant and the past, especially the affective life he now misses. Steuding is right to note the "sad but somehow strangely pleasant melancholy."

I once considered this a satori poem, giving the sense of what the journey of *Riprap* had earned. Now I see why it is the initial poem. Snyder has no more achieved enlightenment than Han-shan at this stage of his journey. In seeking safety by reclusivity and ritual discipline, Han-shan avoids spiritual risk, and though he has forgotten the way by which he came, he has forgotten neither time nor self. As for Snyder, though high on mountains, he is suspended there, still looking downward, to the valley.

16 October 1982   Perhaps #6 explains this. Here Han-shan speaks to the reader more smugly, I suspect, than a Buddhist should. He remarks the inaccessible way and that *he* has found it. Snyder's Beat phrasing ("How did I make it?") also points up the difference between reader and poet. Being Beat, he has found the way:

> My heart's not the same as yours.
> If your heart was like mine
> You'd get it and be right here.

The pun on *right* is telling, even better the grammatical lapse of *was.* This verse insists less on the rightness of the Way than on the rightness of his choice.

The seventh verse is comparable because its boast of contentment is complacent. "Freely drifting, I prowl the woods and streams / And linger watching things themselves"—this would be admirable in another context, were it not undercut by "Men don't get this far into the mountains." Even in the next verse, where prowling yields to arduous ascent, the following is boastful: "Who can leap the world's ties / And sit with me among the white clouds?"

I am reminded by this verse of Snyder's determination, in *The Dharma Bums,* to scale Mount Matterhorn. Here this verse follows Snyder's explanation: "Han-Shan . . . got sick of the big city and the world and took off to hide in the mountains." This is the explicit motif of the book, which tells of Kerouac's world-weariness and desire to drift freely. But Kerouac's passivity is not shared by Snyder, who is attractive to Kerouac chiefly because of the masculine character of his discipline and striving. He presents Snyder as a leader—"He was being very serious and leaderly and it pleased me more than anything else." Though he finds this boyish and is reminded by the leader's didacticism of Natty Bumppo, I am reminded of the patriarchal authority of Snyder's letters to Lew Welch, another world-weary drifter, and of Snyder's superior seriousness in the discussion with Welch and Phil Whalen in *On Bread & Poetry.*

Perhaps the desolation that swiftly follows acknowledges this boastfulness. The rough terrain of #8 becomes a landscape of vastation in #9. Snyder's version is more agitated than Waley's, and "Bleak, alone, not even a lone hiker" belongs to Snyder's experience. Cold Mountain *is* cold, and conscious endeavor doesn't always avail. The force of environment by which he as well as the snow is "whirled and tumbled" is a force of negation, made so by reiterated negatives of absence. Which is why I said *vastation* and think now of Hart Crane's "North Labrador."

What Crane found absent in the icy landscape was the female presence that I suspect moves Han-shan in #10 to return to the lowlands after "thirty long years." He has not escaped the burden of time and has become aware of its power to *consume*. Snyder brings this out where Waley and Watson don't; also links this verse to the preceding verse by repeating *lone*; and, more important, with *suddenly* gives Han-shan's tears, sentimentalized by Waley and Watson, the force of enlightenment. Returning to the lowlands, it seems, is necessary to the Way, in this instance serving as a foil for #11, which images enlightenment as a goal still to be attained.

17 October 1982   So another stage of the journey begins. The quest is resumed when he recalls what has gone before in terms of the aimless and distracted roaming of his thirty years of lowland life. Again, mountain and lowland are contrasted, and the mountain is turned to as the place where the values of the lowland are overcome: "Today I'm back at Cold Mountain: / I'll sleep by the creek and purify my ears." Thoreauvian, even in respect to sound and silence, is *purify*, a better choice than Watson's *wash my ears*, even though, as often in Chinese poetry, Watson incorporates earlier poetic lore.

To sleep is to give over striving. But the next verse (#13), paired with the previous verse by both Snyder and Watson, tells of the difficulty of doing this. The poem is an agitated response to emerging spring. Both Watson and Snyder convey the irrepressible natural activity with which Han-shan is not in harmony. Though both have learned Fenollosa's lesson, Snyder's verbs are more forceful and contribute to the troubled sense of disturbance. Han-shan wants to rest in his hut because the *bird-songs* (Watson is better: *chatter*) and the activity (*flowers out*, *shoots up*, *drives over*, *wash* are noisy, their sibilance that of process) remind him of the *dusty world*.

The transition from spring to fall, in #14, brings with it a different perspective and deeper understanding of nature. No longer disturbed, Han-shan observes that "Cold Mountain has many hidden wonders." *Hidden wonders* is better than Watson's *weird sights* because it suggests a profound recognition of the invisible process that accounts for such visible wonders as "On the bare plum, flowers of snow / On the dead stump, leaves of mist." The hidden process that makes these wonders wonderful is noted by the absence of verbs. The natural phenomena of the previous verse are just as wonderful, but Han-shan associates them with the dusty world because he does not see them as part of the network of things; sees them merely externally, or sees in them only the tropic force of physical life. Lowland and mountain, accordingly, represent ways of seeing. To see the related nature of things is to climb the mountain. Isn't this why Thoreau, evoked here by the magical rain, was as much on a mountain as Han-shan, had Olympus at Walden?

Because it respects this sense of wonder, Snyder's verse is more "poetic" than Watson's—though by now I should have said that it is "poetic" chiefly because it gives us at once both poles of its vertical axis. Bachelard defines *poetic* in this way in "The Poetic Moment and the Metaphysical Moment." The poetic moment is "a harmonic relationship between two opposites," an "ambivalence" not an "antithesis." Poetry is concerned with vertical rather than horizontal time, with simultaneity rather than succession. In a poetic moment like "Who knows that I am out of the dusty world / Climbing the southern slope of Cold Mountain?" the "two terms are born together" and may be said to be "androgynous." Poets who realize this, do not "unfold" but "knit" their poems, make them "a tissue of knots"—not only knots, as Hugh Kenner describes patterned energies, but the knots in wood, since *fushi*, the

Japanese word for song, means "a whorl in the grain." Vertical time is really a psychological dimension, an axis on which one descends to distress or ascends to consolation, or has both at once; a fitting dimension for a Buddhist because it contains "everything . . . that loosens the ties of causation and reward, everything that denies our private history and even desire itself, everything that devalues both past and future."

19 October 1982

The way is *laughable,* as Snyder said at the start, and Han-shan, who comically inspects himself in #15, does so because he now respects the unerring nature of nature's wonders. In the previous poem, "At the wrong season you can't ford the creeks" troubled me because nature has no wrong seasons. Now I see that *wrong* applied to his need to find the *right* way. Here he is a *naked bug* with only the *Tao Te Ching* to guide him. Careless of dress, indifferent to self, he is militantly vigilant over "senseless cravings"—cravings of sense.

The fifteenth verse situates the self in regard to the cosmos in both #14 and #16. In the latter, Han-shan cosmitizes (indispensable Bachelardian term) Cold Mountain and thereby realizes the positive nature of emptiness. When he says, "At the center nothing," *nothing* is not *nothingness* but the energizing center of all things. He cosmitizes by likening Cold Mountain to the open house of the cosmos itself, and so for him cosmic space is not hostile but intimate. He is *at home* on Cold Mountain; this moderates the boastful gibe at the end of the second verse. Not only has he realized the nature of the cosmos but he has learned the lesson of its sufficiency.

He has, it seems, learned to *dwell,* living, as he says in #17, off plants and berries, forgetful of time, sitting happily in the mountain landscape. Yet to tell us this is to suggest the op-

posite. The conditional questioning assertion—"If I hide
out . . . why worry?"—and the imperative to "let the world
change" link world to trouble. Ascent is withdrawal, from
trouble: "Once at Cold Mountain, troubles cease" (#19);
"My home was at Cold Mountain . . . far from trouble" (#23).
I read this verse more favorably in respect to Han-shan than to
Snyder and Kerouac. In their case, doesn't renunciation come
too early? They would be forest sages before serving as house-
holders. Can this responsibility be avoided by appealing to
one's karma and present happiness?

Subsequent verses proceed on the assumption that this question has been asked. In #18, Han-shan is misunderstood because lowland and mountain are unaccommodating, as polar
as different orders of being and mind. This, it seems, justifies
withdrawal. Of course, *up* is always valorized more than *down*,
and troubles come from below. "Once at Cold Mountain,
troubles cease— / No more tangled, hung-up mind." The Beat
jargon tells the Beat solution: get high on mountains. And
when, in #20, a critic tries to "put [him] down," Han-shan's
response is Beat, laughter at such foolishness ("He misses the
point entirely") and a reciprocal put-down ("Men like that /
Ought to stick to making money").

So #20, which may be read as acknowledgment of attainment,
may also be read as justification. Doesn't *utterly without regret* protest too much?

Yet the enlightenment of which it speaks is warranted by #22
and #23. Han-shan realizes that in coming to Cold Mountain,
he has come back to his original nature. Cold Mountain was
always his *home*, the cosmic house. Now self and cosmos in-
terfuse: light flows through both *the galaxies* and *the very*

mind, and he knows the "boundless perfect sphere." Sharing the circulations of being (Emerson), he knows that being is round (Bachelard).

Why didn't Snyder end here? The concluding verse is anti-climactic. The difference between Han-shan's way and that of others has already been established. Why remind us again that we should "Try and make it to Cold Mountain"? In reading this verse, I recognize the posture of the dharma bums and re-member the translator's youthfulness. None of the other trans-lators puts it at the end and thereby foreshortens and trans-forms the journey of a lifetime.

20 October 1982   A remark by Snyder on translation explains why I read *Cold Mountain* as essential autobiography. In a letter to Dell Hymes, he says, "It is not a translation of the words, it is the same poem in a different language, allowing for the peculiar distortions of my own vision." *Vision:* both ocular and mythic. Surely he was moved, as we are, by the myth, the quest, of these poems. The quest is not unusual for a Bud-dhist—this truncated version of the myth of the hero, of withdrawal-initiation-return—and I read it as essential autobi-ography because it tells the story of the soul, "the true story," as Robert Duncan says, "of who I am." Still I find the story curious, not for its aspiration, but for its renunciation.

Charles Altieri, who recognizes many reasons for treating Snyder and Duncan together, overlooks the extent to which both are (like Olson) poets of lore and have found in myths the scenarios of their lives. He grants that the story of Psyche and Eros serves Duncan in this way, but mentions neither *Cold Mountain* nor the study of a Haida myth (a version of Psyche and Eros), which, together, become Snyder's essential story.

He Who Hunted Birds in His Father's Village is now the
title of the undergraduate thesis on myth that Snyder wrote
at Reed College in 1950–51. Nathaniel Tarn, another poet-
anthropologist, who now prefaces it, rightly says that it is "a
short, elegant and confident document." I understand why
Snyder values it: it is his groundwork, demonstrating the *digging* he advises us to do (for *lore = loopings = feedback*); and
it is his link with others, like Eliot and Pound, who had already undertaken this modern task. Yet why has he chosen to
publish it now, that is, in 1979? Is it that, having learned from
critics its importance in explaining his development, he sees
no reason not to disseminate it?

The double negative allows him a certain disinterestedness
that may not be warranted. At a time when he was publishing
little poetry he may have wished to add to his prose work—to
the didactic push of *Earth House Hold* (1969), *The Old Ways*
(1977), and forthcoming, as he knew, *The Real Work* (1980).
Wished, that is, to come up with other poets whose prose
work has been substantial and distinguished: Olson, Ginsberg,
Creeley, Duncan, Rothenberg, among others. In regard to myth,
one thinks of Duncan's *The Truth & Life of Myth* (1968)—and
there is always Olson, the *muthologist*. If territoriality is in
question, it is probably a matter of claiming priority and importance in respect to *ethnopoetics*, the enterprise begun in
Alcheringa by Rothenberg and Tedlock. Take Tarn's preface:
professional endorsement, one anthropologist certifying another even as he certifies himself by noting Snyder's omission
of Lévi-Strauss. As for Snyder's preface, it gives him a chance
to speak again, this time not only for his political concern for
the destruction of indigenous culture by Western monoculture
and for the ecological import of myths (they tell us how to inhabit). He also addresses what *Alcheringa* has brought forward: the primacy of the oral mode, of performance, of telling

stories. Much is gained by putting the book in the present context. I am also glad to have it available if only as admonishment to those poets who have made a vogue of source work and have not come to it out of necessity.

What necessity? As the photographs of the "green would-be scholar" and the mature poet tell us, there is the autobiographical impulse of connecting an earlier and a later self. Then, in the curious self-consciousness of "the seeds of the self o'er leaping," there is reference to soul making, the psychic function of myth. Finally—he, too, places it last, as if it were an afterthought—there is a confession: "In scholarship we often don't understand ourselves well enough to know why we *really* do something. The one dimension of the myth . . . I didn't clearly state, was that it's a story of lost love."

That he acknowledges this now speaks well for his development, and I don't want to forget it in going back to beginnings. *Cold Mountain* compensated for lost love, but the myth of these poems is incomplete and needs to be filled out by the Haida myth that preceded it. Filled out, too, by the subsequent meditative work of poetry suggested by Snyder's belief that myths are "the kōans of the human race."

23 October 1982   Snyder found his kōan in John Swanton's *Haida Texts and Myths.* Even if he didn't come to this essential myth in childhood, as Duncan came to his, it belongs to childhood by virtue of his "strong sense of the North West." It belongs to the sense he may have had then but certainly has now of being a child of nature, self-taught, and compelled, as it were, to explore the high country. He may have published his thesis because now he sees it as an essential part of his legend.

Legend? See the interviews in *The Real Work*. What should be said of the editing that, among other things, normalizes the language and presents a somewhat humorless sage? The presence of a "collaborator-editor" troubles me; he models Snyder's work on the *Lin-chi-Lu* and thereby asks us to accept it as a wisdom-book. In the best of the interviews, with Peter Barry Chowka, Snyder gives us a portrait of the sage as a boy caught between country and city, native and white, natural and destroyed, landscape and urban "ghost." "When I was young," he says, "I had an immediate, intuitive deep sympathy with the natural world. . . . In that sense, nature is my 'guru.'" *Is*, still is. And since *nature* now is *Gaia*, as in *Songs for Gaia*, he means that his sympathy is for the "great biosphere-being," the Mother of us all.

Did he intuitively know the "answer" to the kōan all along? Is he telling us the "answer" now?

26 October 1982

The myth, as Snyder sets out its elements to enable us to recognize the type to which it conforms, is as follows:
1. Man wins supernatural [swan] maiden for wife.
2. She is insulted, and leaves.
3. Man goes on quest for her.
4. They are united.
5. He wishes to return to his home. He is transformed into a bird.

The type: "the supernatural wife loss-of-wife quest-for-wife pattern," which involves the "archetypal divisions of marriage, loss, quest, and reunion," or, in terms of basic human content, "the winning, loss, and regaining of love."

What is especially interesting—and little commented on—is the vertical axis, and the fact that the hero returns home, to the lowlands, to the shore, and becomes a sea gull. In becoming what he has hunted, has he fulfilled the quest, attained reunion, regained love? Or does this version of the myth spell failure? Snyder addresses this resolution in the preface:

> To go beyond and become what—a sea gull on a reef?
> Why not. Our nature is no particular nature; look out
> across the beach at the gulls. For an empty moment
> while their soar and cry enters your heart like a sun-
> shaft through water, you are that, totally.

The last sentence is the most wonderful in the book, an authentic expression of being, equaled only by the underwater fishing on Suwa-no-se Island. It tells of a subsequent sense of unity with the world, *that* reunion, *that* regaining of love. Cosmically, too: sunshaft and water, corroborating Tarn's insight, that for Snyder "love is liquid, made in water." I cannot read this sentence without recalling all that Bachelard says about birds and being; and Olson's chii-mi, Duncan's doves, Lowry's gulls (in "The Forest Path to the Spring"); and Creeley's "The Birds" and, most of all, the initial verse of Crane's invocation in *The Bridge,* a poem about the quest for love. Here, too, is the vertical axis and a being who compasses it, a liberated being, alone yet at home in the world, soaring in the service of love.

Crane's poem is about childhood loss and the journey that brings him home, to reunion not with his mother but with the Mother of us all. As with Whitman, love is found in an answering cosmos.

Passion becomes ecological. *Eros* and *ecos* join in intimate space. Love is inhabiting, dwelling.

The kōan involves Snyder's sense of childhood and what he
learns about it from Freud and others. It opens to the terrify-
ing world of Kali. The dimension of myth that most engages
him is the psychological; the primary concern in all of his
work is mind, and his journey is chiefly an inward one, into
its depths.

Living with Lew Welch, as well as his own experience, probably confirmed what he says of formative childhood experience,
the family, and the Oedipus complex. By relating this complex
to Jung's study of the Demeter-Kore myth, he is able to account for Swan Maiden as one aspect of a triune goddess and
to see her "as the projection of [the] mother—beneficent and
forbidding at once." This explains the popularity of her story,
"particularly as she appears in those versions in which she
enigmatically gives in to the man, only to leave him for a
slight reason and require an elaborate and dangerous journey
of him before returning." But Swan Maiden is only one motif
of a larger quest myth, the one set out in Joseph Campbell's
The Hero with a Thousand Faces, and this quest ends with
the hero resolving the Oedipus complex by replacing the father and entering into a "mystical marriage with the Queen
Goddess of the world." The study of myth introduced Snyder
to the matriarchal world, and he accepted the poet's work proposed by Robert Graves' *The White Goddess.* Yet the myth of
the hero whose marriage "'represents the . . . total mastery of
life [woman is "'the totality of what can be known'"]'" is
patriarchal. Does this account for Snyder's difficulties in
marriage?

Relevant asides.

> You mentioned . . . that there were certain aspects of
> your life which you had excluded from your poetry, cer-

tain explosive potentials that you had never acted out in it—like the relationship with your mother which you said was very much like Allen Ginsberg's [in *Kaddish*]. (Ekbert Faas)

Poets are the sons of witches. . . . Living with the image of the Teeth Mother was the darker side of Lew's songs . . . [songs that ultimately were] devotional songs to the Goddess Gaia. (Snyder, preface to Lew Welch's *Selected Poems*)

In regard to his past, everything Snyder writes, the book on Haida myth and *Cold Mountain,* is to some extent, as he learned from Abram Kardiner, a "projective screen" that reveals as much as it hides.

28 October 1982   According to Graves, there is only one story. It is suggested here by the question (*quest*ion), "Do you know the trail that leads to my wife?" The way of the shaman's soul-journey is the way of *eros,* the oldest, most difficult, most needed way in the world. Journey to love. Healing and making whole.

13 March 1983   Snyder told Robert Ian Scott, who recently brought out ten poems that had been published at Reed College in 1950–54, that "these poems . . . show that I (and all of us) read Pound and Eliot. Plus the Mother Consciousness first stirred up by Robert Graves."

What's important in these poems is the profound melancholy that made Eliot's waste land the fitting geography of Snyder's spirit. Also: the poems belong with the myth of loss treated in his undergraduate thesis and show both his extreme valorization of descent and ascent and the confusion that prompted him to serve the matrifocal values of the one by means of the patriarchal transcendence of the other.

The first—the key—poem puts his predicament. This is not merely sexual but involves *eros* in relation to *ecos*, to family and generation(s) of life. He feels guilty not only of "concupiscence," given Eliotesque weight by the allusion to Prufrock in the last poem, but of an act, as Pound would say, *contra naturam*. The *errors*, which in another poem distress the Great Goddess and bring sterility, are, as the pun tells us, of *eros*.

> walking lonely on a fall day
> in a long meadow, slanting open to the woods
> where the frost chilled
> the dead grass, a year ago
>
> peer sharply through the brown grass:
> the slim thin white thing rotted
> long ago
>
> build now a squat stone tablet
> for ants to sun on
> and hide it in the dead grass:
> "Here lie My Children."

The meadow is "feminine," a place of love, doubly desecrated: by the life-denying use of a condom, the snakelike thing, the surrogate penis, whose rot bespeaks revulsion, and by his return to find it. His loneliness is probably the result of physical absence, as in the Robin poems, but the injunction to build a gravestone, which, like the poem, will not hide but reveal his fault, complicates matters. It declares a primary violation of the female, even as, in "My Children," it insists on patriarchal possession. At least, in "A Stone Garden," where he is still working out the issues of these early poems, he says, "What became of the child we never had?"

The loss is genuine, of the anima, as the next poem tells us.

> Her life blew through my body and away
> I see it whirling now, across the stony places.

I lost her softly through my fingers.
Between my ribs in gentle gusts she
Sifted free.

She is breath (voice), an energy such as he celebrates in *Regarding Wave,* and he lost her by grasping, though she, it seems, also sought to be free.

Many of these poems tell of the displacement of matriarchy by patriarchy, the violation and death of the Great Goddess at the hands of gods who come from "the pitiless velvet sky." They also tell of Snyder's desire to serve the Goddess by sacrifice and by overcoming lust in following the Buddhist way to the "transcendent land." So Han-shan comes to mind, as he does in the poem on George Leigh-Mallory, who died climbing Chomolungma (Mount Everest). Not that Han-shan was moved to make such a Western ascent, but that Snyder was. The meaning he ascribes to it is readily seen when the poem is placed in the context of the other poems. Leigh-Mallory surmounts the "rank valleys" and with "practiced skill maintained his life / In that translucent cold." Snyder admires this conscious endeavor, even though the sky-gods did not welcome Leigh-Mallory. He found a "hideous demon" whose gender, I suspect, is female because *mists* ("He fell beyond the mists of Chomolungma") are associated with women. Besides, in Snyder's view, the Great Goddess rules in spite of patriarchy and will not be "mollified."

28 October 1982   *Riprap* (1959). When you open this book, with its strange title, you know something new has entered American poetry, even though Pound and Rexroth had already taken up Oriental poetry. For poetry, identified with both work and Way, is part of the practice of life, "a good way to be," as Snyder says of zazen. Oriental in resonance more than form, its underlying

tone, its stillness, is of the kind Snyder appreciates in Chinese poetry and landscape painting, and in haiku. When you open this book—and *Earth House Hold,* too—you've entered a different time and place.

For most of us, the world of work in these poems is also strange; perhaps, even *work,* associated with his teachers in the dedication, is. "Riprap," the titular, concluding poem, is a metapoem in which the hard work of "roughs" (Whitman) is assimilated to a poetic practice which, in turn, belongs to the pursuit of the Way. Connected with men like Blackie Burns and Roy Marchbanks, poetry becomes "man's" work; the insistence on care and craft, on the physical rhythm of work itself, respects this, too (as when Thoreau recommends work to remove the palaver from our style). Duncan's figure for his art is weaving, loomcraft—think of spiders and spinsters—which Snyder does not seriously consider, though his work becomes an art of knots in which he "knit[s] old dharma-trails."

The initial and concluding poems—"Mid-August at Sourdough Mountain Lookout" and "Riprap"—seem to be the most Chinese, though the latter is not meditative. Its imperative mode of willing enjoins the poetic work that will enable Snyder to continue the journey recorded in this book and to move beyond the troubled serenity of the initial poem.

30 October 1982

Words are rocks; and, later, rocks are words. Their placement in "Riprap" is careful and solid, visually a veritable "riprap of things," a collage or ideogram in which each word is distinct, its weight acknowledged, its fit notably achieved. Sometimes this is a matter of position (*i.e., set* in the fourth line, *place* beneath *placed, thoughts* rhymed with *things*) and repetition (*solid* and *Solidity*); often it is a matter of assonance and consonance ("Before the body of the mind"; "These poems, people"; "placed solid, by hands"). The most brilliant instance is "Granite: ingrained," where etymology is both visual and phonic and, in a look ahead, the *grain* of *Regarding Wave* appears. *Riprap of things* restates Williams' "No ideas but in things," and in asking us to attend both the most diminutive things ("ants and pebbles") and the most cosmic ("Cobble of milky way"), the poem reaches back to Whitman. The baffling syntax forces us to consider "the complexity far beneath the surface texture," interfusion of "straying planets, / These poems, people, / lost ponies," all interchangeable. The universe, here, is as wonderful and unimaginable as "an endless / four-dimensional / Game of *Go*," where this Japanese game is a kind of riprap and, in keeping with *straying* and *lost*, a game in which one may trip or fall. So we need "sure-foot trails"— and *we make them* as we go, by choosing granitic words that are solid because ingrained with our experience, with our *thoughts, things*, and *torment*, and fused by processes like those of cosmic creation.

This poetry of experience isn't confessional. Its creation calls up Blake as Crane remembers him in "fury fused." It also reminds us that liberating ascent, however transcendent, requires the hard ground of one's life, traverses it.

5 November 1982   Chronologically ordered, yet dialectical, the poems play off each other, converse over his valorizations of ascent and descent, his ups and downs. As always, composition is by book, which is more than the sum of its parts and a greater achievement than any poem. The poetry itself works, enables a (re)education in how to live (love).

Take the second and third poems, "The Late Snow & Lumber Strike of the Summer of Fifty-four" and "Praise for Sick

Women." In the first, ascent and descent have economic and political meanings. One strikes because one is exploited, but unemployment and the need to look for work deny its natural necessity and positive value. *Contra naturam* in "Praise for Sick Women," also about repression, links both with Pound's usura canto and joins the mountain work of men to the lowland work of women. Logging—man's work—is countervailed by standing in line in the city, the lowlands of woman's work, fertility. *Arbeiten und lieben,* as Freud said, thinking of the difficulty men have in accommodating both. (So Snyder, in "After Work," a poem that belongs here, accommodates them as separate activities, each in its place, and much to his satisfaction.)

"The Late Snow & Lumber Strike" also plays off the lookout poem. Stillness now hovers over an entire landscape; its psychological equivalent is not serenity but quiet desperation; it tells the absence of work. Hitchhiking is now frantic: *blown like dust* is infernal, and *drifting* does not have the minimal positive meaning of *Cold Mountain,* evoked by Shuksan, whose ascent fails to lift Snyder above his troubles. This is also true of the ascent of Mount Baker, which explicitly evokes the lookout poem because he gazes down valley, disturbed now, however, by the need to work.

Was his economic situation so desperate? Or is desperation the measure of how much manhood for him is equated with work? Is there too much extremity? "I must turn and go back / caught on a snowpeak / between heaven and earth." Aren't *betweenness* and *turning,* as in "Nooksack Valley," the pivot upon which the book turns?

"Praise for Sick Women" is juxtaposed to a poem about work and followed by others concerned with work in the moun-

6 November
1982

tains, not because the primitivity of the menstrual taboo belongs with the temporal vista opened by this landscape, but
because work and women are aspects of Snyder's axial thought.
Women are the reward—the compensatory amelioration—of
work. To think of one calls up the other.

These valorizations are explicit in *Earth House Hold*. Even
the journals, mostly about work "in the woods [mountains]
& at sea," to cite the dedication to *Riprap*, are preoccupied by
concern with women. The men to whom he dedicates *Riprap*
speak up in *Earth House Hold*, their talk the common talk of
manly men without women. Finding their teaching valuable
in regard to work, does Snyder find it valuable in regard to
women, and as requisite to manhood?

Blackie Burns teaches new foresters that forestry and women
do not mix. The pun in "the *recreation* side of it" points up
his view of women as sex objects, and other comments, of
Swiftian cloacal revulsion, further degrade women. One of the
puns in *lookout* involves avoiding women ("Should I marry? It
would mean a house; and the next thirty years"), though for
the lookout Buddhist, nonattachment is difficult because his
mind is not empty of thoughts of women (a photograph of a
nude woman hangs in the lookout window) and one thought,
it should be noted, denies the values of ascent and the male
reluctance to take up domestic life: "Or having a wife and
baby, / living close to the ocean, with skills for / gathering
food."

Why does Snyder record the macho humor of foresters and
sailors, so much of the latter concerned with whores and the
male folklore of women? Did he find it funny? Does he think
we will? Or is he acknowledging a part of himself, trying to
set it straight, reverence, as in "Praise of Sick Women," being

a way to do this that doesn't compromise the male point of view in which menstruation is seen as sickness? What to say of a young man who balls in Samoa and weeps when contemplating the mosaic of Virgin and child in Hagia Sophia? Nothing concerns him more in the early sections of *Earth House Hold* than love and the "net-network of things." As much as Zen, he comes to Japan to learn a way of love. When he reads Lawrence (an early influence), this is what he ponders. Kwannon is the goddess whose shrines he visits. Love relationships and the need to give up "personal fearful defenses and self-interest strivings" are what he considers most—to yield "fruitless competition," which evokes for him the juxtaposed image of "logging camp morning."

Poetic aspiration complicates all this because aspiring is a form of ascent and the Muse demands devotion. When he entertains the poet's choice of ways—either to become "sane and ordered" or to "step beyond the bound" (as becomes a shaman)—he opts for the former, chooses to yield neither himself nor his masculinity. Though he values the poem of inspiration granted only by the Muse, he settles for the poem of "artisan care"—"the contrived poem, workmanship [it is all in this word]; a sense of achievement and pride of craft." The Muse he would like to serve is associated with "cool water," with Buddhist emptiness of mind, with neither extreme of intellect (thinking ego) or dream (unconscious). Yet, though reluctant to risk abandonment, he understands its necessity: he begins to record dreams and speaks of the need for "a higher responsibility to holy ghosts and foolishness and mess."

"Praise for Sick Women" is impersonal—a more impressive poem, "To a Far-Out Friend," records his own experience—and speaks didactically for all mankind. Female is expressly defined in terms of fertility and the "difficult dance" of repro-

7 November 1982

duction through which she leads the male, though the sexual experience, told in terms of her *topos*, is the male's. Woman's *dance* is set against man's *discipline* and *mind*, which do not lose their hierarchical value because only in respect to woman, some wholly other, are they *contra naturam*. They *confuse* her. But the dance serves the male, enabling him to *see*. The verse fills out a journal entry on "true insight [as] love-making" and the rightness of representing Prajna as a female.

The two parts of the poem stress the conflict introduced by *discipline* and *contra naturam*. Like Pound, who evokes the Eleusinian mysteries in Canto XLV, Snyder uses *contra naturam* to declare the priority of matriarchal society and ground his view of patriarchal society (civilization) as repressive. Much of the second part of the poem catalogs the superstitions and taboos that, universally, follow from man's fear of women's sickness. The culture of fear; *ressentiment*. Hence, "our Mother Eve: slung on a shoulder / Lugged off to hell," like Kore, raped, made queen of the underworld, of death not life. Snyder knows that such myths—and the Hindu myth of "kali/shakti"—are the work of the male imagination. Men have transvalued values, clustered *moon* (with its *changes*) with *hell*, with *evil*, with *woman*, thereby denying her a life-giving-renewing function.

This poem questions both poles of the vertical axis, but only to inspect the problem. It is not necessary to have the female viewpoint of "To Hell with your Fertility Cult" (in *The Back Country*) to confirm Snyder's ambivalence. He evokes Kore; he doesn't become her as Williams and Duncan do.

And he quickly reestablishes the values of ascent. His appreciation of geological time, in "Piute Creek," is really an appreciation of timelessness. In this moonlit mountain landscape,

"All the junk that goes with being human / Drops away." Now
the moon is associated with enlightenment rather than change,
with "A clear, attentive mind" whose seeing does not require
the female's physical agency. Even so, thoughts of love in-
trude: "No one loves rock, yet we are here." Which is to say,
out of place. Mountains are sacred, not human, places. One
doesn't inhabit mountains; human dwelling (*ecos* and *eros*)
belongs to the valley. So the movement from "Milton by Fire-
light," which depreciates the story of Adam and Eve, to "Hay
for the Horses" is one of descent. It brings us to the shore of
"For a Far-Out Friend."

Is *far-out* used in praise or censure? Personal to the point of
confession, this poem reveals a masculinity at once usurping
and mean. No *discipline* or *mind* here. Having been drunk
and beaten up his "friend," Snyder admits that he "was less
sane than you." This apology would be acceptable—even
more the explanation of his "torment"—were it not for the
fact that, "hooked on books," he sees his friend not as she is
and may wish to be but in terms of the pictures of deva-girls
in Zimmer's book on Indian art. Mind, here, is force because it
assimilates her to an archetype in the recollection of her running naked in the surf—which also figures the anima and the
unconscious. This is why, when he finds her again, it is in
Zimmer's book and why, when she refuses to act her part in
the "wild Deva life where [he says] you belong," he resentfully
relegates her to what he disclaims, "this dress-and-girdle life."

Sick women? What of sick men? For a long time I thought the
middle generation of poets—Lowell, Berryman, Roethke—
especially hung up on and sick with sex. Not so. Yet in fair-
ness, mustn't it be said that the subsequent generation of
poets has tried harder to understand this sickness?

8 November
1982

He is not proud of himself as depicted in this poem, and in two anecdotes, told at his own expense, immediately brings himself down. In "Thin Ice," where he falls through the ice, he mocks his sureness. Have the previous poems been *skating!* In "All Through the Rains," he cannot catch the mare he wishes to ride.

His descent is marked by confusion and a sense of failure. A valley poem, "Nooksack Valley," tells of darkening weather and depressing thoughts. He has come to a "far end," a "mind-point" on which he turns, and gives over much that his native place means to him, including "schools, girls, deals," in preparation for his trip to Japan. This poem belongs in *Mountains and Rivers Without End*—is part of that journey: Highway 99, down which he will go, is a vertical axis. Japan is *down;* what he goes home to find but can't find he will search for there, having now relinquished the popular myth of the hero in quest of love that he disdained in his study of Haida myth.

This deep interior poem of disquiet is especially fine. It significantly marks a turning because its tone and situation recall the lookout poem.

"Migration of Birds" treats his remaining days with Kerouac and announces his own migration, which will be neither to the north, which he just left, nor explicitly for the purpose of nesting.

Only four poems on Japan, one of them long, all of them subdued. "Toji": his attention moves from the sleeping men to the statue of the goddess of compassion and love and the "loose-breasted young mother," both linked with *shadow* and *shade,* with the unconscious. "Higashi Hongwanji": in this temple poem, he notes the relief of a buck watching a "sleek fine-haired Doe." "Kyoto: March": he imaginatively explores an entry in his journal on returning to Kyoto by train and observing the little houses in the snowy landscape (*Earth House Hold*, 42); he exploits the contrast of outer cold and inner warmth, which sets the solitary observer longingly outside the circle of family life, of generation and generational love.

"A Stone Garden," the most ambitious poem in the book, consists of four large blocks of verse, the four main islands of Japan, set in the sea. Stone, not rock; no riprap here, not even prosodically. And garden, a made place, of love. This is what he meditates on, on the *Sappa Creek*, a wanderer again, whose brio is subdued by thoughts of inhabiting. The dream of the fertile countryside he had on the train to Tokyo is still present; the *echoes*, too, and the perturbations that troubled him. The landscape is one of descent: "Centuries of leading hill-creeks down / To ditch and pool in fragile knee-deep fields"— "Glittering smelly ricefields," he says later. What is remarkable in this *ecos* is the union of male and female and how, as he pursues his thought, this relates to *eros*. Men and women *work* together in this ancient, established way. But another valorization of work breaks the dream in which he enjoys this prospect ("I thought I heard an axe chop in the woods"). This opens the poem to problems of work *and* love and, initially, to the frenzy of "excess poets" (poets in excess) and "unwed girls" in Tokyo, which is neither a "high" town nor a goddess like San Francisco in *Mountains and Rivers Without End*.

9 November 1982

He goes on to "recollect a girl I thought I knew"—probably Robin, conspicuously present in the enlarged edition of *The Back Country*—and does so in terms of fertility; in terms of motherhood, reverenced in Japan, and the continuity of generations that nullifies the "impermanence and destructiveness of time." For him, women-as-ground stands to men as blooming ricefields to cities. This is why the Great Goddess, who "warms the cow and makes the wise man sane," is invoked in the next section.

Like the others, this section proposes its meditation in the opening line ("Thinking about a poem I'll never write"), one that recalls the journal entry on the poet's alternatives. Why *never write?* Hasn't he, not the Muse, as he claims, "gone astray," or, more exactly, *Not gone astray?* The loss of which he speaks might be figured by the Shekinah in exile, and it follows from his reluctance to serve the Muse with the requisite abandon, to go the shaman's way as in the primitive examples he cites. The confusion here is the truth of the case. "The hand is bare" not because the Muse, like a "long-lost hawk," has flown away but because, like the young man in the Haida myth, he has lost the love of the Swan Maiden. Nor is "the noise of living families" a reason, since a family might be recuperative.

Section 3, even prosodically, responds to the control of sections 1 and 2; and section 4 responds to section 3. The first line ("What became of the child we never had?") ties back to the "living families" of the previous section and, by also recalling the girl of section 2, enables Snyder to resume the meditation on *eros* and *ecos*—"Let's gather in the home." Not yet able to assimilate wife to Muse, the accomplishment of *Regarding Wave;* having two kinds of relation to woman, that of erotic fulfillment in marriage and that of poetry, he chooses the former at the cost of his ambition for the latter. Insofar as he repudiates the aspiration that explains the loss of Robin, this is salutary.

Section 4, a sonnet, evokes family life and the *delight* (replacing ecstasy?) that accompanies the continuity of a "marriage

[that] never dies" because it is both generative/generational and built (yes: formally made) of "flesh and wood and stone" (synonymous with "the woman there"). Now he will not escape in Buddhist fashion but bind himself to the burdens and limitation of time, bind himself with delight to birth and death, in recognition of the forever-renewing agency of marriage.

The poem repudiates the rectilinear way and proposes marriage as a way to enter the eternally recurring, the network of things. The conclusion, "A formal garden made by fire and time," acknowledges the primary lesson he has learned in Japan. The culture that he depicts here gives woman and domestic life a central place (he notes that Japanese men are "better at home than at work"), founds itself on *eros* and *ecos*. Moreover, *fire and time,* reminding us of granitic rock, tell us that this ground is sure and solid, that a stone garden in the sea is as good as a rocky summit in the sky. The constant, finally, is *formal:* trails, marriages, cultures—all must be built with care.

With three poems under the heading "The Sappa Creek," Snyder returns to the masculine world of work. All, however, are modulated by what precedes them. In the first, work has become responsible for the maintenance of life: "we wander greasy nurses / Tending sick and nervous old & cranky ship." In the second, he captures a moment of danger in which the femininely valued shore-light-nature has ascendancy over the masculinely valued sea-dark-machine. In the last, a Williams exercise, he is self-depreciatory: spilling the paint is both humorous and colorful, a needed accent after much self-preoccupation.

10 November
1982

But "T-2 Tanker Blues" picks up the meditative insistences. This Beat poem is confessional in the manner of *Howl*, but otherwise fails the comparison. It lacks the electrifying imagery and the syncopation of Ginsberg's poem, and its nouns and dashes of consciousness don't jump with "sensation of Pater Omnipotens Aeterna Deus." The poem owes nothing to jazz— to Kerouac's choruses, for example—though Snyder is blue and suffers "America's naked mind for love": "My wife is gone, my girl is gone, my books are loaned, my clothes are worn, I gave away a car; and all that happened years ago. Mind & matter, love & space are frail as foam on beer. Wallowing on and on." Yes.

"Tanker Notes," in *Earth House Hold*, gives a better account of this experience than the poems do. Perhaps the reason is to be found in "Cartagena," written in 1958, but telling of a sexual episode during his first passage in 1948. Though he is one of the whoring crew, Snyder leaves us in doubt about his initiation and reports only his drunken response: "And cried, 'Cartagena! Swamp of unholy loves!' / And wept for the Indian whores who were younger than me, and I was eighteen." By recollecting, is he measuring in terms of a decade's experience, pointing up his adolescent sentimental naïveté? Or, since the response transforms *unholy* to *holy*, is he recalling his youthful—still constant—reverence for women? Is this, even in respect to drunkenness, a representative anecdote?

In any case, the masculine world is not compromised, and to end with "Riprap," which reflects on what he has made, declares his commitment to ascent. So does what is omitted from this account of his experience. Leaving things out, ellipsis, is a formal property answering to emptiness, but the troubled poems of love he could not find a place for in this scenario, tell another story.

Myths & Texts (1960) is a concurrent work, going back, at least, to Snyder's study of Haida—as indicated in the title, which also names concern with "symbols and sense-impressions," the inner transformation of facts, their flowering, as Thoreau says, into truth. This book puts him with the ethnologists, but, more important, tells us that myth is foundational, work still to be done, not merely the means of structuring that Eliot advised, though that, too, is evident in this carefully made book. Myths here are elements of his own vision, his own story of destruction and creation. The injunction of the book is "See or go blind!"

11 November 1982

In every way—scope, organization, program—this is a very ambitious poem, especially for the twenty-two-year-old who began it and must have known that such a learned poem asks comparison with—and challenges—the long, cultural poems of Eliot, Pound, and Williams. Snyder spoke of it recently as one of his best books, as well he might since Robert Bly said it was "one of the two or three finest books of poetry" of its decade and Robert Kelly put it with the *Pisan Cantos*. Snyder even measures its success in terms of sales and is pleased that it sells well without footnotes, though he authorized Howard McCord's notes in 1971, and must surely know how much more available the text is now that William Jungels has written an excellent dissertation on it. Is it only one of the best because he places it with *Mountains and Rivers Without End*, a perhaps even more ambitious poem begun at this time?

The dedication now acknowledges other teachers, Lloyd Reynolds and David French of Reed College. Subsequent books will be for Kenneth Rexroth, Oda Sessō Rōshi, his wife Masa, his mother—a significant reversal of the usual order.

12 November   Snyder's epigraph comes from Acts 19 : 27; he uses it as a par-
1982   tisan of Demetrius, the silversmith who made shrines for the
goddess Diana. With it he countervails its Pauline import,
condemns the Judeo-Christian tradition, and announces his
service to the Great Goddess.

His myth is both personal and archetypal, one of *ecos* and
eros, because the forest is for him, as for the Amer-indians,
the actual body of the Mother, intimate space, not the hostile
space of the destroyer. He begins in the present with the destruction (desecration) he has participated in as a logger. But
"Logging," to cite the participial title of the section, is a continuing process, ever-present and archetypal, a fact of ancient
China as well of the last American frontier. Yet insofar as the
process involves what Raymond Dasmann considers an attack
on an eco-system-based culture by the imperialism of a biosphere culture, it calls for a halt; prefigures *Turtle Island*.

Even as he tells of its probable irretrievable loss, Snyder goes
in search of the primitive, proposing just such understanding
and practice of life as a remedy. Isn't this why he denies chronology by working backward (for feedback) and why the book
is formally circular, enclosed by references to the morning
star? To repudiate the rectilinear denies progress; to advance
the cyclical opens and recovers another kind of world. Not a
growth model, as in economics, but a steady-state model.

13 November   For Pound's auspices, read the exquisite opening poem. It is
1982   ideogrammic, representative of the art of the entire book.
Not only are the lines carved in Pound's fashion, the tone is
Poundian, elegiac and sweet, especially in the reiterated "Io."
The Great Goddess accords with Pound's dedication to the
Eleusinian mysteries, and her invocation is evocation, since
she is present again in experience. Myth is significant because

it enables us to recognize this, to behold, as Pound says, the crystalline light, "the light not of the sun" in Canto XVII, where Io, Diana, and Kore figure. Snyder insists on this in the cyclical nature of the poem, its form following the natural pattern of death and rebirth and conforming also with the annular pattern of the cosmos. This, too, is the form of the book.

There are *insistences* in *Myths & Texts*, that is, elements of what Barthes calls a writer's "secret mythology." They are finally of greatest importance, but they are not formally important here. *Themes* is a more exact term for the premeditated elements that are the formal means of creating the coherence of a spatial, closed poem of this kind. The opening line ("The morning star is not a star") and the closing line ("The sun is but a morning star") are thematic and formal. To read the first is to recall the last, the closing line of *Walden*, another cyclically formed book. And to recall Buddha, who when sitting under a bodhi tree (trees are important) was enlightened, but not by Pound's crystalline light. This may explain the negative declaration with which the poem begins and asks us to remember the planet Venus. But what does this mean?

Lack of punctuation, the formal disposition of lines (*i.e.*, "The May Queen" under "Io, Io"), enforce the significance of juxtaposition. So we read "The morning star is not a star" in terms of "Two seedling fir, one died"—that is, in terms of death and, in a suspended way, rebirth, though loss is its burden, as "Io, Io," sometimes only an outcry of woe in Pound, tells us. But Io is linked with the May queen, who, the quoted material (from Frazer?) informs us, "Is a survival of / A prehuman / Rutting season." Is it, then, that only when we recover the vista this verse opens, of a matriarchal culture close on the natural world of trees and animals, answering to generative-sexual renewal, we will see the morning star as Venus? Is this book—does it owe anything to Olson's treatment of Venus and concern for *Der Weg* in *Mayan Letters*—proposing such a path of enlightenment?

Spring is evoked in the first verse, autumn in the second, for the spinning year brings the Pleiades to rest at San Francisco. (This reminds me that Duncan's "Evocation" is the poem with which Snyder's poem bears comparison.) Yet May revives in the present of this verse because *dream/dream* is an agency of renewal, whether merely entertained or, preferably, brought into being by efficacious shamanist technique. In a cosmos as harmonious as this one moved by the stars, where renewal is concurrent and complete ("Green comes out of the ground / Birds squabble / Young girls run mad with the pine bough") and vegetable, animal, and human are not divided from one another, isn't it likely that dream is not divided from reality, unconscious from conscious? Living in the roundness of such a world, wouldn't we be whole—hale and holy?

The poem remains open, opening the book. Its seedling and pine bough are important thematically. Though it laments loss, it celebrates the powers of Dionysus. The young girls who run mad are his votaries, but they are also linked with Io, the cow maddened by a gadfly, who prefigures the animal-human world of "Hunting."

After this prefatory poem, "logging" may be said to begin, in Snyder's present, in the Northwest woods. The difference in voice and resonance is startling. There is no myth here, for the groves are cut down. *Logging* names ruthless destruction and consequent ecological disaster; man's work, done, as Exodus 34:13 commands, in order to supplant the matriarchy with patriarchy. And Yahwist demythologizing goes on; it is the biblical legacy of our national history. This theme also be-

longs to Snyder's secret mythology because defending the
groves is the work of poetry. He says, in *The Old Ways*, that
"the long 'pagan' battle of western poetry against state and
church, shows that . . . poetry has been a . . . not particularly
successful defending action." In 1956 he was more confident
that it might be than he was in 1974, when he would no longer
wait out the kalpa, but draw a line and take his stand.

Does *Myths & Texts* sell well because it demands so much
exegesis? I find myself resisting the compulsion to write out
a "reading" of it. Say only what must be said, at whatever cost
to its richness. For example, that the third poem establishes
both a central motif—by defining (in found material) the re-
generative power of the lodgepole pine—and the vertical axis
of valley and mountain and time and eternity. That the fourth
poem also joins Northwest and Orient, not only because of
their similarity of landscape, but for the reason he discovered
on his first trip to Japan ("the subtle steady single-beat of the
oldest American-Asian shamanism"), which, in turn, may inform *dream/dream* in the first poem. That the fifth poem
stages a debate over Snyder's loyalties—and perhaps needs a
fuller gloss.

14 November
1982

The learned poet rehearses his repudiation of an academic
career by impugning the "meaningless / Abstractions of the
educated mind." As woodsman and logger, he tells us, in the
image of the book in the privy, that learning is shit. Out-of-
work, exploited, he disdains the "summer professors" and
places them, with the powerful, at the top of the social tree.
Kenneth Burke's *victimage* and *hierarchy*. But the proletcult
proceeding would be Burke's despair because its symbolic
action isn't purgative-redemptive, is too simple- or single-
minded, melodramatic. Snyder would have us believe that loggers destroy the forest against their will, yet are free, as he is,

to choose whether or not to work for (Professor) Marx. And when the machine (the rapist mistaken for a "sick whore") breaks down, the loggers, neither Luddites nor revolutionaries, tinker, having the pragmatic, inventive skills of the men (good Americans?) he claims them to be.

The sixth is a found poem: Snyder's father's recollection of the abundant berry-picking that followed the first logging. It provides a somewhat folksy pastoral interlude (like "Ma," not yet incorporated in *Mountains and Rivers*). The seventh poem, also historical, presents the causes and consequences of workers' unrest that erupted in the Everett Massacre, but is especially interesting because it, too, is an example of oral tradition.

With the eighth poem, much of what has been rehearsed finds memorable expression. The short, direct, stabbing lines are serially ordered from dawn to dusk to tell of the violation of nature, even of ants and bees, by a D-8 tractor. The verbs evoke the enormity of mechanical violence, an unequal battle from which small animals and insects flee. The details are exact and resonant: "Each dawn is clear / Cold air bites the throat"—worthy of Han-shan, who is mentioned in the twelfth poem; "Thick frost on the pine bough / Leaps from the tree / snapped by the diesel" recalls the young girls of the first poem and the fate of dryads in others; "wild horses stand / beyond a row of pine"—never could they destroy as tractors do, the lesson Wendell Berry, for one, has been trying to teach us. The motionlessness and endurance of the horses belong with the "Black lava of a late flow"; both are evidence of life and *natural* violence. But then in "Taurus by nightfall," the D-8 becomes a bull, pastured for the night. This recalls the Pleiades of the first poem, but also ties to the next, which brings the

logger "home" at night, down from the mountain, back to his
"girl" and the reward and restoration of love.

The distance between work and love is conspicuous here, and
the girl in the bath is as vivid as anything in "Logging." Prose
statement and syntactical economy establish the honesty of
this small poem, a reminder perhaps that in a demythologized
world, dream (*dream/dream* echoed now in *dreaming of home*)
is followed by diminished sacramental experience. When
Snyder says of the Western tradition of romantic love that
"the lovers['] bed was the sole place to enact the dances and
ritual dramas that link primitive people to their geology and
the Milky Way," he may have had this poem in mind. The
mode of recollection fits its joylessness.

In the tenth poem, there is a ghost logger, an IWW bindle stiff,
buddy of the derelict in Ed Dorn's *By the Sound,* a book of
this time and territory. Both writers "dig" the West and are
deeply engaged by the Western hero. "Boys without fathers
and mothers" too, a characterization I take from Snyder's
"The Incredible Survival of Coyote," where he remarks that
"Heroics go with first phase exploitation" such as logging.
The *ghost logger* belongs to the history already set out but
gets his power from dream. Perhaps he is an ancestor, an eternal one of the dream. He prompts the outrage (a verbal surrogate for political action) that Snyder also shares with Dorn
but found the model for in Pound.

> Them Xtians out to save souls and grab land
> "They'd steal Christ off the cross
> > if he wasn't nailed on"
> The last decent carpentry
> Ever done by Jews.

Machines and horses are again juxtaposed in the eleventh poem. The emasculation of the latter is readily seen as caused by the former—or, more to the point, since horses must be castrated to be domesticated, the emasculation of Indian and logger alike, in the person of Ray Wells, a Nisqually. Emasculation is vividly evoked because, like the girl in the bath, it bears a complex burden of meaning: to destroy an *ecos*, as the Amer-indian references remind us, is to emasculate its inhabitants, destroy its *eros*; it tames them, and makes them instruments of their further destruction.

Perhaps Snyder's compromised role—he has "set a choker," the butt logs themselves great fallen phalli—prompts the subsequent wonderful collage of shamanist material. Brought together are the prophecy of Drinkswater and the vision Crazy Horse had, as reported by Black Elk, whose greatness, as he says of Crazy Horse, was "the power of his great vision." Included also is Haida material that makes it fitting to add Hanshan. This is the visionary company Snyder would like to join, as "Looking off toward China and Japan" suggests. A more significant detail reminds us that the vision quest (as in *The Bridge*, which anticipates so much in recent poetry) involves watching the morning star.

Black Elk, whom we should honor as one of our poets, said that "Sometimes dreams are wiser than waking." In regard to Drinkswater's " 'You shall live in square / gray houses,' " he said that "there can be no power in a square." Before Bachelard said that being is round, Black Elk said that "the Power of the World always works in circles, and everything tries to be round." Snyder's book, too; and for the time being, the vision quest for roundness will be his political action.

Just as the seals in Tomales Bay and the bear still in the "wet 17 November
brush" in the fourth poem prefigure the animal world of "Hunt- 1982
ing," so the fires in the thirteenth and fourteenth poems prefigure "Burning." The concluding couplet of the first—"The
crews are departed. / And I am not concerned"—echoes the
ironic "The nymphs are departed" of Eliot's "The Fire Ser-
mon," and the detachment probably prefigures the reliance on
the kalpa with which the section and the book end. But the
smoke of the sawmills—the incense to Jehovah—is cause
again for outrage, for a summary, melodramatic alignment of
the forces of good and evil, the latter, in the march of civilization, destroying the groves of the former: "Cut down by the
prophets of Israel / the fairies of Athens / the thugs of Rome."

There is the incontestable truth of "Creeks choked, trout
killed, roads." I won't argue about what he says of "suburbs,"
but question *roads*. What is the way to Kitkitdizze?

Perhaps the concluding poem moderates matters? There is
still contempt in the verse on "men who hire men to cut
groves," but other verses suggest the amelioration of waiting—
for the end of the kalpa, where the destruction necessary to
renewal is of atomic force; for the power resident in natural
resistant things: the cone-seed of the pine and the flower that
cracks the pavement.

But will destruction of atomic force prepare new birth? Even
when thin forests of lodgepole pine return, will the Amer-
indians return with them? More than the nature cycle is
needed: the intervention of men and women. There is no community in *Myths & Texts*, "no meeting together" of any kind.
Are we to console ourselves, as he seems to, with the example
of the Chinese painter who witnessed the fall of the Ming
dynasty, lived in a tree, and stoically said, "The brush / May

paint the mountains and streams [Nature] / Though the territory is lost"?

18 November
1982

The book, remember, was written in the 1950s. And though Snyder belongs to the poetic generation of Olson and Duncan, he is their junior, especially in political experience. If he read *Mayan Letters*, a pioneer text for poets in search of the primitive, he attended the archaeology more than the will to change it served for Olson. The movement backward in time in "Hunting" and "Burning" may follow Olson, and may answer the despair and impasse of "Logging," that is, though the book is formally indebted to Eliot and Pound, may acknowledge the limits of their usefulness.

Digging also respects place, not the heroics of exploitation, and in moving to "Hunting," he finds his model in the shaman. He begins a vision quest that, in time, will become a politics of vision; heeds the injunction to *dream/dream*, aware of the Papago teaching that the reward of heroism is dreams. But "Hunting," in evoking the shaman's culture—a culture respecting the relationship and sacrality of all things—is itself the vision. It fills out an entry in Snyder's Japanese notebook ("two days contemplating ecology, food-chains and sex") and deals less with killing than with "making love to animals," to cite a section of the essay "Poetry and the Primitive," in which we learn that hunting, like the quest for vision, requires disciplined and loving attention.

The shaman is the exemplary hunter. He has the greatest negative capability: "The Shaman-poet is simply the man [or woman] whose mind reaches easily out into all manner of shapes and other lives, and gives song to dreams." Practiced in the discipline of both inner and outer worlds—of unconscious and wilderness, themselves equivalents—the shaman teaches us how "to become one with the other." His, the "basic mind-science," teaches the lesson of love.

So, *first shaman song,* and all the other *songs for animals* in this section.

The Poundian disposition of verses in this poem makes even the remotest past present. Snyder is the shaman who sits "without thoughts by the log-road / Hatching a new myth / watching the waterdogs / the last truck gone." He has begun the vision quest ("two days without food") and entered the trance in which he participates in the practices of shamans ("In the village of the dead, / Kicked loose bones / ate pitch of a drift log") as well as the seasonal movement of food-gathering from mountain to seashore. The geography is that of the Haida, and logging stands against it, telling us why "Hatching a new myth" has become something other than masculine work and why, in undertaking it, he may also be searching for the anima.

Most of the poems are ideogrammic and may seem relaxed and flat unless they are entered by one's doing for oneself the work of recovering Snyder's sources. The learning gathered here is considerable. Even more notable, this method abolishes the presence of the poet, and regards the animals to whom he gives voice. *Gelassenheit.* As before, there are found poems, one on making a horn spoon, its materials taken from Boas but, as Jungels notes, brilliantly condensed and made active. It is the first of the ritual/making poems Snyder likes to write. The concluding line, in Kwakiutl, is a fine touch, both enacting closure and confirming the (ever) present of the poem. There are also catalogs in a poem for birds and a poem simply listing the food the Jicarilla Apache ate. This is another mode he favors. Yet having recognized these formal

20 November
1982

means says nothing about the way the poems work in relation to each other.

The poem for birds, for example, stands to the following poem as text to myth, joined by the injunction "See or go blind!" (The fundamental discipline is attention, for reader as for shaman.) Birds, having remarkable vision, have immemorially been associated with vision: the eagle feather ("Brush back smoke from the eyes, / dust from the mind, / With the wing-feather fan of an eagle"), the "hawk's wing / of vision." The representative anecdote alludes to the myth of Raven, who stole the sun and threw it in the sky. The lore of the poem, some present, some historical, most of it mythical (as in the foundation myth of the Flathead), respects the network. The reason for augury is cosmological; seeing is always a matter of seeing relationships.

Turning to the longest, most accomplished poem, that for bear, I remember that the hen-pheasant told her children that their father was a log. The boundaries of the natural world are not as tight as we have drawn them. And with the bear— sacred, even supernatural—we enter the world of animal marriage, where making love to animals is not exclusively a matter of hunting, though that, too, is part of the story.

In keeping with the universality of bear ceremonialism, the poem is a composite of various tribal rituals and lore. All of it, however, relates to the story of the girl, who, while hunting berries (recall the berry picking in "Logging"), is abducted by a bear and taken to the mountains (now a place of love). Here she becomes the mother of bear-children. Years later her brothers rescue her, the rescue itself following the propitiary rituals of the hunt. All of this is present, available to us in ar-

chetypal experience. If we wish, we can make a horn spoon or,
as Snyder proposes here, hunt bear. According to McCord's
notes, the poem incorporates his encounters with bears; and it
concludes as follows:

> —I think I'll go hunt bears.
>   "hunt bears?
> Why shit Snyder.
> You couldn't hit a bear in the ass
>   with a handful of rice!"

The lines startle us out of mythic time and are full of ironies.
For after a fashion the logger doesn't understand, Snyder has
been hunting bears. The only requisite of hunting the logger
knows is marksmanship (underline *man*); he may not know
that you can track bears by their scat and that "handful of
rice" evokes the very relationship with which the poem makes
us familiar.

In wanting to hunt bears is Snyder proposing to rescue the
Swan Maiden? (One marriage-fable recalls another.) Is the
myth of abduction a version of Kore, the mountain replacing
the underworld, life replacing death? Is this displacement
significant?

The seventh poem is especially lovely, as delicate as the spiderwebs it depicts. Or maybe it's the innocence of the dewy morning, the ceremony of the death dealing (hunting) of man-made
snares and spiderwebs. Snyder's evocation of the network has
nothing in it of Frost's "design of darkness to appall," is not
sardonic like "Design," with its "Assorted characters of death
and blight / Mixed ready to begin the morning right." Snyder
is present only in the evocation of the objects of his attention;
he neither comments nor metaphorizes, as Frost does. His
speculation is not meditative, like Frost's, but literally visual:

21 November
1982

he sees relationships, the web of the veritable network, and doesn't impute design only to question it ("If design govern in a thing so small").

Form confirms this test of poets. Frost's use of the sonnet is also sardonic because it is a formal means of governance, its design playing against that query. Indeed, it is the thinking ego that can design in godlike fashion that accounts for the querulousness with creation. Frost's sonnet is perverse (it represents a reality it denies), a design itself of darkness to appall, telling us no more about creation than we already know from received opinion.

In his open poem, Snyder opens a morning vista to an earlier but still present world. Dancing with rabbit, hasn't he "dance[d] us back the tribal morn" and restored our confidence in creation? Isn't the evocation of this trickster—capable of transformation, snared but alive again—cause for celebration?

The closing verse, with its details of the Shuswap *ecos*, makes it all present in the colloquial remark, "Our girls get layed by Coyote / We get along / just fine." It tells us that the network is not a snare and a delusion, and cause not so much for satisfaction as grateful acceptance.

(Take time here to read Antin's "The Death of the Hired Man," in *Siah Armajani* [Pasadena: California Institute of Technology, 1982].)

22 November 1982   The poem for deer is equally successful if only because by now a context has been established that measures the morality of hunting as we practice it. The verses that frame this poem set off the incidents of gratuitous killing and, as symbolic action, expiate the sacrilege; and the verse that depicts

a deer in motion is every bit as good as "Picasso's fawn, Issa's fawn" evoked in it. This should tell us how much of the logger's world Snyder has repudiated. But, in addition, the poem has the same central place as the poem on the D-8 has in "Logging"; and "Home by night / drunken eye / Still picks out Taurus" asks that we connect them and, thereby augmenting the confrontation of values, *see* the enormity of the sportsmen's ways.

The ninth poems also play off each other, the sad romantic love of the one and the "ecological eros" (Jungels' phrase) of the other. This is not invariably the way of the poems in the three sequences, though each sequence works out a comparable argument involving death and life, destruction and creation.

Buddhist material begins to appear toward the end of "Hunting" and, with it, an increment of cosmology and wisdom. In the fourteenth poem, which picks up the primal necessity of hunting introduced in "But a man's got to eat" (second poem), the question of following the example of Buddha, who fed himself to tigers, and of changing our ways, is considered. This would require that the overreachers, who would snare the sun and burn the world, learn generosity and yielding from the Kwakiutl woman and climb mountains for other than the usual masculine reasons. Here, as frequently in these poems, the closure "saves" the poem by providing a key: "'Stalk lotuses / Burst through the rocks / And come up in sevens.'" *Stalk lotus* is a variety of plant, but I read *stalk* as an imperative verb—it juxtaposes with *start to climb*—and even as *stalking* since hunting is the overall concern. Hunting of this kind, of course, is shaman's work, for the lotus is the Great Goddess Padma and all the lore associated with the Mother of us all. It is also the flower, cited earlier, that cracks the pavement, a power (worthy of the number seven) of the kind Williams identifies with poetry in the poem on the saxifrage.

In the transposing of the usual values of the vertical axis, the poem asks for radical transformation, but not merely the kind proposed by *Cold Mountain*, which is recalled in the next poem by "high on poetry & mountains." Read this poem with the twelfth, which puts distinctly the spiritual difference between lowland and mountain, and tells of a descent to be considered, perhaps, with Maudgalyâyana's. He is now exemplary, not "That silly ascetic Gautama." And asceticism, the value hitherto associated with mountains, is forgone. Instead, mountains evoke the "First day of the world," not only creation and fresh sensation, but rebirth ("new born"), that is, natality, the warrant of beginning something new. This is why the concluding poem celebrates the birth of a baby, the ever-renewed promise of life; and, just as important, why it reads out the lesson of compassion in terms of nurturance. The concluding verse links the girls who nurse animals with "bacchantes, drunk"—with the girls who run mad with the pine bough. The vision it attains affirms the sensuous life of matriarchal culture. Yet since the poem closes with such a questionable priapic figure as Coyote, it remains open to "Burning."

24 November 1982

With "Burning," its title taken from *The Waste Land*, Eliot's asceticism—his view of sexuality as the cause of the wasted land—enters the poem. It does so because the previous sections have not resolved the issues that most concern Snyder.

Coyote, who laid all the girls, is said to lack the "buddha-nature." This representative of the irrepressible life of the body, whose phallus is his double, is no more an accidental feature of Snyder's poem than Saint Augustine and Buddha are of Eliot's poem. Hunger and sex, the moving forces of "Hunt-ing," are instinctual, and Coyote represents both, "an abso-lutely undifferentiated human consciousness," Jung says, "corresponding to a psyche that has hardly left the animal level." Which is why, as Snyder says, Coyote is "the most ar-chaic and widely diffused figure in world folklore." And why, as Jung adds, he belongs to the shaman's world. Yet for us his value is great because he reminds us of contradiction and am-biguity, of good-and-evil and suffering-and-health, which, ac-cording to Stanley Diamond, patriarchal theodicy and order try to deny.

Snyder acknowledges this as of most personal interest to him in his essay on Coyote. So Coyote figures at this turning be-cause now the poem will be primarily psychological, and, as the transposition of values that has already occurred suggests, he recognizes that the way of *either/or* is not as helpful as, and must be compensated for by, *both/and.* Having undoubt-edly read Radin's *The Trickster* (1952) and Jung's commentary, he would have learned that the vertical axis in his work ex-pressed "the polaristic structure of the psyche" and that to accommodate "the tensions of opposites," he needed an *enantiodromia*—opposites, incidentally, that Jung speaks of as *shadow* and *anima.*

Self-transformation is the work proposed by "Burning."

To compare the *"first"* to the *"second shaman song"* is to see how far he proposes to go on his interior journey. There is now no vestige of the world of "logging," only the present ter-rifying experience (initiation) of death and rebirth, of disin-tegration and merger with the primal mother-stuff (*seawater, green slime of bone marrow*) and restoration in the sun. I am reminded of the prefatory poem of Rothenberg's *The Seven*

25 November
1982

Hells and of Schwerner's *The Tablets,* the fullest and most profound re-creation of the psychic experiences of the primary world.

But he is not the shaman of this song; he has yet to achieve emptiness, he still *clings,* or *clutches. Clutching* might have been the title of this section.

Take the next poem. Each verse provides a more complex transcription of experience. The first, concerning meditation, tracks consciousness. The second presents a delirium of *falling* and *clinging* in which what is falling in the void are "a hand, a breast, two clasped"—tokens of love. (The breast, obsessive with Snyder, is synecdochic, evoking both the nurturing and the sensual woman.) *Scuttles* calls up Prufrock's predicament, and the question and answer, as much by the shift in tone as by indicating a divided consciousness, give us the heart of the matter: "Loosely, what's gone away? / —love."

The third verse evokes the natural cycle to which he's not attuned and presents a moment of thought in what seems to be the lonely life of a lookout. Of most importance are the inset lines: "wearing a thin sweater / & no brassiere / in the failing light." They belong, formally, with " 'have no regret,' " and both are enclosed by books, among them *The Waste Land,* summoned by "chip, chip," Snyder's modification of Eliot's *jug, jug.* Yet Snyder has regret, if only for not learning how to love: "& not a word [in the books] about the void / To which one hand diddling / Cling." The image is striking, and *void,* at once *emptiness* and *cunt,* tells his confusion.

What follows, "*Maudgalyâyana saw hell,*" refers to the fifteenth poem in "Hunting" and depicts "the hells below mind" of its tenth poem. It is not as bad a poem as Jungels thinks—

he refuses to gloss it—and belongs here because it rehearses the agon of ascesis and desire, heaven and hell, life and death, dark interiority/dream and bright exteriority/reality, all disposed on vertical axes. The mind here is not empty but overwhelmed by consciousness, the ego's substance. The posture is meditative, not the result, which is why Snyder prefers to open his eyes and look at the clouds, the image of heaven *and* "wind & rain / Realms human and full of desire." The explicit moral of the poem is "We learn to love, horror accepted," where horror belongs not to the Other but to oneself. What Snyder says of the Great Subculture applies: the poem looks into "the negative and demonic potentials of the Unconscious" in order to be freed of them. It confronts the shadow, a necessary descent on the journey to love.

The obliquity of the next poem, *"Maitreya the future Buddha,"* indicates its importance. It speaks for rebirth and love, for emptiness and egolessness, and seems to me to be a patent fable of lost love, a counterpart of the hyacinth garden episode in *The Waste Land.* Whoever *who* is, he is characterized by refusal ("refused / To kiss you long ago") while *you*, who once *fed* him berries, is said to have *fled* him and refused to console him when he found "the world a Wheel."

Poems of love and enlightenment. Sometimes they are considered separately, as enlightenment in the poem on jimson weed, sometimes together, enlightenment the cure for the battered heart in the sixth poem. Here, the clutchings that batter the bough are best overcome, as in the anecdote of Red Hand, by realizing that the bough is dead and by yielding—crossing the river. Snyder does this by going to Japan. But the discipline of Zen fails him because, like Ananda, he grieves, in his case for the death of love. This is the burden of the seventh poem.

27 November 1982

The word *breasts* occurs in every verse of this ideogram. Sometimes it is an image, sometimes a metaphor. The poem, it seems, moves toward resolution by turning image into metaphor, assimilating the girl with "her cool breasts" and the little girl who wonders if she will still be loved when her breasts get big to "The Mother whose body is the Universe / Whose breasts are Sun and Moon." The last verse seems to be conclusive because it puts the eternal nurturance of this Mother over against the nurturance of "Earthly Mothers." But in a crucial instance, metaphor becomes image: the Mother of the Universe calls up "the statue of Prajna / From Java," the statue of wisdom that Snyder noted was fittingly female. In his journal, the evocation of this "girl statue" prompts speculation ("True insight a love-making hovering between the void & the immense worlds of creation"); in the poem, it is followed by "the quiet smile, / The naked breasts."

Tantra unites spiritual and sensual, wisdom (enlightenment) and love, ascent and descent. It asks us to recognize that love is not solely *eros* but regard for the being of another. Its ritual puts *eros* (and ego) to this extreme test.

The poem about John Muir on Mount Ritter fables an extreme test, where what must be let go is the clinging of the ego, the striving of ascent. This found poem belongs to the mountain world of Han-shan and tells of spiritual crisis, when the way up comes to a "dead stop" and the descent beckons. Yet (only) such impasse is transformative. Muir speaks of it in terms of smoke and clarifying fire, and of the acquisition of a "new sense" that enables him to resume the ascent. This sense involves sharpened perception into and trust of the network and, with them, the wisdom to rely on "the boundless compassion / Of diatoms, lava, and chipmunks," as Snyder counsels later.

To rely, that is, on the Mother of the Universe, as Buddha is said to have done at the end of "Hunting."

The political turn in the ninth poem is curious. Is he diverting himself, refusing Muir's example and choosing other heroes, men whose activity is consistent with clutching, "grabbing hold"? Or is political action part of the Way, a corollary of compassion, itself an expression of love? "*Amitabha's Vow,*" the next poem, answers affirmatively. This parody, with its vows rendered in Beat lingo, is fit for dharma bums, or "dharma revolutionaries," to recall the subtitle of *Earth House Hold,* where, in "Buddhism and the Coming Revolution," Snyder says that "Wisdom without compassion feels no pain." The final lines also affirm Muir: "we should go back / we don't."

And isn't the eleventh poem a meditative version of Muir's experience?

> Q. What is the way of non-activity?
> A. It is activity

The dialogue addresses the issue of the previous poem, but enacts Snyder's response to a kōan. Meditating in the zendo, he experiences "Sudden flares . . . / Netted, fitted"; and this dialogue tells what he's learned:

> Coyote: "I guess there never was a world anywhere"
> Earthmaker: "I think if we find a little world,
> "I can fix it up."

There is also the significant Thoreauvian image of transformation and rebirth: "In the dry, hard chrysalis, a bug waits hatching." Not *awaits* it; waiting enables it. Nonactivity, then, is the way of activity. "Hatching a new myth"? Zazen as shamanist technique? Hatching a new self.

Installments of a Zen diary in the twelfth poem, only Snyder's
are not philosophical like Paul Wienpahl's, and the *flares*, recalling the previous poem, now belong to "terrible meditations," of deliquescence and rejection in love.

The longest installment, and most notable, follows, this one
doubly dialogical since the verses converse and some end
with parenthetical remarks. It begins with intense sensation
("Spikes of new smell driven up nostrils"), with the recovery
of what the Nootka lost when they sold out to traders. So:
"(What's this talk about not understanding! / you're just a person who refuses to see)."

The Nootka may be said to begin the history of which "Logging" is a chapter. For now he recalls the world of *Riprap* and,
with it, the poetic work that provides surer ground than the
metaphysical speculation in which he has been engaged. The
recorded speech of a forester evokes this masculine world, his
youthful world of fresh sensations and bodily being. "No more
depth—but the same (macho) freshness and noun-rich structures"—a remark in yesterday's letter from Cid Corman. In
turning back, is he turning from complexity of thought and
emotion, trying to recover those "simple emotions, be they
dark or bright" that Hawthorne preferred to the "lurid inter-
mixture . . . that produces the illuminating blaze of the infernal regions"?

In any case, he deprecates himself, thinks of the terrible
mother and equally terrible virgin huntress, and hesitates to
yield himself to the Mother of the Universe.

As long as you hesitate, no place to go. This is the crux of the
poem and those that follow.

A skin-bound bundle of clutchings
        unborn and with *no place to go*
Balanced on the boundless compassion
Of diatoms, lava, and chipmunks.

Love, let it be,
Is a sacrifice   (my italics)

This, the beginning of the fourteenth poem, pretty much says it, though the recollection of marriage, when the "two of us" descended Mount Tamalpais, says something more. It does so by recalling the refrain of Lew Welch's "The Song Mt. Tamalpais Sings" (*"This is the last place There is nowhere else to go"*) and by the logic of the concluding lines: "Thought of high mountains; / Looked out on a sea of fog. / Two of us, carrying packs." Thought is balanced but superseded by immediate observation; the lookout is now at sea level, not high on mountains; still aware of separation, he is also aware of unity and a common burden. These lines point back to the close of the previous poem and have an equivalent in an earlier verse recalling the marriage: "Green shoots in the marshes / Creeks in the proper directions / Hills in proportion."

Apocalyptic closure. The implicit contrast of the Siwash past and present is a correlative of his own loss, which is cosmitized by observing the spoliation of earth, "This whole spinning show," from Indra's lookout. From this cosmic vantage, "It's all falling or burning"—forest fires, then, in 1919, and now, and "flares," a verb which, when read as a noun, recalls fires of another kind and the spiritual transformation evoked by "The hot seeds steam underground / still alive."

30 November
1982

The vision of destruction and creation that structures this book is essentially consolatory, and of immediate psychological rather than political consequence. The recovery of a matrifocal vision is of most importance. The penultimate poem, composed entirely of Amer-indian materials, calls up previous seascapes and fog, previous Great Goddesses, and, with them, a sufficient natural world and the sea-womb of life. Its injunction, "Get foggy," is telling. So is "Dream, Dream," which reminds us of the initial poem in the book, brings all of the book forward again, and may even name its quality. Coyote, who enjoins "Earth" to dream of a happier time, now figures in his role of culture hero. He, too, has a vision, one in which death is beneficent because transformative.

The explicit use of *text* and *myth* in the last poem serves two purposes: it tells us that "The mountains are your mind"— outer is inner, and fact is psychological "truth"—and that myth cosmitizes text. Both are correlatives of the transformation he seeks and feels promised if he fights fire and suffers, as in fact he does in the text. Thunder Creek, an actual place in his home region, becomes mythic by way of association with *The Waste Land*, with "What the Thunder Said" (the "cloud mutters"), "Falling towers" ("troy's burning"), "a damp gust / Bringing rain" ("sweet rain"). And like the close of *The Waste Land*, the myth of *myth*, in this instance the myth of a purified world following cosmic destruction, comes from Indian scripture. But Snyder is hopeful, where Eliot isn't. He takes his optative mood from Thoreau, citing now "The sun is but a morning star," and keeps the poem open by omitting the period. Surely, in recalling Thoreau, he wants us to remember the story of the wonderful bug that came out of a dry leaf of apple-tree wood as well as the sentences that qualify this faith in time: "Only that day dawns to which we are awake. There is more day to dawn."

2 December 1982   I do not think *Myths & Texts* a "sacred text," as Thomas Parkinson, in the 1960s, said it was. Nor would I say, as Steuding does, that Snyder's reputation rests on it. Too much

is granted the mythic structure and not enough what Eliot finally acknowledged in *The Waste Land*, the "personal grouch." We are impressed too much by the "epic" and mythic aspects. The poems with which I would compare it—*The Bridge* as well as *The Waste Land*—also respond to the crisis of civilization and involve tales of the tribe; but all are conspicuously personal, and more profoundly concerned with sexuality and love and psychic reintegration than we usually admit. These poems celebrate not civilization but the poet's heroic survival in it, and their success as "epics" depends on the representative significance of the poet's encounter with civilization, the intersection of self and history.

Like *Cold Mountain, Myths & Texts* provides a scenario, this one of vocation, the shaman's. Snyder says, in the *Cottonwood* interview: "Well, most poets are not poets [because they have] no vision that is really a larger vision."

Thinking of Snyder's praise of Duncan—"the great American shaman poet"—I see that *Myths & Texts* stands to Snyder's later work as Duncan's *The Venice Poem* stands to *Passages*. Snyder himself gauged it by turning to the open form of *Mountains and Rivers Without End* and the more inclusive form of *The Back Country*.

The Back Country (1966, 1968) is a journey book, where *back*, among its several meanings, is *down*, in search of the feminine. This capacious book is ordered by numerals, later by titles: I. Far West, II. Far East, III. Kali, IV. Back. Four, a good solid number, of the cardinal directions, fits the world-circling that brings him home. These sections, initially called *books*, are pigeonholes ready to accommodate whatever Snyder wishes to add; open containers, as it were, keeping the book open. So the interest now is in what he adds to the second edition—

3 December 1982

how, by revising, he re-visions, re-members his experience. The rearrangement of material is minimal; what is added is not: ten poems in I, three in II, twenty-four in III, two in IV. These poems do not seem to be new, written in the interval between editions, but poems that he now sees fit—is fit enough—to include even at the expense of symmetry. He adds most to III, and names it *Kali*, name of neither place nor direction, but an evocation of what troubles him most and is farthest back. Having acknowledged this, he can return, go back, where *back*, spelled backward, suggests mirroring, not only the retrospective but the introspective character of the book.

To cite Bashō in the epigraph suggests a kind of exploration other than that, say, of Tennyson's Ulysses. The roaming poet-wayfarer follows another way, a *narrow* path (as in Buber) and "the deep and difficult way . . . the *selva oscura*" (as Corman says in his translation of Bashō). Though *roaming* recalls Hanshan's first thirty years, it is finally not of that aimless horizontal kind. "Through the Smoke Hole," giving it vertical representation, indicates its spiritual significance.

21 January 1983   *Far West* rehearses the previous work. The introductory poem, "A Berry Feast," immediately recalls *Myths & Texts* and comments on it. Now the lore of bear and coyote and animal marriages is set against city people as well as loggers. The poem declares the primacy—and resilience—of wilderness over civilization. Berry picking reminds us of the recollection in "Logging," only now the association with bears evokes sexuality, the direct, natural, earthy sexuality insisted on in *The Back Country*—with nurture, clearly, one of the values of the back country. There is no feast in the poem but a celebration of natural functions and "satisfaction" (Whitman). Perhaps the movement from mountain to shore prompted Snyder to close the book by adding "Oysters," where a veritable feast at the

seashore rounds the book, encloses it, so to speak, in a food chain, token of his ecological understanding.

Yet "A Berry Feast" is not a good poem for the same reasons the book falters. The poem is overextended; it works cumulatively, but the parts often lack distinction. This is true of the book, which in some sections, especially *Kali*, seems padded. Then, the valorizations are often *either/or*, though the excitement for me on this reading lies in Snyder's concern with ameliorating just such rigidity of mind and the assurance and righteousness that accompany it.

Valorizations. Take "Marin-an," a poem about work. Here, Snyder's attentive leisure and satisfaction (with just enough to suggest that they are disciplined yet as easy as a mare grazing) are set against the noise from the *far valley* (far from him, from his way) of men going to work. This is pointed up by putting it last and by the force of the closure: "thousands of cars / *driving* men to *work*" (my italics). The men are not free, as he is, and work loses its satisfaction. The highway is not a freeway but a system in which the men are caught. True enough, generally speaking. Yet the valorization is too easy, made without negative capability. He makes us feel the rhythms of his content, but not those of others.

Or take the companion poem, "After Work," which shows the relation of work to manhood. Work, here, is identified with ax and rake and the cold outdoors—it is "masculine." And the man so employed hasn't been driven to work, though his work, like that of the other men, is defined by the indoor, warm, nighttime, domestic, "female" world of satisfaction (wine, food, sex). In both poems, Snyder is deliberate and ritualistic, and savors his experience. Yes, *his*. But what of the girl? He knows his work, accepts it and its male distinction. Does she know and accept hers, getting supper ready, slaving, as we say, over the "hot iron stove"? We know what comes after his work, but what comes after hers? There's the reciprocity of their leaning against each other, though *against* may tell a story such as Joanne Kyger tells in *The Japan and India Journals, 1960–1964.* Her portrait of Snyder—her own self-portrait, too—isn't flattering, corroborating what one suspects: that the shack to which he returns after work is as Victorian as the old houses in the West, that the male is dominant, the female ancillary. Early in their marriage, Joanne Kyger notes Snyder's assertiveness and disregard for her desires and identity. She wonders if his masculinity is threatened. "As far as I can recall," she says, "he has always treated women this way." (Such behavior is true of almost all of the men mentioned in her journal; it is not unusual but common, and easily disturbed by the restlessness of women beginning to question it.)

Far West, like "Logging" in *Myths & Texts* and *Riprap,* is almost exclusively male.

22 January 1983
There are many work poems, of forest and sea. In the former, the polarization of values is contained within the single, isolated male experience. As in "A Walk," a notable poem exemplifying the disciplined *play* Snyder puts against *work,* satisfaction belongs to the balance or complementarity of the poles of experience. Not that work isn't intrinsically valuable, but that satisfaction is a reward for its ascesis—comes after work, in the "feminine" terms of cool water and food. Now where "A Walk" is an analogue of making a poem, that is, of the way of creative experience, "Fire in the Hole" is an analogue of another kind of making, the explosive sexual activity of the male, which is comparable in its rhythm of intensity and release to the experiences of creation and play.

The poems of work at sea speak for the human isolation of this work-world. This is especially the case because they are preceded by "August on Sourdough, A Visit from Dick Brewer," where the lookout's isolation is extreme. With "Rolling in at Twilight," this poem commemorates male friendship and prepares for the complicated issues treated in "For the Boy who was Dodger Point Lookout." How complicated they are may be seen in "How to Make Stew in the Pinacate Desert," where Snyder's compulsive need for ritual is imposed on "woman's" work. The poem calls up the lonely cookouts in *The Dharma Bums* and may admonish Kerouac's easier way. For recipe is ritual, recited here for men, Locke and Drum; and fidelity to ritual, it seems, enables men, when isolated, to hang on. Who chooses to eat by himself? The poem omits the satisfaction of the feast and makes most of the satisfaction of following a discipline. There is also a certain satisfaction in satisfying oneself. And though he buys the ingredients in town and borrows equipment, and does this in a warm communal way; though he is passing on a tradition and enacting a sacrament, following a way is also a way of getting away.

Was. Everything in "For the Boy who was Dodger Point Lookout" is retrospective and, by coming last, puts this section in perspective. It tells us what has not yet been told but is essential, and, in giving reasons for the quest, opens into the next section.   23 January 1983

The poem is also for the *boy* Snyder was fifteen years ago (*ca.* 1950–52) and is unusual for its candor—confession of perplexity—and self-pity. The incident recounted here belongs to the generative source of the book; it is the *back* he seeks to understand. Like the logger (wise old man?) in "Sather," he hopes that travel will make him big. What he learns of Zen and Indian religions is not conspicuous: his is a journey not so much of learning as of love—learning to love—and the lore in his work, as in Duncan's, cosmitizes his world in its service.

The headnote, an unusual feature of the poem, tells of an earlier ascent with Alison Gass, a central female figure in the book, and of a lonely descent years later that "brings it back." Even its brief terms evoke the Swan Maiden myth alluded to in the poem.

Two verses, one of the past, the other of the present. The first rehearses the incident of making camp, of Alison bathing and Snyder ascending farther to talk with the lonely lookout, with whom he identifies. The arduous ascent is referred to only in "We / had come miles without trails." He omits the details told later in "Alysoun," the initial poem of *Kali*, where he remembers cursing her blisters, the reason she "whimpered all night long / with evil dreams." ("I always wanted a girl who would go hiking with me" [letter to Will Peterson, 8 September 1957].) The ascent to the lookout predicates two distinct worlds, nicely elaborated by the different referents of *we* and *our*, sometimes Alison and Snyder, sometimes Snyder and the lookout. The preferred location/relationship, even in recollection, is the lookout's world, "our / world of snow and flowers," there in the "gleaming snow peaks" above "the foaming creeks / and forest valleys," the meadow and the pond "feminized" by Alison's presence. From the lookout's *perch* (has he already recalled the sea gull?), he sees her as Swan Maiden, recognizes her loveliness, even perhaps his loss, but appreciates more his talk with the lookout (as in the visit with Dick Brewer), the "quiet meeting in the mountains," he says later, that "helps keep me sane."

In the second verse, he scores the extremity of feeling by the first-person declaration of his double loss: "I don't know

where she is now; / I never asked your name." The semicolon
relating them suggests that self-concern is the cause of both.
Why didn't he ask the lookout's name? Isn't it "crazy" that he
doesn't know where she is when he so badly wants to know?
And just as "crazy" (I play on his use of *sane*) to read personal
difficulty in the exorbitant terms of "this burning, muddy, ly-
ing, / blood-drenched world"?

The best poem in this section is "Sixth-Month Song in the
Foothills," another work poem, in this case one in which work
is truly a way of being-in-the-world. It tells us what he has
learned to this point and provides the measure of other com-
petences—love, for example—that he has yet to acquire.

24 January
1983

June, named in Whitman's fashion, may also, as Altieri suggests, allude to pregnancy, which would place the "masculine"
activity of the poem within the organic round of Mother Nature. I think of Whitman, his participial universe, his songs of
occupations, and poems such as "Sparkles from the Wheel."
Following "Marin-an," the poem defines work not according
to the imposed mechanical routine of the city (see "North
Beach Alba," where the work he drives to is in the "feminine"
countryside) but according to the natural rhythms of the season, entered, moreover, not reluctantly but in readiness, as in
a dance. Here, he is getting ready to ascend, literally and figu-
ratively "sharpening [his] tools." The poem belongs with such
rituals of preparation as described in "Bubbs Creek Haircut";
it involves attention, attending to and opening to what is outside the *shed* (*head*). It is predicated on interior and exterior
space as well as up and down, and composes a cosmos.

Working meditation. Like Thoreau, hoeing beans, only Snyder
isn't doing this for the sake of tropes. Nothing is symbolic
here: words are things, or, more exactly, in Fenollosa's terms,

actions, processes. So in sharpening his saws and axes, by attending to that, he is sharpening his attention. I think of Williams' "By the Road to the Contagious Hospital," and also because Snyder has learned the lesson of junctures.

The "I" is absent because it has become the *eye*, "a locus of experience," as Creeley says, "not a presumption of expected value." Notable also is that his particular activities unite him with the natural process, the melting snow, the packhorses grazing new grass, the returning swallows ("all processes in nature are interrelated," Fenollosa says); do this by turning his attention *out*, to something other than self. Emerson says that "the eye is the first circle; the horizon which it forms is the second." So the circle, centered in the shed, widens to the yard, the meadow, the low hills, the mountain. And the *cold shed* is transformed; it is neither hostile nor dead/empty space, but intimate space, *my shed.* And in every verse, the swallows move in and out, the very emissaries of this transformation. Since they are said to "fly in to my shed," transformation may be thought of as a gift, like the descent of the dove.

This is the way in which things answer us and the way in which we attain being. *Shed-head-nest:* by this calculus the empty nest near the door has been filled. The nest is a primary image of intimate space and being, since being, as Bachelard says, is round, enclosed, well-being. The poem itself is circular, with the initial and terminal *shed,* the latter, like a door, securely closing the poem. The nest is also a reminder of activities that belong to the complete rhythm of life and of the fact that Snyder is not yet ready to enter that dance. As the heavily stressed initial word of the last verse indicates, he is not readying himself to settle down (should *down* be underlined?) but to move *Beyond,* to ascend once more to the logger's world.

Far East. Japan. Juxtaposition to the previous section tells of
radical change, descent, the spirit subdued because of a new
relationship to women. Japan begins to turn his relations
around, old Japan against the new, present in the ways and
work of old women like Mrs. Kawabata who, in the introductory poem, gives him flowers and outperforms him in cutting
weeds. Her work, the care of the earth, is handwork comparable to his with ax and rake, work whose "feminine" character is evident in contrast with mechanization, the roto-tiller,
for example. Such evidence of modern civilization, associated
also with blue jeans, is "masculine," and its ultimate image is
the American fighter plane whose vapor trails threaten the
dharma trails he has come here to follow. In some ways he is
like those "young expert U.S. pilots" with whom he contrasts
himself ("I stumble on the cobble rockpath, / Passing through
temples"). He realizes this in the public bath when, watched
by the bath-girl, he wonders if he is different. His masculinity
is not in question, but he is a white American, an invader (in
this domestic place) not easily distinguished from those who
made atomic war.

Every section of the book, and the book as a whole, is ideogrammic in composition. Each section presents an image
of self. This method is also employed in individual poems,
in "Vapor Trails," to cite an excellent instance, where what is
contrasted—the twin vapor streaks and the twin needles of
the pine—has a common form that belongs to the design of
nature. "Watching for the two-leaf pine / —spotting that design": *spotting* is a military term transferred to nature study.
Does it acknowledge that war is in the nature of things?

Such "nature" poems—"Foxtail Pine" is another—represent
filiations, continuing activities and aspects of self.

Another, "Mt. Hiei," tells of an aborted ritual, moonwatching, that reminds him of a mistake he made as a lookout. His awareness of isolation, of the hostile space of both the "dark house" and the universe, joins present and past. This small, skillfully executed poem is Creeleyesque in form and feeling.

Like "Yase: September," the poem about Mrs. Kawabata that "December at Yase" calls up, "Mt. Hiei" prefaces "Four Poems for Robin," the central poems of this section. Not Joanne Kyger, to whom Snyder was married in Japan, but Robin fills his thoughts because he has not yet accepted what he admits were "the pointless wars of the heart."

27 January 1983   Even when he most tells his love, he gives himself away, not by yielding but by revealing his fault. The quiet, direct speech of "Siwashing it out once in Siuslaw Forest" is resigned ("I don't mind   living this way") and accords with the fractured, internally divided lineation. *Siwashing*, a derogative use of *sauvage*, both tells and mocks the bravado of his cold night alone in the forest. His recollection, which is only of their sleeping together in a warm bed, is spelled out in "But sometimes   sleeping in the open / I think back   when I had you." The personal pronoun is prominent in all of these poems. Here it is not quite the same as in "I remembered," but determined and active, in keeping with the ego of "when I had you," where possession and sexual mastery are one.

To say, in "A spring night in Shokoku-ji," that all he wanted "Is forgotten now, but you" is lovely but untrue since what he remembers now and wants is her "cool body / Naked under a cotton summer dress." His loneliness seems always exclusively a matter of sexual longing. I can't recall any poem in which he has with women the kind of meeting (in Buber's sense) he has with men, nothing comparable to the visit of

Dick Brewer or his visit to Les Blakebrough and John Chappell in "The Firing," where art and immortality are celebrated in terms of sexual mastery.

His dreams of love are troubled by the ghostlike (Nō-like) appearance of Robin, "wild, cold, accusing." This, from "An autumn morning in Shokoku-ji," where "Bitter memory like vomit / Choked my throat" and he wakens from his dream "shamed and angry."

"December at Yase" completes the sequence by fully rehearsing their difficulties—and passing them off. The issue, centrally, is one of individual destinies that, like Venus and Jupiter in the previous poem, are rarely in conjunction. When he says (for this is his account), "you chose to be free," he imputes blame, makes the separation her fault, though *free* calls up the *possession* from which she sought release. She was willful, then. But he, equally so, "was obsessed with a plan," so obstinately that in all this time he never chose to go back to her: "I didn't. / I thought I must make it alone. I / Have done that." The force of the insistent "I"! The boastfulness in admitting a fault! The plan was only something he thought was the case, yet he approves of the fact that he carried it through; and, in terms of *making it,* he suggests that his determination on spiritual goals is not unlike his determination on sexual goals. If he can be said to have succeeded in the one, he has without question failed in the other.

Were it not for dreams he would be untroubled. They, however, awaken guilt and desire—the love, he says, they left behind at nineteen, that "all crave and seek for." This establishes the value of love, his present sense of its importance, but his way of putting it suggests that each of them went on to better, "higher" things. Now, however, he is not sure, no longer knows what his karma is, even though he excuses himself by saying that he thought he was serving his daimon, doing what his "karma demands." *Demands.* The finality of that!

A Zen monk told him, in 1959: "You only climb a mountain to see what's around; only a fool wants to stay up there."

28 January
1983

The major addition to this section is "Six Years," a loose sequence in which the cycle of the year is used to order the miscellaneous yet representative attentions and experience of his residence in Japan. Though temple activities are part of it, the sequence in its entirety may be read as a Zen practice of life that to some degree restores the "peaceful heart" whose lack troubles him in the initial poem. This poem is among his best, as quiet as its snowy landscape and solitary, meditative walker. It speaks for a perfection like that of the pine tree—that is, as the perfection of "Hieizen wrapped in his own cloud" tells us, of a solitary excellence or sufficiency. Everything in this poem calls up Han-shan and Cold Mountain. None of the subsequent poems has the clarity and stillness of what, were it not for the interfering mind, would be a perfect vignette of unmediated attention. None but the last, which records the stages of meditation at Shokoku-ji. Here the enclosing of the poem in terms of his awareness of "a far bell / coming closer" respects the endless round also figured by the calendric cycle. The subtle change in the line at the end—it is neither broken nor part of a verse but, like "the pine tree is perfect" of the first poem, set apart ("A far bell coming closer")—marks the transformation of which Zen discipline is the means. Set on the page, surrounded by space, without period, it is the single attention in the open space of consciousness that is called emptiness.

An ego records the episodes of this poem but it has yielded

to the objects of its attention, as in the comparable discipline of the householding catalog in "February." The sequence tells of the education of the ego. The ideogrammic presentation is anything but peaceful, but the round of events teaches one to take and attend to things as they come.

Why an *envoy?* In *Earth House Hold,* he juxtaposes "Tanker Notes" and an essay on Zen discipline. So here. Zen and the art of engine maintenance. Back at sea, he continues the journey; he is in "the belly of the ship." But the resonances of this are defined by the next section, *Kali;* by the need to get to India and to be delivered from the terrible mother.

Kali names a religious tradition, still vital in Tantrism, that Snyder says goes "back to the Stone Age," to shamanism and nature mysticism, but is of concern here because it restores the worship, avoided in Buddhism, of the Great Goddess. The calligraphic figure and epigraph on the title page of this section evoke the Black Kali, the devouring, demonic goddess depicted in plates 68 and 69 of Zimmer's *Myths and Symbols in Indian Art and Civilization.* I cite Zimmer because he, too, reverences and restores the goddess, the female cosmic energy. Another epigraph, actually the first poem on the verso of the title page, tells of a hunter's return to find his wife dead and the village empty. It calls up both the Haida myth and Hanshan's experience—that is, the scenario whose losses Snyder will subsequently make good.

29 January 1983

The juxtaposition of these elements indicates the primary concern whose origin the first, added poems establish. "Alysoun," "To Hell with your Fertility Cult," "Robin"—Kali is less a presence than Swan Maiden. If the sections of the book were seasonal, this would be autumn, the season of the Reed College poems. He has indeed gone back.

Nothing in what follows surpasses these first few poems or
presents so vividly the still troublesome conflict of matrifocal
and patriarchal attitudes. This conflict may account for the
hopelessness of a poem of social and political revulsion like
"This Tokyo," for the fact that he does not resist social and
political ills so much as internalize them in terms of "masculinity." He knows that the ultimate exploitation is of women,
and is sexual—"The shivering pair of girls / Who dyked each
other for a show / A thousand yen before us men"—but in the
poem that footnotes this he records his own visit to a whore-
house.

Is the appreciation of the courtesy and human concern of the
prostitute free of patriarchalism? Is it to be dismissed because
hopelessness may be ameliorated by human warmth, as in
"The Manichaeans," and however we find ourselves in this
relation, we are Shiva and Shakti?

> We shall sink in this heat
> of our arms
> .   .   .   .
> dreaming as
> Shiva and Shakti
> And keep back the cold.

The issue is variously rehearsed. I like best "Nanao Knows,"
"How Many Times," "Tasting the Snow"—all at the end of
the section. Nanao knows about work and love: that mountains and cities, connected here with masculine striving, are
evanescent; women, too, but "each girl is real," and what is
permanent is the generative process ("In and out of forests, cities, families / like a fish"). What Nanao knows regards the
wave. "How Many Times" acknowledges Nanao's truth, but
does not respect the *we* so much as the *I*, his erotic arousal
and inability to be as open as she is. "Tasting the Snow" admits that "once I had thought / laughing and kissing / how

cosy to be tuckt in bed" but gives over warm family life and "fuss-trust-love" for cold (purifying?) solitary "masculine" ascent.

The concluding poem, "After Rāmprāsad Sen," renders the fact, hinted in "the belly of the ship," that Kali is womb as well as tomb. It expresses Snyder's love of her and his belief that he will be forever born anew of her, but also his fear of birth; and it doesn't cancel what he says in "Tasting the Snow": "Now I can turn to the hunt."

Kali gives the impression that India was as important as Japan in Snyder's education. But he was never at home there, only a traveler in search of spiritual disciplines and erotic art—or so it seems from "Now, India," the book-length letter in which he tells of his journey with Joanne Kyger.

30 January 1983

As for *Back*, it accords with the circularity of the last two poems in *Kali* and endorses their understanding. In this section he returns to his starting place with the wisdom he has gathered, chiefly the lesson of nature's roundness and nurture. The initial poem, "The Old Dutch Woman," ties back to the initial poems of earlier sections and presents his resolution of male and female roles, mountain and garden, wild and domesticated. The old woman—he recollects his Berkeley days—tended "domesticated flowers," where he "knew Indian Paintbrush / Thought nature meant mountains / Snowfields, glaciers and cliffs, / White granite waves underfoot." Yes, a conquering male, he *thought* this then. Now, pondering also the Heian ladies' and his grandmother's gardens, he knows that nature is nurture, in garden or on mountain. So his own clambering recalls the mountain goats that were intent on finding food not tasting snow.

The long poems ("To the Chinese Comrades," "For the West")
are less interesting than the short poems with their incremental testimony. "7. IV. 64": "all my friends have children / &
I'm getting old." "Hop, Skip, and Jump": "we have all trippt
and fallen." "Across Lamarck Col," an excellent poem, rehearsing once more the central love affair of the book, admitting his fault, even as, in understanding now the give and take
of love, he stresses *take*. "August was Foggy," on the restoration and renewing of love, a poem as delicate as its organic
image of leaves of grass. "Beneath My Hand and Eye the
Distant Hills," a consummate poem, in which the mountain
geography of the vision quest becomes a landscape—the
mountains and rivers—of love, where she (whoever she is)
fulfills and feeds his vision, and conceptualizing, which di-
vides, is overcome; yet, even here, in the poem that best represents the transformation that has taken place, the dominance
of "pusht ruthless, surely, down." "Through the Smoke Hole"
not only cosmitizes the journey but speaks again for transformation.

Nurturance, so conspicuous in this section, affirms the mater-
nal beneficence as against the destructiveness of Kali. It prefigures *Regarding Wave*.

The Hasidic fable with which Zimmer concludes *Myths and
Symbols in Indian Art and Civilization* applies to *The Back
Country:* you must journey afar to find the treasure at home;
not only the spiritual treasure of the psyche, as Zimmer has
it, but the treasure of home that comes of inhabiting.

1 February   "Or having a wife and baby, / living close to the ocean, with
1983   skills for / gathering food" (3 August 1952). The equivocation
             of this entry in *Earth House Hold* is gone by 1969, when he

published this book and *Regarding Wave. Earth House Hold* = *ecos* = housekeeping on earth, where *house* and *earth* spell *hearth* and, with it, *heart*. No *ecos* without *eros*, as in Duncan's commune-cluster in *Bending the Bow. Regarding Wave* celebrates this arrival.

Earth House Hold covers the journey and education of the previous volumes of poetry. It is an indispensable gloss. The last essay on the Banyan Ashram and his marriage to Masa Uehara (in 1967) overlaps with the story told in the poems.

Earth House Hold is framed by two important but polar kinds of experience, related in the sense that the discipline begun as a mountain lookout was necessary to the way that brought him to the ashram and the sea. The latter, in fact, provided him the deepest experience of archaic life. Nothing in Snyder's prose surpasses the account of the ashram and, above all, of spear fishing ("I became absorbed in the life of the sea"), where all he says of hunting is borne out. The joy recorded in the essay, as much as the songs of cuckoos and doves, fills "the whole morning world with song." And the marriage with which the essay ends, wonderful and culminating as it is, is only part of that fundamental life, an affirmation of it.

Unlike his marriage to Joanne Kyger at the American Consulate in Kobe, his marriage to Masa was communal and sacramental. Its ritual involved the ascent of a volcano, where the ceremony took place, and descent to the sea. So, as Snyder remarks, surely realizing the meaning of this emblem of his experience, "within one morning we passed from the windy volcanic summit to warm coral waters."

Beginning with "Passage to More Than India," the essays in *Earth House Hold* mark a turning in which the marriage, with all it signifies of archaic/matrifocal ways, may be said to be the revolution (transformation) alluded to in the book's subtitle. The cover photograph is of a conch: "The spiral (think of nebulae) and spiral conch (vulva/womb) is a symbol of the Great Goddess." A conch horn was blown at the marriage. A similar convoluted organic form is pictured on the cover of *Regarding Wave* (1970 edition), and both books feature photographs of the family—Snyder, Masa, and Kai.

Regarding Wave is a central text because his submission to love is one with his understanding of cosmic energy and interdependence. In joining the family, he has, as Corman says in his fine essay on the art of the book, "joined the life-circle again." He has learned in love to love the universe, the biosphere, Gaia, to whom he later sings in *Songs for Gaia*; learned to serve its (her) ends by fulfilling his spiritual aspirations in love, in the daily tasks and responsibilities of householding. This brings him home. The best brief statement of the transformation undertaken in this life-journey is the recent preface to Edward Schafer's *The Divine Woman* (1980). Here, Snyder writes from a secure matrifocal position, having, in deference to the Muse, the yin, the valley spirit, overcome "the one-sided masculine ethos" of Western civilization. One does this, he says, by going in search of the primitive, by learning about the "archaic matrifocal roots" and, as he says of men, by learning to "touch the woman in themselves." One must acknowledge the "sexual fire" of creation and regard the wave ("she moves through us") if one is "to demonstrate and celebrate the interconnectedness."

3 February 1983   Snyder glosses the title in "Poetry and the Primitive," where he develops a poetics of voice in terms of the *eros* of self-and-

world. In going to the "root" of the matter, he reminds me of Olson, who represented the relationship in his letter to Elaine Feinstein:

the Muse ("world"
the Psyche (the "life"

Both, of course, respect the physiology of speech: to breathe is to exist in the world by virtue of its energies. Now *primitive* (primary, first) names this requisite nakedness and contact, a nature-related way of life, like that of the ashram, that in all of its particulars is close to life and makes one aware of "the sheer fact of being alive." Snyder insists that the poet have such "authentic experience" and acquire the shaman's "knowledge of connection."

If "poetry is the vehicle of the mystery of voice," the mystery resides in the fact that in breathing in the world, we are empowered to breathe out the song of the self. Song (speech) is, as Olson knew, the primary self-act; it enables the self to appear. *I sing myself* (Whitman): not the ego, but the me-myself. Song celebrates this intimate relationship and also gives us the word that thereafter becomes its place: self-word-world. No wonder voice, this *eros* of being, figures as Muse and that Snyder appreciates the Indian tradition in which voice (vox) is Vāk, a goddess, who, as Sarasvati, wife of Brahma, represents his creative energy. Sarasvati is also the name of a *river*, hence "the flowing one," which reminds me that the root of *rhythm*, measured motion, is *rhein*, to flow—the measured rhythm exemplified by breathing, "the most perfect exhibit of physiological rhythm" (Susanne Langer); the measured motion exemplified physically by the wave. Snyder comes to this by way of the etymology of *wife: wave, vibrator*. And here *vibrator* recalls the Hopi belief in a resounding world, one whose axis vibrates to Pögánghoya's call—a "universe [that]

4 February 1983

quivered in tune" and that he was to keep in tune, the universe itself his voice and instrument of praise. So Amerindians do indeed sing, for songs echo the Creator who created song "to implant joy in life."

Regarding Wave = Regarding Wife. That is: the deepest self, the anima, the voice that speaks through me, animates me.

7 February 1983   The book is dedicated to Masa and appears under the sign ⋺∈. This identifies her with the "Queen of the Vajra-realm." No mistaking the "Thunderbolt in the Dark Void," which Snyder mentioned in explaining yab-yum in *The Dharma Bums,* a graphic representation linked by Zimmer to the intertwined triangles of Solomon's Seal.

So poetry, as Rothenberg says, is copulation with the Shekinah. As in Tarn's "La Traviata" in *Lyrics for the Bride of God,* Oppenheimer's *The Woman Poems,* Kelly's *The Book of Persephone.*

Yet I am more impressed by the fact that *Regarding Wave* is a communal and domestic book, demonstrating the truth (and poetry) of an early statement: "The movements of the triad of mother, father and child can be made to express any device of mythological or metaphysical thought."

Triadic, like a wave. And wavelike lines, some triadic, stepping from right to left (in "The Wide Mouth"), others free flowing, like these on Kai's conception:

> Waves
>   and the
>   prevalent easterly
>   breeze.

whispering into you,
>
> through us,
>
> the grace.

The book relates the experience that led to this. Another journey-book, but enclosed by his awareness of the wave, the *Ur-Phänomen*, visible energy of all things. "Wave" invokes it:

Ah, trembling spreading radiating wyf
>
> racing zebra
>
> catch me and fling me wide
>
> To the dancing grain of things
>
> of my mind!

Dancing grain, as in "tree grain" and "every grain a wave," belongs to both *things* and *mind* as well as to the things of his mind, and evokes the actual grains of sand of the seaside. A subsequent poem, "Sand," refers to "'all the grains of sands of the sea'" and establishes a fundamental fact of this book of natural elements, that all belong to Gaia ("I slept up on your body; / walkt your valleys and your hills"). Ubiquitous elements, too, as Far West and Far East, no longer separated, indicate.

Then *seeds*. From the sands to the seeds of his "fucking head" (seeds, later on, sacramental elements in "Song of the Taste," for the world is to be eaten, oh taste and see) to his "dreaming of / babies," this, however, in the context of eco-female violation. "By the Tama River," which contains an instance of this, literally surrounds the gravel trucks in its own rounding, and gives us the first glimpse of Masa and of the community and a measure of natural good: "Friends and poets / Eating, drinking in the rain, / and these round river stones." This is the good he misses in "The Wide Mouth," a poem of emptiness as absence (compare it with the domestic sufficiency of "Not Leaving the House"); the good he sets against the war in Vietnam, which is associated here with the end of his previous marriage—with his inability to love ("will I ever learn to love?") and his killing the sick cat, which, in turn, connects with what he tells us of the disemboweled girl and disemboweled still-living wolf bitch in "White Devils."

The songs of the second section exorcise these demons. They restore an erotic sense of "Great majesty of Dharma turning / Great dance of Vajra power" and show the extent to which Snyder's dream of love is one of fecundity and family. Still I am disconcerted by such images of "crude force" (Williams' phrase) as "Ferghana horses archt / rearing, fucking" (in section one) and "I swung you / around and came into you / careless and joyous" (in section three). Even "Song of the Slip," perhaps the most exquisite poem, consummatory in so many ways, may be prouder than reverential:

> roaring and faring
> to beach high on the dark shoal
> seed-prow

> moves in and makes home in the whole.

The puns of the last line are good ones and speak as well as anything in the book of Snyder's holistic homecoming. Yet the dream in which these lines occur is a male fantasy consonant with the assertive participles and verbs of these lines. Is this song itself a "slip"?

8 February 1983

Is this "masculinity" less disturbing—to be accepted as natural, like the rearing horses—because he thinks of babies, of generation, the cunt he praises in the subsequent poem the "hollow you bear / to / bear"? In any case, it's generation, family, and community that matter to him, and it's good to know he appreciates the leaderless democracy of the ashram. And

good to know that he knows what troubles me here: the learning to love, as he says in "Bedrock," a later poem to Masa.
"Teach me to be tender," he asks of her, getting down to bedrock, to something more foundational than riprap, remembering perhaps that in an earlier poem on the wars of love, he saw
himself as "stony granite face."

Regarding Wave is the book of water, which makes stones
smooth and round.

The third section is devoted to the ashram, to Kai's conception and birth (like a dolphin leaping), and to the new (way of)
life, the rounding this establishes: "Not leaving the house /
From dawn til late at night / making a new world of ourselves
/ around this life." For which the praise of the closing, title
poem, telling of the voice he hears "*now* / / A shimmering
bell / through all." The far bell has come closer in the realization that the voice/wave has indeed become wife, "a wife / to
/ / him still."

Some poems in the New Directions edition might have been
included in the original Windhover Press edition. Among
other things, there is prosodic continuity, poems of wavelike
interpenetrating phrases, representing a reality of interpenetrating energies, the chief cosmological fact of these
poems. Even such minimal poems as "Hiking in the Totsu-
gawa Gorge" is not out of place. Its four words—"pissing / /
watching / / a waterfall"—name "physiological," "mental,"
and "objective" natural phenomena. "Watching" may or may
not join with the subsequent phrase, but it names an activity
of mind consonant with other activities, a mind no longer
concerned with meaning but with relation, connection, with
becoming the place (site) of an event. The title is longer than

the poem and contributes to it by calling up old ways in a landscape appropriately associated with water.

The New Directions edition opens the Windhover Press edition by reducing the force of its triadic form and by carrying forward the story begun there. It brings Snyder back, ready now to inhabit. In this respect, "In the Night, Friend," is the focal poem, transitional, "West Coast bound," and for this reason both richly retrospective and wonderfully prospective. The collage—situating Snyder in contemporary culture and suggesting its profound antipathy to the ways of the poet—is a summary of much of his life and work. But of most importance, in connection with *Regarding Wave*, is the faith in renewal, the redemptive possibility, told in the conclusion. Beginnings are small, like these verses, but as the creation myth of Genesis revived here reminds us, they are everpresent. Ever-present also because, in keeping with his service to the Great Goddess, he reads Genesis with regard for the face of the waters, for sensitive chaos (to cite the title of the cover photograph). He remythologizes what the Yahwists had demythologized, and even establishes the face as *ground*, which is why, as the rhyme indicates, land looks *round*. He has come home to nest. Life, for this American Adam, begins anew in marriage, the birth of a child, settling. "How rare to be born a human being!" (*Myths & Texts*) might simply have been *How rare to be born*, how wonderful natality, beginning, "making a new world . . . / around this life." The peach tree— the fruit tree—resonant here of *eros* and domestic, settled life, is the measure of worthwhile human life from the Pleistocene to the present. As Emerson says, build a house, beget a child, plant a tree.

21 February 1983   *Turtle Island* (1974). The book of inhabiting (or *reinhabiting*, to use Peter Berg's term), of marginal thought and marginal

place, calling up Wendell Berry, a preeminent poet of place, exemplar of rural reconstruction, the settlement, finally, of America, of Turtle Island. The lineage? Thoreau first, this aspect of his life of more importance now than adventuring in the wild. Then Whitman: study out the land, its idioms and its men. Williams (and Lawrence): "the spirit of place," which figures with John Dewey's "The local is the only universal." Olson, of course, who also taught us how to relocate and renew our places, to settle *down;* who did not practice life in the old (rural) ways of Berry and Snyder, but knew as well how to dig in by learning the lore and by loving attention to land-and-life, the areal appreciation of man in the landscape he had learned from Carl Sauer.

The book of "domesticated or domesticating Love that governs the creation of a household." That's Duncan. But Snyder joins him (and Berry), knowing that "the heart's fuel is love" and that our hearths belong to the great household: "great / earth / sangha."

The book of the family, the family itself the resistant force against "the marches of relentless power" (Duncan).

Kitkitdizze. The home place in the "home country," on the western slope of the Sierras, not far from Ishi's region, where the manzanita and kitkitdizze are reclaiming land once mined, logged, and homesteaded; abandoned land that Snyder is reclaiming by living intimately on it, in a more archaic way, "as the Indians do." Pole-frame log-house, no electricity, bottled gas, study-hut—pretty much like our "place" in the woods, essentially backcountry-rural, toward self-sufficiency, in close contact with things, nature-related. Located, local and communal, with all the direct political action that being involved involves. Sociality, too; community workdays. The spirit of it all like that of the ashram on Suwa-no-se Island: "We all went there [Yuba River] one Monday in the summer with a ruck-sack of dinner picnic things and spent the afternoon at lazy swimming . . . the ridge and the river. Back up again by dark."

So the search for the primitive ends in place (in a place, in a family); in inhabiting, in being *grounded*; in looping back to learn the old ways, "ancient human fundamentals." Nothing less now than learning how to survive.

The companion volumes are *The Old Ways* ("tasting the berries / greeting the bluejays / learning and loving the whole terrain") and *The Real Work* (healing the "sickness of civiliza-tion," which, Stanley Diamond says, is "its failure to incorpo-rate . . . the primitive").

Turtle Island demonstrates what Snyder says in "The Politics of Ethnopoetics," where he seems adversary to much proposed by *Alcheringa*, preferring not to study the primitive so much as to become primitive. This speech, the fullest gloss of *Turtle Island*, ends with the prospect his own poetry begins to fill: a landscape poetry not unlike the Chinese and songs that "sing for plants, mountains, animals and children," poetry itself a primary means of helping us to inhabit our places. And the cosmos: for inhabiting, finally, means completing the "net-works and webs of energy sharing," achieving a climax cul-ture, a stable, diverse culture in which art, notably the first arts of song and dance, are the "climax of consciousness." This is of political importance because nothing matters to our future so much as inhabiting, which would rid us of the sense of world alienation by restoring, as Hannah Arendt says, the love of the world and, with it, the common sense of a com-mon world.

With Duncan, who said that "Maximus calld us to dance the
Man"; yes, with Olson, who said that "dance is enough to
make a whole day have glory," Snyder may be said to interpret
Crane: dancing restores the tribal dawn.

Looping back as far as 300 million years. But also looping   22 February
back to his own past, this providing measures of change in   1983
himself that speak well for the possibility of human transformation he outlines in "Four Changes."

Two poems belong to the period of *Riprap* and *Myths &*
Texts. "Walking Home from 'The Duchess of Malfi'" is dated
Berkeley, 1955, and once more rehearses the central experience of his journey to love. *Thought-fought-taught* tell what
he learned but took so long to act on; how the first brought
the suffering from which he freed himself only to experience
"Pains of death and love" and realize that love itself—more
love, not less—is the cure. The second poem, "I Went into the
Maverick Bar" (read it with "Dusty Braces"), acknowledges a
frontier-masculine heritage not easily forsworn; a world, too,
still very much with us, evidence of the kind educed in Dorn's
Hands Up! that readily results in political polarization.

From short hair to long hair:

> That short-haired joy and roughness
> . . . .
> My long hair . . . tucked up under a cap

> The return to marginal farmland on the part of long-
> hairs is not some nostalgic replay of the nineteenth
> century. Here is a generation of white people finally
> ready to learn from the Elders. How to live on the con-
> tinent as though our children, and on down, for many
> ages, will still be here (not on the moon). Loving and
> protecting this soil, these trees, these wolves. Natives
> of Turtle Island.

Put "By Frazier Creek Falls" with "Mid-August at Sourdough Mountain Lookout" (*Riprap*). Now the title does not merely place the poem but belongs to the placing that has become the work of poetry. More important, the poem does not present a psychic landscape; the "I," as Duncan has it, has passed into "sIght," has been absorbed in the activity of looking that belongs with all the other activities of the "living flowing land." The appreciation here is areal, the realization and injunctions ecological. Up and down—"looking out and down— / / The creek falls to a far valley"—are no longer valorized. When they are in the figurative terms of graphs in "For the Children," it's down that matters, the "valleys, pastures" where, if we survive "the steep climb," we may someday meet in peace. The valley spirit moves in *Turtle Island*.

This is why I mention the adjacent poem, "On San Gabriel Ridges." It is not about ascent, though "O loves of long ago / hello again" may refer to that. Instead it is a dream of love and death in which nothing is lost: "all of us together / / twining and knotting / through each other." I am reminded of Creeley's "People."

The book of everything together.

23 February Put "Straight-Creek—Great Burn" against "A Walk" or
1983   "Sixth-Month Song in the Foothills" (*The Back Country*). More meditative now, and not solitary. And not testing himself by difficult ascent or preparing for ascent. Watching the spring come in as before, and birds again quite as important. But his attention—*watching* is now the primary activity of participation (one of the ways he is teaching his sons)—is both remarkably close and wide, aware. So he relates the sluicing water to the flow-wear lines on boulders and these, in turn, to the wear on the human heart—and "in shapes the

same" summons the thawing clay and what Thoreau made of it in *Walden*. Now he notes the "chartreuse lichen" and its use as a dye, and the "geosyncline," the downward flexure of the earth's crust that in the fairy-tale time of earth history ("Once on a time") was the bottom of the sea. The birds and sky are the great thing, heaven itself a bird, the clouds its feathers, and the poem (others, too: "It Pleases," "Magpie's Song," and "As for Poets") cannot be read without recalling "The Blue Sky," the consummate poem of *Mountains and Rivers Without End*.

Again, no ego. The mind's activity is comparable to the "tumbled talus rock," part of a process he shares. Similarly, "us resting on dry fern and / watching," though visually separate, is inseparable from the pecking birds, sluicing water, writhing clouds. The pronoun in the objective case accords with the fact that now the self is a thing among things, its activities of a negatively capable kind; it also respects plurality, the fact that we can no more *watch* than *think* alone and have our being in a common world.

Inseparable because the entries (observations) that are the poem are themselves like the birds, "almost always flying all apart / and yet hangs on! / together." The verbal activity is comparable to the organic order, the "order held / in constant change," spoken of by A. R. Ammons in "Corsons Inlet."

The poem closes with its recapitulation, with the intertwined activities of the birds, the mind, and the poem. It would be inaccurate to distinguish these activities, to speak of them as natural, mental, and verbal; for the birds' flight is the mind's dance and a poem, just as the mind's dance is both flight and poem.

> They arc and loop & then
> their flight is done.
> they settle down.
> end of poem.

Formally this verse enacts what it says. The indefinite pronoun includes all of the elements mentioned earlier, elements
whose activities belong to—take place in—cosmic space. To
settle down (like resting and watching) and to end the poem
are not conclusive because the universe represented here is
eventful, its verbs of stasis and completion readily becoming
participial in nature.

Buddhist teaching of totality and ecological study inform this
awareness, not absent, of course, from previous work, but now
the foremost concern. "Earth-sky-bird patterns / idly interlac-
ing / / The world does what it pleases"—this pleases him in
"It Pleases." (See his definition of *delight*, which spells out
the interdependencies of energy in Blake's "Energy is Eternal
Delight.") He believes, as Duncan said before we came into
our present sense of the fate of the earth, that "the cosmos
will not / dissolve its orders at man's evil." His cosmic trust is
the basic trust he sees in his second son's nurture, where the
boy at the breast also takes in the universe, much like the
Apache children who, in Dorn's account, learned to appreciate
landforms from the observation platforms of their cradle boards.

In this poem to Gen, "whales of cool and dark" reminds me
that in Snyder's flowing and dazzling world, where "sliding
by" is the "real work," the whales, as endangered as bears,
have become a totem animal.

> The whales turn and glisten, plunge
>   and sound and rise again,
> Hanging over subtly darkening deeps
> Flowing like breathing planets

in the sparkling whorls of
    living light

And Turtle Island is kin to whales, swimming, as he says, "in
the ocean-sky swirl-void."

This sense of the cosmos also belongs to "The Bath," Snyder's
finest poem of family life, where the bath is sacramental and
eroticizes the world. If he speaks of delight in ecological terms,
it is because *ecos* and *eros* cannot be separated; nor can *ethos*,
as Olson says. Which is why the bath, along with other practices brought forward in this book, is important. To have
an ecological conscience one must love the world. *This is
our body.*

Hopi has replaced Haida. The book opens with a naming
poem, "Anasazi," that evokes the "ancient ones" and makes
present the round of Hopi life represented in its circular form.
The pictographs by Michael Corr also evoke this early time.
But the most important, because Snyder also employs it in
"The Blue Sky," is not by Corr.

24 February
1983

Kókopilau, the humpback flute player of the Hopi, is the
locust *máhu,* whose story is a fable both of place and of the
power of song to resist and heal. He is the shaman-figure who
now defines Snyder's work.

By meeting the eagle's test, the wounded *máhu* wins for his people the privilege of inhabiting the eagle's land, of living "here with you." Both the communal power of song and its connection with suffering recall the story of Gassire's Lute, but according to the Hopi, the power of song resides in the concurrence of its vibrations with those of the earth's axis. That Pögánghoya and Palögawhoya sit at the poles and "give warning of anything wrong on the planet by sending vibrations along the axis" explains one of the uses Snyder makes of song. The others concern fertility, that is, culture, since Kókopilau carries the seeds of plants and flowers in the hump on his back and is sometimes represented with a penis to symbolize the seeds of human reproduction. He is a culture hero not unlike Coyote, who carried his enormous penis in a box on his back and whose penis, when broken and discarded, became plants.

Snyder himself connects Kókopilau, Coyote, and Buddha in "The Blue Sky," where all are masters of healing, medicine men, and old. This configuration transforms Coyote and speaks for Snyder's own transformation. Coyote is no longer the trickster antihero, and Snyder now advises poets against identifying with this "lustful breaker-of-limits," though he says that those who can "handle" him, as he presumably has, may acquire the power of healing. In "The Incredible Survival of Coyote," Coyote survives the exploitation of the West and becomes its spirit of place, which is why in "The Call of the Wild," where he realizes that Coyote cannot survive a "war against earth," he resents the government trapper who will silence Coyote's song, the music his sons have just begun to love.

25 February 1983   It is not easy to characterize Snyder's material imagination because at various times, one or another element is conspicu-

ous—the hard earth, the rock of *Riprap*, broken and placed by willful man; the liquid world of *Regarding Wave*, where the rocks in their riverbeds have become round and smooth. If anything is conspicuous now, suggesting the prominence of water, it is the *flowing* all things share, the *fluidity* of both his universe and his verse. Though the poems speak of place, place itself is "a swirl in the flow, a formal turbulence, a 'song.'" It is probably needless to decide because, even though he speaks of Earth Poets, Air Poets, and so on, he thinks that all the elements are requisite to the discipline of the poet. He concludes *Turtle Island* in a double way by commenting on the last poem, "As for Poets," in the last prose-piece of the book. Of course he is codifying and explaining his own practice, what the elements have taught him, not only the four elements but the additional elements of Space and Mind. The order in which he treats the elements is not hierarchical, even though one could not become a Mind Poet, that is, a cosmological poet, without the foundation the others provide. So we begin with the fact that Earth is Mother, nurturer; that Air is breath (Vāk); that Fire, which thaws the frozen oil, is "fossil love," the "deep-buried sweetness"; that Water is creation. (This does not suggest an order such as Neumann's growth of consciousness. All of these elements are "feminine," even Mind, spoken of in the Mohawk prayer as *wife* to Space.) The Space Poet is a poet of space only because of the homing instinct or intuition of his poem which "like the wild geese of the Arctic . . . heads home, far above the borders, where most things cannot cross"—the poet whose intuition of the universe enabled him to write "The Blue Sky," which ends with the eagle flying out of sight. And the Mind Poet? He

> Stays in the house.
> The house is empty
> And it has no walls.
> The poem

Is seen from all sides,
Everywhere,
At once.

This poet has learned much about the inner structure and
boundaries of the mind, that the mind is the place (and the
verbal space of a poem may be) where "we are both in, and
outside, the world at once." By a long and roundabout way, he
has come to Cold Mountain.

Cold Mountain is a house
Without beams or walls.
The six doors left and right are open
The hall is blue sky.

Having done this real work explains why he relies now on
"the power within," manifest in song, to make him at home in
the universe as well as to resist the State.

In "Without," he says that song is "the proof of the power
within." Is that power kin to imagination which internalizes
things by representing them in mind? And is song, which depends on taking in breath to make the self appear, the communal agency of imagination? Or is it that song, empowered
by Vāk, exemplifies the primary relationship of self and world
and is proof that the poet is not an ego-poet but an eco-poet?

He comes home to the world not as a recluse but as a house-
holder, ready to fulfill domestic and public duties. He now
serves on the Arts Council of his home state and speaks at
home and abroad on environmental issues. Political action, in
fact, may be the most significant measure of his love because
learning to love has taught him what to defend. It has also
made him joyous. This political book is remarkably joyous
and serene; hence, its authenticity.

Nothing troubles critics so much as the political mandate
of Snyder's poetry. His work has always been political, a
counterstatement to the counternature of civilization, to use
Kenneth Burke's term for its symbolic action. Now the mandate is explicit. The very title challenges us by renaming a
continent we little appreciated and rarely inhabited (unsettled,
as Berry says); is as challenging, say, as the renaming of the
Amer-indians: Native Americans. In view of Snyder's definition of himself in relation to place, Turtle Island names his
homecoming. But the naming disestablishes most of us and
asks us to do what he has done: give over a mind-set ("erase
arbitrary and non-existent political boundaries from your
mind") and acquire instead an *areal* knowledge of land and
life, of actual relationships, that is closer to the *reality* of our
lives. "Turtle Island," he says, "is *good* metaphysics because it
points in the direction of real seeing." Good politics, too, because it opens cracks in our conception of reality, introduces
possibility.

26 February
1983

Inhabiting a place and taking a stand there is a political act.
Pound admonishes us to stand by our words; Snyder, to stand
up for our places and to dig in there. This is an act so fundamental that it is not considered political at all. To change
one's life, to practice life in another way—isn't the mandate to
do this the reason why Snyder's politics is impugned? Snyder's
is a politics of direct encounter; the mediation of "politics" is
minimized, its reification also. "Sweep the garden"—do what
is needed, here and now. Even the blurb on the book is disin-
genuous, claiming that only "a few [poems] are frankly political," when the book itself is notable because it moves beyond
his previous work by including prose—the formal equivalent
of drawing the line—and is wholly political and intended to
be. Can it be that readers of poetry (the shelving word is *Po-*

etry) still want poetry pure and are not yet mindful that the lyre is also a bow?

When he was a lookout, Snyder pondered "poetry & nature in our time" and considered two things: that there wasn't an audience for the poetry of nature and that such a poetry must "articulate the vision." Much has changed since that time. Now art increasingly speaks for nature, and the shaman, in giving voice to a constituency hitherto neglected in our politics, has become political. And by virtue of his vision, his profound awareness of the *ecos-eros-ethos* of life.

So it seems fitting to think of Snyder's lifelong work as a vision quest. Seen in this way, it does not readily divide between the work of the seer and the work of the prophet. Charles Altieri, who makes this distinction, approves of the former but not the latter, overlooking what Mark Schorer recognized in Blake, the politics of vision itself; overlooking, too, the fact that the quest for vision is necessarily followed—fulfilled— in its social reception. I am not questioning Altieri's discomfort with bad political poetry; some of the "frankly political" poems yield to polarization and stereotypes that betray the complex relationships Snyder usually acknowledges. But I do not agree that proposals such as "Four Changes" are simplistic: the interval since its publication, having brought closer the crisis it addresses, does not support such a view. In fact, it is Altieri who may be said to be simplistic, and for the reason he admits: that he "readily aestheticize[s] Snyder's poems" and thereby ignores "any possible consequences his vision may have for guiding my moral and political actions." By refusing to be moved by Snyder's vision, he is able to deny its political force. Yet he is one of the best readers of Snyder's poems and must have been moved by them, moved to resist them and discredit them by specious arguments. He claims that Snyder is politically ineffective because "his images depend so much on 'primitive' custom very foreign to the area of contemporary moral and political discourse he wants to influence." On the contrary, doesn't the leverage come from this, working, say, as anthropology does on parochial minds, to incorporate the primitive we forget at our peril?

Critics, whose politics are sometimes merely speculative, often dismiss the politics of art because art is seldom, in their sense, politically "realistic" and "pragmatic." But the political work of art needn't be of an immediately programmatic instrumental kind, as those who jail poets know. Surely, what John Dewey says of poetry as a criticism of life puts the essential point. It works "not directly," he says, "but by disclosure, through imaginative vision addressed to imaginative experience (not to set judgment) of possibilities that contrast with actual conditions." Criticism of this kind, he adds, is the most penetrating because it makes us aware of "constrictions that hem us in and of burdens that oppress" by opening before us a "sense of possibilities." It appeals, that is, to the most explicitly political values: freedom and justice.

When Chekhov says, "Ah, my friends, you live badly; it is not necessary to do so," *not necessary* gives the sentence its political force.

The book is impure, and without the formal unity of the previous work. Openness, diversity, violent juxtaposition, interpenetrating parts—I read this as an advance, perhaps the formal equivalent of a climax culture.   27 February 1983

Journey's end: mine, not his. He tramps a perpetual journey. So I conclude with *Mountains and Rivers Without End,* which more than any of Snyder's books suggests a serial rather   15 April 1983 than a long poem. It was undertaken, I suspect, because on completing *Myths & Texts*, a formally closed (hence *long*) poem, he needed an open form coextensive with his life. All of his books are journeys—excursions, as with Thoreau—on which he tracks his life; *kinhin*, walking meditation, so to speak, where the actual landscape, the very geography, also belongs to the mind. But in covering the same biographical ground, this book subsumes the others: it is explicitly a journey where journey is both formal means and a metaphor of the Way, and, accordingly, it reveals the figure in the carpet, the archetype, which, he learned from Henry James, "stretches from book to book."

Like the Chinese scroll that proposed this form, the poem is to be viewed not spatially but temporally, a view at a time, as on an actual walk. For the walker in this landscape—landscape signifies Nature: he knows now that Nature is both mountains and rivers—is a spiritual seeker who has entered on the endless journey of life, of enlightenment and love. His Way is primarily Buddhist, framed by the content and ritual of the opening and closing poems, and concerned with what he speaks of in "Dharma Queries"—"acting out the present kalpa through Amitabha through Avalokitesvara through Sakyamuni through you." For the most part, the landscapes of the book belong to America, to his natal geography. This is important because it prompts some of the most profound reveries in Snyder's work, among them the deepest, according to Bachelard, the reverie toward childhood. The inclusivity that it seems he needed does not involve the kind of ecological and historical information he mentioned when speaking of the book in *The Dharma Bums* so much as the exploration of psychological/spiritual experience first undertaken in the last section of *Myths & Texts*.

Of the many analogues, probably the most significant are the following: 1) the Chinese scroll that shows "two little men hiking in an endless landscape of . . . mountains so high they merge with the fog," the landscape Snyder assimilates to his region and peoples with Han-shan and Shih-te, the dharma bums of hobo jungles and logging camps, and Bashō's *Journey to the Far North*, from which an epigraph, in *The Back Country*, merges *roaming* and *dreaming*; 2) Whitman's "Song of the Open Road," itself a meditation on *road* and a model of the "free poem" in which it is proposed "To know the universe . . . as a road . . . for traveling souls" and as the largest yet most intimate space; 3) Kerouac's various chronicles of the road, which owe much to Whitman and provide a model of multiphasic expression as found, say, in "Bubbs Creek Haircut"; 4) the Hopi petroglyphs, the migration symbols of their journeys, one of which figures on the cover of the second edition of *Mountains and Rivers*; 5) his own journals, ideogrammic in form, in *Earth House Hold*.

The practice and poetics of journeying (and journals) belong to the spiritual vocation of what Emerson, in "Circles," calls "the onward way." Whitman also names this direction (of life) when he says, "Forever alive, forever forward." They, among other Transcendentalists, remind us of the spiritual hunger so conspicuous in our literature, of its concern with spiritual destinies, with self-culture. That is Emerson's term for the soul, which, by becoming spheral, is not necessarily aggrandizing itself but coming home to its original relation to the universe. By his re-orienting us, this is what Snyder recovers. By identifying the poet with the shaman—and by assimilating Buddhism—he acknowledges the extremity of the poet's work and the extremity of our need.

It is understandable, then, that Steuding, with Snyder, considers this book a magnum opus. In speaking of it, Snyder refers to *The Cantos;* and Steuding, assuming parity, refers to *Leaves of Grass,* wondering if it will last for the same reason Whitman's book does and be cherished as "a record of a spiritual journey." This, I think, might better be asked of all of Snyder's work rather than this small, albeit *interesting,* book.

16 April   Why? Well, as I see it, "The Blue Sky" is a consummate poem
1983   that, as Snyder suggests by adding it alone to the second edition, concludes the work. Not that Snyder's journey ends here but that it is impossible to go beyond the beyond of the cosmic space it opens. Form, in this instance, might be said to be cosmos: not only does the poem represent the jeweled network but, in giving us the ultimate vertical, it provides the vantage from which it can be seen. Here he attains the view from "high above" that "makes sense" of "the crazy web," a view, he says in "Bubbs Creek Haircut," that "few men see." I don't know what Snyder meant when he told Ginsberg that this book was going to be "the first complete poem of SPACE" (did he spell it large for Olson's reasons?) but the space of "The Blue Sky," the vault of heaven itself, encloses (closes) the whole book, as does the blue cover of the second edition. And the summit of the journey may be said to be reached when temporality yields to spatiality and, in our contemplation, we realize the absolute for which blue stands in Buddhist thought.

This is appropriate because *cosmos,* by definition, is whole and harmonious—"complete," as he says he wishes his poem to be. And all the more so because the poem itself is a meditation on healing and wholing in which Snyder fulfills the shamanist work nominated here by Kókopilau and the work of enlightenment proposed in *Cold Mountain,* where Han-shan, we recall, at last comes home to the blue sky and in its all-pervading light discovers "a boundless perfect sphere."

"If the universe is circular, which it is, does that not mean it is a closing world? . . . I would like to have the poem close in on itself but on some other level keep going."

It does close in on itself, but the poems that follow "The Blue Sky" falter or merely add to it; and the book may yield not so much to closure—Snyder intends to end it—as to design. He speaks of its "necessary plan" and of working from an "overall intellectual structure" that he tries to forget yet spontaneously write "into." When he says that he finds the material "intractable" and must "punch it all up and drive it into the corral," it seems that he has lost sight of the open poem he once proposed. Why does he speak of the completed poem as comprising twenty-five—sometimes forty—sections?

Because of its multiphasic interconnectedness, *Mountains and Rivers*, even as it now stands, surpasses the previous work. The book is a composite of composites, ideogrammic in part and whole. This is the point of it all because the ideogram here demonstrates the fundamental truth (representation) of the form and of Buddhist thought: that fragmented materials, at some level, are connected; that nothing is unrelated in a universe of interdependence. This close-grained book is formally tighter than *Myths & Texts*, and richer. But we realize this only by deeper participation, by discovering and attending to what Snyder calls *ku*, focal images of structural import like the double mirrors in "Bubbs Creek Haircut," and "content points," like "Goodwill," also in this poem.

17 April 1983

I think now of Duncan's "Passages," a supremely multiphasic, truly open poem, because it, too, takes passage and is essential (spiritual) autobiography that resonates beyond itself, that is, requires and calls up his entire work. It is as if Snyder already knew that the scenario of *Cold Mountain* was limited and proposed another that would answer the fullness—the several "quarries"—of a life still to be lived. It is as if he knew a poem of the road Duncan had not yet written: "Come, Let Me Free Myself." For the onward way, after all, is entered, as Emerson says, by abandonment. That's what an open road (and open poem) means; that's the ontological possibility it opens to us. And Snyder knows this. The paradigmatic journey of this journey-book is at its center, "Night Highway Ninety-Nine," and its *ku* is

> —Abandon really means it
> —the network womb stretched loose all
> > things slip
> > through

This is what makes *Mountains and Rivers* so *interesting*. No other volume includes such diversity of language and form, and such a range of materials—such concern for the fullness, in William James's phrase that Duncan employs, of "what is." And no other advances as far as this book in going in where Snyder says Buddhists and poetry go in: to birth and death "as the condition of the universe in the psychology of [our lives]." This means, as he explains, that the light and the dark, first known in infancy, are the beneficent and terrible mother, and that to be a poet, to be creative, one must be "willing to grapple with the *feminine* side of [his] own nature," that is, with the destructive and death-dealing mother. This is what the open form of *Mountains and Rivers* opens to: the scenario is not one of retreat, as in *Cold Mountain*, but one of encounter, and if we follow its way, enlightenment is reached because the lowlands Han-shan fled have not been denied, and, in not denying them, Snyder has found the basic trust that may have been lacking in his childhood. "The Blue Sky" is not merely about healing and wholeness; it is their achievement, the essential requirement of being a shaman. Trust comes of seeing the interconnections and exchanges of all things and of every level of reality; it is the reward of realizing, to cite the title of Garma Chang's book, the Buddhist teaching of totality.

Or call the journey one of individuation because the service to the Great Goddess that is central to it goes beyond the praise in *Regarding Wave* and *Songs for Gaia*; indeed, the "grapple" of these poems—"The Blue Sky" was published in 1969—makes possible the concurrent and subsequent books.

20 April
1983

The service begins in "Bubbs Creek Haircut" because shaving the head, as Snyder explains in "Dharma Queries," is an offering to the Goddess and, though emulating the Buddha, declares his own Tantric allegiance. This is also evident in the fact that the ascent for which he prepares involves a deva world of goddesses ("—the valley spirit / Anahita, / Sarasvati, / dark and female gate of all the world") and that all he ponders of Heaven and Hell, Goodwill, and patriarchal and matriarchal ways is problematic, ready to be, if not already, transvalued. Even his undertaking to journey in mind—in memory—respects his service, belongs to descent. The poem, which Anthony Hunt, in an excellent essay, calls Snyder's "Great Departure," is exceedingly complex. Its rich materials—haircuts are later recalled—connect it with subsequent poems; I miss only the buttermilk not so much because it evokes the Buddha as because it is associated with nurture, with the Goddess/Cow whose milk was prepared by priests with shorn heads.

There are other indications of comedown in this poem: the episodes of Moorehead and McCool, foresters, whose machismo the poem impugns; and the concluding episode in which the old scab barber (Jung's wise old man?) comments on Snyder's meditation on *chair* by cranking him down. This brings him to "The Elwha River," to the anima that had long ago escaped him and that belongs with the lost things, still possessed in memory, of the second part of this ideogram.

I was a girl. In the first part, Snyder encounters the anima, enters the female consciousness, becomes the Other, even as the girl of this mysterious dream poem is a returning, accusing valley spirit, as it were, out of a Nō play. The reflection of event and the theme in which the girl rehearses it figure the "double mirror waver" of the previous poem, the dimensions open to mind also explored here in terms of the real and the dream river. This sad lost girl—pregnant, abandoned by her boyfriend, and reproved by the schoolteacher—tells her grievance by developing the detail of the sleeping (indifferent) fisherman in her theme and by explaining that the river conspicuously eroticized in her dream is not the real Elwha she has taken pains not to recollect. Taken pains because it is painful, as everything associated with the Elwha is for Snyder, here and in all of his work. In "Night Highway Ninety-Nine," this is noted by "High Olympics—can't go there again." Yet he does in order to recover the lost things for the most part associated with women. In the third part, he descends from source to mouth, identifying its "milky confluence" with the goddesses of the previous poem, praising it, and, arriving at Whiskey Bend, where, long before, he had lost a tobacco pouch, acknowledging gratefully "that lowland smell." We remember that in "A Stone Garden," this smell belongs to an *ecos* of *eros,* of fertility, and remember it because the fact of trail making in conjunction with the lowland smell recovers the ways *Riprap* had not resolved.

He journeys down, always down, as in the next poem, "down /
that highway ninety-nine," and since he doesn't travel only by
night, perhaps *Night* in the title is intended to call up night
journeys, as initiatory rites of passage. This graphic poem is a
composite of journeys past and present, the present journey,
like the meditation in "Nooksack Valley," essential to the
turning that takes him to Japan. In fact, as he approaches San
Francisco, glimpses of the landscape remind him of the Orient
and at the same time the road, the American Way, "gets more
straight" and his resolve to try the "six great highways" in-
creases. He abandons himself in this poem, exultantly opens
to experience, which includes driving the L.A. whore, a modern replica of the Goddess. If he doesn't explicitly repudiate
the foresters with whom he has worked, he leaves them behind and, with them, much of the exploitation and despair associated with the history of his region. The book on Japan
that he finds at the Goodwill may be an augury of good will.
It occurs to me now that in his arriving at the city he has seen
"gleaming far away," his passage, like Crane's in "The Tunnel,"
has been redemptive.

He is not high on mountains in "Hymn to the Goddess San
Francisco in Paradise," where the sacrality of woman's nakedness may belong to "the blue sky" because legal repression
produces a "plain sky." This polarized poem of Beat consciousness connects ecstatic consciousness with his immi-
nent passage to the Orient. When high, he believes that "we
live in the sign of Good Will," but he himself lacks this will
in respect to "damned square climbers." Moreover, he under-
cuts the celebration by ascribing the epigraph to Nihil C[as-
sady] and by expressing his disgust with the "fake front strip
tease." Hart Crane again. Maybe Williams. America versus the
back countries. Descent to "the flute and lute and drums."

Nothing shows that the back country is back and down so much as its association with the market, the only evidence of Snyder's passage, notably, to India. "The Market" might be said to be a lowland version of the network. But what strikes me most is that, in recollecting his childhood experience of getting the milk ready for the milk train, he suggests his earliest (incompetent?) service to the Goddess, and that the concluding experience of buying bananas while waiting "for [his] wife," all the while fascinated by the exposed genitals of a beggar (a shadow figure?), seems to question the value of his marital exchange, a husband's dissatisfaction—erotic appetite, perhaps inadequacy—reason enough to remember the terrible mother and enter on the darkest journeys.

22 April 1983   "Journeys" refigures the preceding poems; it is another instance of the double mirror waver. By figuring the deepest descent, a harrowing of hell, it prefigures "The Blue Sky." In tonality, among other things, it belongs with "The Elwha River," and I am reminded by it of Lew Welch, mentioned here, who said that for poets, breakdowns are breakthroughs. His unsent letter to Duncan on his breakdown ("Up and down. Up and down. Through. Below. Above") provides essential commentary on what Snyder undertakes and achieves in these poems—commentary that I find excruciating because Lew Welch measured his lack of strength and discipline against "Mr. Snyder," who, he thought, had all the virtues by natural endowment.

"Journeys" is a dream sequence, much of it involving underground, labyrinthian ways and the lowlands. One needn't read beyond the first line ("Genji caught a gray bird") to see its relation to Swan Maiden. It would be foolish to explain a dream of such complexity—as foolish as the dream-hero's attempt to chart the complex way. Note only that the wounded bird he kills becomes a woman, that he repossesses the anima and puts himself in its keeping, to learn what is uncertain—the knowledge of evil or love? More likely of evil *and* love. Note also that in the following poem, which evokes a Dantesque journey, he finds himself alone in, yet curiously outside, the Olympics landscape of the Elwha River.

Like Rothenberg's "Sightings," the sequence, in its various juxtapositions, offers several readings, while filling out a fairly certain trajectory. Poems III and IV, for example, juxtapose violence and love, the experience of lowland and loft, but the neolithic hunters of the one may be the ancestors of the logger who comes to mind in the other. Poem VIII, which treats a comparable experience of love (another double mirror waver), seems to corroborate and elaborate it. The juxtaposition of V and VI is also significant because loss of home and family in the childhood landscape in V is both measured and transfigured by the fertile ricefields of the Japanese landscape in VI. Here, the insistence on descent and the capitalization of lowlands ("LOWLANDS"), as if it were a discovery or recognition, declare the value that replaces ascent. And this is more fully realized by the juxtaposition of VII, a poem of the underground (the vertical axis is now complete: heaven, earth, hell) linked with the basement in "Bubbs Creek Haircut," but also recalling such hells as Crane's "The Tunnel" and Ginsberg's "A Meaningless Institution." For hell here is not so much the excrement of the place, though that is significant testimony, or its likeness to Plato's cave, but the fact that a space reminiscent of a kiva is wholly without women and the redemptive power of love.

The progression of the sequence involves deepening, as with multiple, receding reflections in a double mirror. The concluding section now makes ascent preparation for something else: for an ultimate abandonment and loss, the falling, told here in terms of life and death, that is transformative and frees the spirit to continue its journey. Not only is the way up the way down, but awareness of death is the necessary condition of life because, as Coyote says, "then you really have to take life seriously, you have to think about things more."

23 April 1983

"The Blue Sky" is morning work, the work of a mind liberated from its own darkness. And morning work like Olson's in "Tyrian Businesses"—a scholar's concern with etymology, the "etym-smashing" that enables him to go back to the root or truth of things. Here, it serves ritual, becomes a language event, an authentic shamanist poem whose closest analogues are Duncan's "Spelling" and "Chords." To say the poem is it- self healing since sound, as Kókopilau reminds us, restores the harmony of the universe, the wholeness this poem invokes and evokes: "Whole, Whole, Make Whole!" Kókopilau liter- ally figures in the poem, a repeated petroglyph marking the stages of its journey—the Hopi journey to the center, that founding? He is the humpback flute player whom Snyder, in a subsequent poem of that name, con-fuses with Hsuan Tsang (he brought the seeds of Buddhism to China) and with himself in his role of disseminator of nurturing truth.

Healing and making whole recover what has been lost, *tie back*, as the etymology of *religio* indicates. So we find here not only the buttermilk and good will (evoked by "charms against the evil eye") of previous poems but a "strange girl poet" whose dream, unlike that of the girl in "The Elwha River," is one of cure and reunion. And there is Amitabha, whose vow Snyder took in *Myths & Texts*, its political aspect played on now in the meditation on *kam* and *comrade*, where "bent curved bow" calls up the commune of society and cos-

mos in Duncan's *Bending the Bow* (1968). And doesn't the
eagle, whose flight ends the poem, suggest the recovery of
Swan Maiden, and all the more when we remember the "sick
old seagull" of an earlier section?

"The Blue Sky"—"shades of blue through the day"—attributes transcendent value to daily life. It describes an arc from
sunrise to sunset and includes the etymology of *azure*. And so
when I come to the end of the poem, I think of *The Bridge*,
another circular journey poem, whose closing questioning
lines portend redemption:

> The serpent with the eagle in the leaves . . . ?
> Whispers antiphonal in azure swing.

Portend because Crane knew that redemption is an experience endlessly earned. Perhaps in saying that " 'The Blue Sky'
raises a question which is the Eagle," Snyder, too, acknowledges the endless journey.

Or search. By now, what he seeks is certainly clear. He has
made the "invisible counter-player" visible, and in *Songs for
Gaia* connects the blue of the *bios* with the blue sky. He already told it in *Myths & Texts*:

> "Earthly Mothers and those who suck
>   the breasts of earthly mothers are mortal—
>   but deathless are those who have fed
>   at the breast of the Mother of the Universe."

But the dream he told Ekbert Faas, of a cave or underground
room entirely covered with breasts that nurture him, is more
recent and confirming. It is not, I think, a regressive dream because his guide is Duncan, who, in a comparable dream of poetic vocation in our time, is led by Olson to the springs, the
source of renewal in myth. Duncan finds, as Snyder does, that

the work of poets is to "restore the Milky Way, the spring of stars that is our mothering universe." Or, to cite Francis Ponge, "It is to nourish the spirit of man by giving him the cosmos to suckle." And since Snyder believes that language does this—that poetry is love because it enables us to participate in the very world it represents—he knows, as Hsieh Lingyün said when meditating on the magic of the world and the need to transmit this truth, that he must "make the most of the years by nourishing life."

Back to Sherman Paul
Kitkitdizze

> It's an odd feeling, to be out where you thought you were pretty much alone, and then realize somebody's over there. Not a bad feeling; so here's Sherman Paul setting up camp not far down the lake and he clearly got here by the same trail. This country belongs to everyone, but a lot of people don't know it or just aren't interested.
> In this case Sherman was tracking me, but it's not really me he's interested in, we're both here for the fishing. So we're brothers at heart, and I listen to his thoughts closely—his cautions and critical comments, his meditations on the route I took, mis-steps and dead ends and all.

> I'm not Han Shan, or Japhy Ryder or particularly even Gary Snyder. I translated Han Shan only half-knowing what I was into—always keeping my own distance though I recognized the affinity. But Paul is correct in seeing that I have—in my personal stubborn path—deeply held on for both: solitude and community, *vajra* and *garbha*. The idea that they are separate is a literal function of occidental restlessness, colonialism and imperialism—solitary and cranky men without women or children on fur-trading expeditions. Athabaskans or

Eskimos in the arctic seldom worked or lived alone. In wild nature the human unit is not an individual but a family band, working together.

The Mahayana, Great Vehicle, Buddhist path opened this as spiritual life "possibility" centuries ago. Its implications are still to be fully actualized. Poetry is a mode of the "middle way" between solitude and total involvement. I stumbled onto it while breathing out my song about climbing the icefields of Mount Hood, age sixteen.

Paul probes my restless early love life and I suppose that's fair. But Kerouac's novel *The Dharma Bums* is a novel, not biography, and it is certainly reckless to draw conclusions about real people from it. I was never the great lover Japhy Ryder is made out to be, and not all that solitary or patriarchal, either. Legends flourish on extremes.

I'd rephrase it slightly: "To serve the matrifocal values by (not patriarchal but) solitary transcendence." Remove the question of gender. As above, the unit is a band, a family, a village, a watershed. But we are also totally alone, each a separate final fate, each responsible for our own deeds and life. Boldly and firmly tasting *that* (the vision quest of adolescence comes to mind) enables us to bring clarity, focus, and courage back to the group. This also is political, it is the courage of self-sufficiency and subsistence and self-governance, in other words the ability to say "no" to the idea that we need a nation-state, or centralized hierarchical religious authority, to valorize our lives.

"Patriarchal values" are values of hierarchy, domination, and centralization—definitely not transcendence. True transcendence *completes* one, with the return to the preciousness of mice and weeds.

This tension between the solitary eye and the nourishing kitchen is the root of the strength and magic of the Old Ways. "Patriarchal" societies, lacking this tension, become one-dimensional, neither transcendent or communal—just materialistic and violent.

Han Shan could well have been a woman! There were a number of tough old Zen lady wanderers and hermits in China. Shih-De would have been her boyfriend!

The (matrilineal) Apache warriors war cry was "for the young girls!" This is also the cry I'm sure of the older women who dressed those youngsters up and led them through their weeks of initiation in the tipi.

Women too, "drink at the breast of the universe." Shakyamuni the Buddha touches the Earth. She shudders, in witness. Everything shakes.

Too much searching concern for motives and meanings. It's simpler than that. In spite of all the learning and deliberateness, a fair portion of my poetry is "beyond me." I just did it, and saw that it worked.

At some point everyone has to go on their own. Does my body of poetry ensnare or liberate? I'll have to keep doing poetry until I'm pretty sure that it has gone past being a snare and is truly a guide to a path. Sherman Paul is working on himself in these meditations more than on me. Isn't this what it's all about? So I'll say he's doing a new kind of literary interpretation and explication here. He's trying to break the blocks down, digest some, return the nutrients to the little ones. The poems pass into the detritus cycle, the cycle that supports "climax." A coyote-name for Sherman Paul's admirable method: "Decomposition Criticism."

GARY SNYDER
20 : X : 40083

Emendations and Comments by Gary Snyder

Page 191 (9 October 1982): I was married to Alison Gass . . . but we were only together 6 months. The woman I had some grief over was different and her real name was Robin.

Page 191 (9 October 1982): There was no particular problem
over my mother in regard to her health and welfare. We
didn't get along too well then, it's true.

Page 258 (27 January 1983): "To siwash" means precisely: to get
through the night without blankets, tending a small fire.

Page 289 (17 April 1983): *Ku* here is "a phrase" or a "notable
utterance."

GARY SNYDER